HJ-

HJx

22/-

(12)

13/11/68

GLOUCESTERSHIRE COUNTY LIBRARY

Headquarters: BERKELEY STREET, GLOUCESTER
Tel. Gloucester 21444

Readers are requested to take care of the books
while in their possession and to point out any defect
that they may observe in them to the Local Librarian.

Date of Return	Date of Return	Date of Return	Date of Return
31/12/68 SWRLB			
-8 JUL 1969			

Experimental Psychology: its scope and method

I History and method

Experimental Psychology: its scope and method

edited by Paul Fraisse and Jean Piaget

Experimental Psychology
its scope and method

edited by Paul Fraisse and Jean Piaget

I History and method

by Jean Piaget, Paul Fraisse
and Maurice Reuchlin

Translated by Judith Chambers

Routledge and Kegan Paul   London

Translated from the French

TRAITÉ DE PSYCHOLOGIE EXPÉRIMENTALE
I HISTOIRE ET MÉTHODE

© *1963 Presses Universitaires de France*

*First published in Great Britain 1968
by Routledge & Kegan Paul Limited
Broadway House, 68–74 Carter Lane
London, E.C.4*

*Printed in Great Britain by
Western Printing Services Limited
Bristol*

*English translation
© Routledge & Kegan Paul 1968*

Contents

Contents

Contents

viii

Contents

Chapter 1

The evolution of experimental psychology

Paul Fraisse

Experimental psychology is so called because its method is directed towards establishing psychology as a science. If science is the knowledge of the laws of nature, scientific psychology endeavours to extend the area of science to include animals and man—considered as parts of nature. The experimental method is certainly not the only scientific method, and scientific psychology is not, and never will be, based on knowledge derived solely from experiment. Observation of all kinds will always play an important part in scientific procedure and especially in those cases where the opportunity for experiment is limited by the nature of the material or by ethical considerations. The experimental method remains the scientist's ideal, for it is only when we are able to reproduce it that we can regard a fact as having been adequately and properly understood. When this happens, a science can not only predict phenomena but can also point to applications which are, properly speaking, scientific.

This chapter cannot claim to cover, even broadly, the history of psychology. In the first sections of this treatise we shall simply trace the important stages in the birth and development of experimental psychology. This will enable us to learn its true dimensions, stemming from its definition, rather than from the limits set by academic tradition and the false claims made on behalf of humanism.[1]

---

[1] The basic texts referred to in this history will be found in the bibliography, but we would like to mention here how much this chapter owes to E. G. Boring's key work, *A History of Experimental Psychology*, 1st edition, 1929, 2nd edition, 1950.

Paul Fraisse

1 Origins

1 'Before' psychology

On beginning his studies in psychology the student will be astonished to learn that it is a very recent discipline. Certainly there has always been an 'implicit' psychology (P. Guillaume, 1943), corresponding to a practical knowledge of oneself and others, and a pre-scientific psychology, which was the systematized knowledge of men of letters (Theophrastus, La Bruyère), of moralists (Marcus Aurelius, Montaigne, Pascal, La Rochefoucauld) or of philosophers (Aristotle, Lucretius).

Of these, philosophy comes closest to science, since the first advance of the mind must be ontological. Originally, however, the distinction between philosophy and science did not exist. Aristotle's *De Anima*, primarily a metaphysical study of the soul as a kind of living organism, is also a biological work full of notes, many of which were extremely accurate, based on the observations of a philosopher-scientist.

It was not until the decline of Aristotelian physics and philosophy in the seventeenth century that the need to understand man came to be regarded as a specific problem. A new discipline cannot emerge unless two conditions are present: on the one hand the evolution of thought must give rise to new problems, and on the other hand new means of investigation must be available to scientists. The developments from which psychology emerged were both philosophical and biological.

2 Philosophical developments in the seventeenth and eighteenth centuries

The progress made in the theory of knowledge helped in the discovery of psychology as a separate subject. It began with the revolt of *Descartes* (1596–1650) against the established School. Although he considered all sciences as belonging to one tree, with metaphysics as the roots and physics as the trunk, he maintained, against all previous forms of realism, that what is best known and most familiar to us is the soul, of which we have direct knowledge. As Canguilhem (1958) correctly pointed out, Cartesian intuition was not the same as nineteenth-century

2

introspection. Nevertheless, the latter is indirectly related to the former, because Descartes introduced the concept of duality in man; the distinction between soul and body. Although the pineal gland joined them, it did not create as firm a union as that imagined by Aristotle, who could not conceive of form without matter or, consequently, of the immortality of souls. This duality of mind and body engendered a series of developments favourable to a growing awareness of psychological problems, though later it was to lead to considerable obstacles. Two methods of approach emerged, the mental and the mechanical. On the one hand, a direct attack on the soul as a spiritual substance, the centre of innate ideas, and on the other an empirical, not to say experimental, research into the mechanics of the body, which Descartes already claimed to have done.

We cannot follow, as a history of philosophy would, the developments which have since been incorporated into this approach, which is too complex and too composite to avoid distortion by its followers. Instead, we will trace some of the lines of evolution, according to an admittedly arbitrary geographical classification, in those centuries when the intellectual life of Europe was at its fullest.

In England, Descartes' influence brought about the empiricist school, which took from his philosophy the direct intuition of ideas and, in general, of a psychic life, but rejected the idea of innateness. According to Descartes, we had innate ideas of God, of the soul, and adventitious ideas, transmitted to the soul by the pineal gland, which were simply the signals of external reality. According to *Locke* (1632–1704), the founder of empiricism, with his *Essay on Human Understanding* (1690), all our ideas come from experience and are a representation of things. For this school, the problem was to identify the simple ideas and to discover the laws governing their composition—without undue emphasis, it is true—Locke was the first to refer to the simultaneous or successive association of ideas though he did not place particular emphasis on it. English empiricism followed a path which changed subtly from author to author. Associationism had a greater place in the philosophy of *Hume* (1711–66), and *Hartley* (1705–57) recognized it as the great principle of mental life.

Any sensations A, B, C, etc., by being associated with one another a sufficient number of times, get a power over corresponding ideas

3

Paul Fraisse

a, b, c, etc., that any one of the sensations A, when impressed alone, shall be able to excite in the mind, b, c, etc., the ideas of the rest. (Boring, op. cit., p. 197).

Taking into account its postulate of a parallelism between sensations and ideas, it made repetition the fundamental principle of all association.

Associationism flourished with the mental mechanics of *James Mill* (1773–1836) and the mental chemistry of his son, *John Stuart Mill* (1806–73). While remaining empiricist as far as the origin of ideas was concerned, this school developed a psychology centred around the analysis of mental activity. It was, however, indebted to philosophical knowledge, which was based on coherent syntheses. But it prepared a framework of thought for those who, like Wundt and Titchener, were to do research into the birth and association of ideas.

In France the psychological heritage of Descartes was not independent of Locke. *Condillac* (1715–80), a cleric and a doctor, was a friend of the Encyclopedists. His principal work, *Traité de sensations* (1754) reveals the current attitude towards psychology. An empiricist in principle, more so in fact that Locke, he wrote a treatise which was a great philosophical work. Using the image of a statue, made fashionable by Deslandes (see Mayer, 1956), he endowed it first with a sense of smell, and from its smelling the scent of a rose, he deduced all our ideas and even our mental faculties without ever resorting to physiology. The Swiss naturalist and philosopher *Charles Bonnet* (1720–93) was to add this last idea to his own work.

Adhering to Descartes' theory of the mechanism of the human body, *La Mettrie* (1709–51) a priest, and subsequently a physician, published in rapid succession *L'Histoire naturelle de l'âme* (1745) and *L'homme machine* (1748). During an illness, he had noticed that, while draining his physical strength, the illness also diminished his mental powers, and he set himself up as the spokesman of a determinist philosophy where thought was simply the result of the activity of the nervous system.

Cabanis (1757–1808), also a doctor, accepted the sensationalism of Condillac and the mechanism of La Mettrie while preserving his religious beliefs. He regarded sensation as the basis of psychic life and he constructed a synthesis on this principle. Revolutionary as it was, his thinking was directed by the question: 'is the body

4

of a guillotine victim still conscious after decapitation'? Out of these researches came a book, *Rapports du physique et du moral de l'homme* (1802) in which he maintains that consciousness, a higher level of mental organization, depends on the function of the brain, and that the soul is therefore not independent of the body.

Maine de Biran (1766–1824) at first went with the empiricist current, but gradually this meditative man turned towards the observation of his inner life and 'through him psychology became the technique of the intimate diary and the science of intimate feeling' (see Canguilhem 1958), an attitude inherited from Descartes and from empiricism. In preferring to concentrate his studies on inner experience, he was the first of a long line including, in direct or indirect descent, the eclectics, Bergson, Proust and, in one sense, the existentialists.

Empiricism was reborn in France with *Taine* (*De l'intelligence*, 1870) and *Ribot* (*La psychologie anglaise contemporaine*, 1870), in reaction to the official eclecticism and under the direct influence of the English school.

In Germany, the developments of thought were more original, and marked a reaction against English empiricism. *Leibniz* (1646–1716) regarded simple or monad substances, like composite ones, as being capable of activity. This principle, on which he laid great stress, was to become the basic tenet of a whole school of psychology called act psychology (Brentano, Stumpf), a school which stood aloof from experimental psychology till its principles were fully established. During the eighteenth century *C. Wolff* (1679–1754), a disciple and popularizer of Leibniz, suggested that a subject called psychology should be conceived of as a possibility. But, paradoxically, it was *Kant* (1724–1804) who, in the sphere of ideas, was to give considerable impetus to psychological work. He challenged Wolff's view that psychology could be a science:

> The 'I' subject of every aperceptive judgment is a function of the organization of an experiment but it cannot be a science, since it is the transcendental condition of every science . . . we are not free to perform experiments, either on ourselves or on others. And close observation alters its object . . . (see Canguilhem, 1958).

But posterity saw fit to reject this epistemological line and retained only the principle of the transcendental aesthetic:

> Ideas of space and time are not simple tracings of things, but a way of considering them.

5

Paul Fraisse

Kant himself was merely concerned under what conditions these ideas could form the basis of a science. During the post-Kantian era the origin and nature of these ideas of space and time were to be studied. With this framework the first German psychologists carried out researches into and put forward theories on the constitution of time and space.

To summarize, then, it seems that since Descartes thinking on psychic life has developed along two classical lines since ancient philosophy; the first concerned with the origin of our sensations and their laws of combination puts the emphasis on their empirical origins and on association, in which contiguity and repetition are the dominant principles; the second stressed rather the activity of the mind.

Still others—particularly in France, from Condillac to Cabanis—emphasized the importance of the body. They put forward a physiological psychology.

3 Eighteenth- and nineteenth-century philosophers and the idea of measurement in psychology

Science in general and the experimental method in particular are based on observations which become precise only when they are quantified. Also we must consider briefly how the idea of measurement developed and became adapted to psychology.

The first person to mention measurement in psychology was a German, *Wolff*. It was he who first distinguished, in the very titles of his books, between a *Psychologia empirica* (1732) and a *Psychologia rationalis* (1734).[2] Moreover, he introduced into the language the concept of psychometry. He thought is possible to measure the amount of pleasure by noting how many faults one was unaware of, or the amount of attention by the length of the argument that one was able to follow.

This idea of psychometry was vaguely evoked during this same century by philosophers, naturalists (*Bonnet*), and mathematicians (*Maupertuis, Bernoulli*), but nevertheless actual measurements

[2] However, it was not Wolff who created the term 'psychology'. Canguilhem, in his historical research tells us that he has discovered that it was used by Leibniz in notes dating from some time after 1696, published by L. Couturat, *Opuscules et fragments inédits de Leibniz*, Paris 1903, p. 526.

6

did not follow immediately. An article by Ramul (1960) gives some examples of the first measurements carried out at this time. *Ploucquet* (1764) held that degrees of intelligence could be measured, first by the number of objects which could be imagined and secondly by the degree of discrimination involved in the range of imagined objects, and thirdly by means of the brevity of the time necessary to imagine them distinctly. According to another of his contemporaries, the intensity of all attention could be measured by the number of ideas of which one is capable of thinking and by the length of time during which one is capable of contemplating, without discontinuity, one idea in all its complexity (*Hagen* 1734). This same author devised, moreover, completely practicable experiments. He suggested, for example, provoking fear in a person by describing imminent dangers to him, then considering the results. *Kruger* (1743–1756) also conceived experiment possible and a measure of the intensity of sensations would be proportional to the physical strength and tension which acted on the nerves.

But these were only dreams, and not one of these philosophers actually carried out any measurement or experiment. The reader will have noted, however, that the only measurement envisaged was that of mental phenomena considered from the point of view of their intensity and duration. These were precisely the aspects which the emergent experimental psychology was to study first.

It fell to *Herbart* (1776–1841), almost a century later, to maintain—from the very chair which Kant had held—that psychology is a science which must be based on experiment, metaphysics and mathematics (*Psychologie als Wissenschaft neu gegründet auf Ehrfahrung, Metaphysik und Mathematik* (1824–25)). Though he claimed to be founding a new psychology it was, according to him, different in essence from physics since it remained metaphysical. The method was to be observation, not experiment as in the physical sciences; but psychological reasoning must by nature be mathematical. Nowadays we would say that mathematics supplies the models rather than the means.

Although his ideas may seem out of date to us today, Herbart had a great influence in Germany, notably on Fechner and Wundt; this can be seen as much in what they accepted as in what they rejected.

4 The progress of nerve physiology in the nineteenth century

The evolution of philosophy had assimilated the idea of a subject of psychology and it had supplied its first conceptual framework, but it was the developments in physiology which brought the first problems and the first techniques to experimental psychology. Of course, there are still unknown regions in psychology, but it is difficult to imagine the state of our ancestors' knowledge, less than two hundred years ago. Therefore, a brief outline of the ground covered might help the reader to understand why psychology began so belatedly.

If, in so many fields, psychology is dependent on the progress of physiology, in the same way physiology has only been able to make progress as a consequence of discoveries in chemistry and physics.

In the eighteenth century physiology was still dominated by philosophical notions (mechanism, vitalism) and it was only in 1800 that *Bichat* claimed the autonomy of the biological method. During the nineteenth century progress was rapid, thanks both to the recognition of this autonomy and the availability of physico-chemical techniques. These contributed not only a purpose, but indispensable tools: the perfecting of the microscope, the invention of the galvanometer, the induction coil, the kymograph all date from the first half of the nineteenth century.

The great discovery in nerve physiology was the distinction between sensory nerves and motor nerves (*Bell* and *Magendie* (1811–22) from which it was established that reflex movements, which had been spoken of since Descartes, are involuntary and have their seat in the medulla (*Hall*, 1832). Some years later *Johannes Müller* established the law of specific nervous energy, i.e. that a nerve never mediates more than one sensation, that is to say that we never have direct knowledge of objects but only of the excitations of the nerves themselves (1838). *Helmholtz* (1860) extended the range of this law by showing that it differentiated not only the nerves corresponding to the five principal senses, but also the different sensory qualities (colour, pitch of sounds).

In 1848–49 *Du Bois Reymond* established that the nerve impulse was simply an electrical wave, and *Bernstein* (1866) demonstrated that it was only a wave of negativity. Thus, the concept of animal spirits was completely disposed of. As early as 1820 Helmholtz measured the speed of this impulse on a frog's

The evolution of experimental psychology

nerve and discovered that it was only 50 cm. a second. It is interesting to note, with regard to this discovery, the doubts of his contemporary, the great physiologist *J. Müller:* according to him, the soul was unitary and movement could not be temporally distinct from its central control. How difficult it is for a science to rid itself of philosophy! Helmholtz also measured the speed of conduction in the sensory nerves of man by applying a stimulus to the foot and to the thigh and comparing the lengths of reaction time. He was using an elaborate technique which has only just been perfected.[3]

However, the nervous centres were still little known at the beginning of the nineteenth century and metaphysical problems further hindered the development of fruitful hypotheses. Descartes had separated the soul and the body, the first spiritual, the second material and spatialized. This spiritual soul had no extension and no parts. This essentially metaphysical line of thought fell out of favour with scientists and, insofar as they considered soul and brain together, they conceived of the latter as having an undifferentiated unity.

At the beginning of the century *Gall* (1758–1828), a good anatomist, but unfortunately a quack, popularized the idea of cerebral localization, thereby stimulating the scientists to thought; they began by presenting refutations. Thus *Flourens* (1795–1867) established, by the method of excision, the different functions of the brain, of the cerebellum, the medulla oblongata, the corpora quadrigemina, the cerebral cortex. But together with the appropriate actions of these different centres, he maintained the principle of a common action and, for the brain in particular, he refused to establish functional distinctions.

In 1861, *Broca*, doing an autopsy on an aphasic, demonstrated the existence of a language centre in the third frontal convolution of the left cerebral hemisphere; in 1870, *Fritsch* and *Hitzig* discovered (through electrical stimulation of animal brains) the localization of the motor centres in the cortex. In the next

[3] To appreciate the rate of increase in our knowledge, it is interesting to recall that it was only in 1908 that Head maintained that there were distinct fibres for tactile sensitivity and sensitivity to pain. These fibres were differentiated only between 1930 and 1940; and even today the physiology of colour vision is not fully understood. On another matter, it was only in 1889 that Cajal demonstrated that each nerve cell and its fibres formed an independent unit, a discovery which supplied associationism with a physiological model.

9

Paul Fraisse

decade the principal sensory centres were defined. *Ferrier*, who first localized the visual centre in the occipital lobes, was able to write the following lines, which underlined the victories won in experimental psychology:

> The soul is by no means . . . a sort of composite function of the entire brain whose manifestations one can suppress *in toto* but not partially; on the contrary, certain psychic functions, probably all of them, depend on circumscribed centres of the cortex of the brain.

However, the problem of the unity and the multiplicity of the cerebral function was not yet resolved, but *Jackson* (1836–1911) and later *Sherrington* (1857–1952) provided the key by introducing first the concept of integration and second that of structure.[4]

5 The study of sensations

The discovery of the laws of specificity of nerves in the nineteenth century gave great impetus to the physiology of sensations. But it is important to emphasize that this branch of physiology—unlike others where one works on specimens (animals) or on patients—made continual use of one psychological fact: sensation.

When Newton (1704) discovered that a mixture of blue and yellow light appeared as white; when Tartini, (1714) observed that two simultaneous sounds of different pitch seemed to be accompanied by a third, lower, sound, they referred to introspective data. Moreover, this presented no problems since it was a matter of general phenomena in which individual differences and attitudes played little part.

But the questions which concerned the physiologists at the beginning of the nineteenth century were those of the connection between anatomical data and the physical structure of stimuli, that is the connection between the light and the eye, or the sound and the ear. When J. Müller, who devoted about 15 per cent of his *Traité* to sensation, established how the image of an object forms on the retina, he felt that he was not far from explaining perception. But, as the relation between the physical stimulation

---

[4] To conclude this preamble, we would add that knowledge of the functions of the sympathetic nervous system only progressed in the second half of the nineteenth century. The functions of the endocrine glands were established during the same period, the first discovery being the glycogenic function of the liver (Claude Bernard, 1853). The first hormone to be isolated was adrenalin, in 1901.

10

and the physiology of the receptors became better known, truly psychological problems arose.

The breakthrough towards psychology was to come about through research in tactile sensitivity, which is anatomically different from sight and hearing. Pressures, movements and temperatures all act directly on the nerves without the mediation of a complex receptor system. Also the questions raised were directly psycho-social.

Weber (1795–1878), professor of anatomy and later of physiology at Leipzig, contributed greatly to our knowledge in this field (1834 and 1846). He distinguished, in touch, three classes of sensation: pressure, temperature and locality. He carried out numerous experiments in each sphere, establishing that these sensitivities varied considerably in different areas of the body. To prove the connection between pressure and temperature, he set up an experiment with a *Thaler*, an ancient German coin. One of the pieces, taken out of cold water and placed on the forehead felt heavier than two pieces laid on top of one another taken from hot water. To study the locality sense, he invented a compass, still called Weber's compass or aesthesiometer, and he found that the threshold of discrimination of the two points varied with the regions of the skin and that it was 30 times greater in the upper arm than in the little finger.

His most famous experiments were on differential sensitivity. He discovered that if a person is just able to distinguish a weight of 29 ounces from one of 32 ounces, then he is also able to distinguish 29 drams from 32 drams, the ounce being eight times the weight of the dram. The 'just noticeable difference' is therefore in a constant ratio with the weight, no matter what it may be.

An optician, *Bouguer* established this same law in photometry in his *Essai d'optique* of 1729, but it was Weber who generalized this and determined the ratio corresponding to the just noticeable difference for weights (1/40), for the length of lines (1/50) and the pitch of sounds (1/60). With his work we are on the threshold of psychophysics, originated by Fechner in 1860.

6 Personal equation and reaction times

Before beginning the first chapter on experimental psychology, we must quote the story of a particular problem which brought

Paul Fraisse

about the discovery of the importance and the method of reaction times.

The story is well known. In 1796, an assistant at the Greenwich Observatory was dismissed because he had made an error of about one second in using Bradley's 'eye and ear' method. This method consisted of registering the moment when a star passed in front of the cross-wires of a telescope, counting the seconds and evaluating the position of the star the second before and the second after the passage, to obtain a position with a precision of 1/10 of a second. In 1816, *Bessel*, then astronomer at Königsberg, had the idea, on reading this story, that the error had not been due to negligence, and he began to doubt the precision of his own calculations. For 10 years he compared his calculations with those of his colleagues (these comparisons in fact constituted experiments), and discovered that differences of up to a second occurred between himself and his colleagues; he also noticed the variability of these differences. He was thus led to the idea of a personal equation in perceptive activity.

In the following decades astronomers and physicists, Arago among others, invented methods first to measure this equation and then to try and dispense with Bradley's method. Thus, even before the invention of photography, they constructed and used chronographs which registered seconds and the motor reaction of the observer at the moment the star passed in front of the lens. But, while they were making technical progress, they were also interested in explaining the personal equation. Between 1860 and 1870, they reached the conclusion that the problem was a psychological one and that it depended on phenomena such as anticipation and orientation of attention. In 1861, Wundt constructed a pendulum to study this phenomenon called complication, a term taken from Herbart.

Then again, a Dutch physiologist, *Donders* (1868) borrowed from the astronomers the simple reaction time method, and had the idea of complicating it by devising a method called the selective reaction time method which had two forms: reaction *b* 'diverse reactions correspond to diverse stimuli' and reaction *c*: 'the subject must react to one stimulus but not to the others'. The duration of reactions being longer than in the case of simple reaction, Donders thought that he could thereby measure by subtraction the duration of the processes of discrimination and choice. These methods

12

were to be used intensively in Wundt's laboratory after 1880. It was there that *Lange* in 1888 discovered that the reaction time is longer if the attention is focused on the stimulus than if it is concentrated on the reaction itself.

2 The establishment of experimental psychology

The time was ripe; the *Zeitgeist*, as Boring says, had done its work. Philosophers who, since Descartes, had been asking themselves epistemological questions were gradually led to psychological problems. Like the empiricists they were, they began to wonder how complex perceptions were constituted and how ideas were associated. The idealist current acted as a counterpoint to naive realism and forced them to see the role of the organism and the activity of the mind in the origin of our sensations and ideas.

The philosophers still only brought theoretical systematized answers to psychological problems. And although they were empiricists, they did not turn to experimental trials to support their theories, while not altogether denying the possibility of experimentation in psychology.

The scientists were also confronted with psychological problems. The observations of physicists, like those of astronomers (whose case we have given as an example) brought up the problem of sensory error. Moreover, because of the progress in the physiology of sensation the influence of spatio-temporal circumstances and, more generally, of the psychic element in the phenomenal account which the subject gives of his experience was recognized.

What is astonishing is that the first psychologists had often been trained as physiologists (Wundt, Binet, Pavlov), and sometimes as physicists (Fechner, Helmholtz). These men approached psychological problems in the naturalistic spirit of their early training, having been used to submit to facts and to believe in them rather than in their own intuition. Finally they made use of the products of their methodology and sometimes even of apparatus which, particularly in the field of sensation, made it possible to vary the stimuli in quality or intensity. Where apparatus did not exist, they invented it easily enough (Wundt, Helmholtz).

The first great psychological treatise, that of Wundt (1873-74), claimed to be 'on physiological psychology'; the first French laboratory (1889) under Beaunis and then Binet, was called the Laboratory of Physiological Psychology and it was the Natural Sciences section of the École Pratique des Hautes Études which embraced it. Today this section contains three psychological laboratories (experimental psychology, child psycho-biology and applied psychology).

Should we, therefore, be astonished by the nature of the first problems tackled by experimental psychology? Sensations, perception, attention, duration of psychic processes can all be measured by chronoscopes and chronographs which are designed for the measurement of physical or physiological processes and which were readily available to the early experimenters. Some of them found that these were minor problems when compared with those of learning, motivation and social influences. But the emergence of problems in every science has its laws which depend less on their intrinsic importance than on the complex interlocking of questions which arise, and on the progress which is made in the other sciences. Physiology has been dependent on progress in optics (the microscope), and electricity (electrophysiology); and psychology has depended on the development of physiology. We should, before approaching more complex motivations, understand the operation of the needs of the organisms. Let us remember that when Fechner was founding psychophysics, physiology had barely discovered internal secretions, the basis of endocrinology; while hormones were not known until 50 years later.

These remarks should not be construed as indicating a reductionist point of view in psychology. This has its proper place, which we shall outline later, but it must take account of the physiological conditioning of our behaviour.

We shall now retrace these early developments in their historical context and we shall see where the genius of men has in fact been hampered by the complacency or resistance of institutions, and also by chance. We shall deal with the problems confronted and the new methods evolved rather than with theories, since the latter tend to become outdated. However, in the beginning the two were closely linked. We have chosen to present these developments by countries. Of course, the above considerations have a general value, but they apply more particularly to Germany.

It was there that experimental psychology was truly founded and the methods very quickly spread to other countries. The beginnings of experimental psychology in England, France, Russia and America are deeply influenced by the intellectual tradition of each country and of the institutions which welcomed the new science.

Germany

1 Fechner and psychophysics

Fechner's *Elemente der Psychophysik* dates from 1860. This is justly considered the first work of experimental psychology. Its history is somewhat confused. *Fechner* (1801–1887)[5] spent his whole career at Leipzig, where Weber was teaching. First a doctor, then a physicist and even a professor of physics, he published outstanding works on the quantitative measurement of electric currents and on complementary colours. But he was not only a scientist but also a humanist who all his life published philosophical works of a more limited value, sometimes under his own name and often under a pseudonym. This preoccupation with philosophical problems helps to explain why, after a nervous breakdown, he abandoned physics and was attracted to psychophysics: he wanted to demonstrate the identity of mind and matter, two faces of the same reality, either of which was apparent according to whether one took an internal or an external point of view. But as a physicist he was not content to affirm or to reason. Seeking a scientific foundation for his theory, he thought in 1850 that it was to be found in a 'law linking the growth of bodily energy to that of mental energy'. Thus psychophysics was born. Who, nowadays, would define it, as Fechner did, as the 'exact fixing of the relation between the soul and the body and, in a general way, between the physical world and the psychic world'?

The importance of Fechner's work does not stem from his original questioning, but from the way in which he attacked a

[5] Main psychological writings: *Zend-avesta oder über die Dinge des Himmels un des Jenseits*, 1851; *Elemente der Psychophysik*, 1860; *Vorschule der Aesthetik*, 1876; *In Sachen der Psychophysik*, 1877; *Revision der Hauptpunkte der Psychophysik*, 1882.
The most detailed account in French of Fechner's work and ideas is in Foucault (1901).

psychological problem and developed experimental methods to solve it, finally attempting a synthesis which he called Weber's law, and we which now call Fechner's law: a daring synthesis which has inspired, and still does inspire thousands of studies (see Chapter 5).

His problem was to find a means of quantifying the intensity of sensation in relation to the intensity of stimulation. He started from a very sound idea. Sensation cannot be directly measured in absolute values. We have no standard, but we can measure the stimuli and determine the thresholds of sensation, in particular the differential thresholds of which Herbart had spoken, and which Weber had studied. From this came his idea: to take as standard the differential scale, considering that one differential scale is psychically equal to another. He began with what we now call Weber's law: $\dfrac{\delta R}{R} = K$, where K is a constant, R the value of the stimulation (*Reiz*). He then supposed that what is true of the differential thresholds is also valid for every increase of the sensation S. He could then write: $\delta S = c\,\dfrac{\delta R}{R}$, a basic formula where c is the constant value of the proportional relation. We need only integrate this formula to find the value of S: $S = c \log_e R + C$. c is a constant of integration and C the base of natural logarithms.

Fechner was not the first to find a logarithmic relation between increments of different natures, and he knew and acknowledged previous work. *Bernoulli* (1783), discussing the relation between moral fortune (happiness) and physical fortune (riches), thought that moral fortune varied with the relation of the change in riches to the total fortune, which is reminiscent of Weber's law. Laplace (1812) gave this relation a mathematical formula. An astronomer, Steinheil (1831) found that the size of stars, judged with the naked eye formed an arithmetical progression, while their intensity measured with a photometer constituted a geometrical progression.

We shall not discuss this law here (see Chapter 5). For the time being we shall simply emphasize that Fechner succeeded in quantifying—albeit indirectly—psychic phenomena, which was a revolution, as Bergson's objections later made clear.

Moreover, to establish his law, Fechner had to measure, as accurately as possible, the different thresholds. It is justifiable

16

to say that he founded experimental psychology, particularly by developing three methods of measurement which are still used today in research into perception:

a) the method of just noticeable differences, now called the method of limits

b) the method of true and false cases, now called the method of constant stimuli

c) the method of average error, now called the 'adjustment or reproduction method'[6]

The importance of these methods lies more in their exemplary value than in their intrinsic scope. Even today an experience of these methods constitutes a basic training for the future experimentalist. In fact, they are essentially psychological and take into account the difficulties involved in all quantitative determination. They recognize the importance of the variability of momentary estimations and the convenience of using averages; they take into account the distortions involved in the ordering of estimations and the necessity of counterbalancing. Fechner also applied the Laplace–Gauss law, which was just beginning to be used in other fields, to measure errors in psychology. With this law he injected into the new science the idea of probability, which was to see wider applications during the next century. Finally, it must be remembered that between 1865 and 1876 Fechner founded experimental aesthetics.

2 Helmholtz and the psychophysiology of sensation

There are men who, by their genius, have shattered the boundaries between academic disciplines. *Helmholtz* (1821–94)[7] was such a, man. First a surgeon, then a professor of physiology at Königsberg, Bonn and Heidelberg, he was to end his career as professor of physics at Berlin. He was not a psychologist, yet his influence on the emergent psychology was very important.

His *Handbuch der physiologischen Optik* (1855–66) is a work

---

[6] On these methods, see Fraisse (1956).

[7] Among Helmholtz' works are: *Treatise on Physiological Optics* (English Edition 1924). *The Sensations of Tone as a Physiological Basis for the theory of Music.* (English Edition 1885); *Popular Lectures on Scientific Subjects* (English Edition 1893). *Wissenschaftliche Abhandlungen*, 3 vols., 1882, 1883, 1895.

Paul Fraisse

in which physics, physiology and psychology all have their place. This work, still a classic today, was translated into French in 1867 and into English in 1924–25. His other volume on tonal sensitivity is equally important in the field of audition. Helmholtz invented apparatus, and methods of measurement and used (as we have seen (p. 9)) the reaction time technique to measure the rate of nervous impulse in man. His theories of colour vision and of resonance in hearing are still relevant. Finally, as a physiologist he was interested in the problems of perception. As an empiricist, very much influenced by the English associationists, he developed the 'unconscious inference' theory, which was to oppose the nativist theories. According to him each of our perceptions may contain more than the actual sensory data, something which arises from irresistible unconscious inferences formed by experience—association and repetition playing a large part. He came to one very important conclusion on the value of scientific observation, namely, that this value depends on the past experience of the observer. There still remained the scientist's personal equation and the 'laboratory atmosphere' which led investigators to observe certain phenomena rather than others. This point explains many scientific arguments.

We cannot mention Helmholtz without mentioning *Hering* (1834–1918)[8] his junior, who was involved in the same type of work. They were separated by numerous controversies because Helmholtz' empiricism clashed with Hering's nativism.

As a physiologist, Hering studied the perception of space, colour, temperature sense, etc; he ended his career in the celebrated chair of physiology at Leipzig, where he succeeded Ludwig in 1895.

He invented a great deal of apparatus which is still classic in the psychophysiology of sensation.

3 Wundt and the establishment of experimental psychology

Wundt was both the first psychologist and the first master of this new discipline. In his Institute of Psychology, founded in 1879 at Leipzig, all the pioneers of experimental psychology were

[8] Hering's works include: *Beiträge zur Physiologie*, 1861–1964; *Die Lehre vom binokularen Sehen*, 1868; *Zur Lehre vom Lichtsinn*, 1872–4; *Grundzüge der Lehre vom Lichtsinn*, 1905–1920.

trained: the Germans, Kraepelin, Külpe, Meumann, the
Americans, Stanley Hall, Cattell, his first assistant, Münsterberg
(German by birth), Scripture, Angell, Titchener (English by
birth), Warren, Stratton, Judd, the Englishman Spearman, the
Frenchman, Bourdon, the Belgians Thiéry and Michotte.

Wundt (1832–1920) was trained as a physiologist at Heidelberg
and at Berlin. He did research and began to publish in his first
year of studies. In 1857 he was *Dozent* at Heidelberg, where he
was for several years attached to Helmholtz' laboratory. There was
great mutual respect between these two men, but without any
personal intimacy. In the course of his 17 years teaching at
Heidelberg, Wundt's interests were to evolve gradually from
physiology towards psychology. The change is perceptible in the
titles of his works which go from the frankly physiological to the
psychological.

Between 1858 and 1862 Wundt published *Beiträge zur Theorie
der Sinneswahrnehmung* which was not particularly original,
but in it he spoke of an experimental psychology based on personal
experiment. Like Herbart, he realized that psychology must be a
science but, unlike him, he thought that it should be experimental.
His claim, however, was limited. His psychology, based on introspection, proceeded inductively by two means: experimentation
for the lower processes and the natural history of man for the
higher processes. To this second part of the psychology he was to
devote the ten volumes of his *Völkerpsychologie* (1908-20).
For the time being, however, he was completely absorbed in the
first part of this work and, in 1862, he presented at Heidelberg
his course on 'psychology from the standpoint of the natural
sciences', a course which gave rise to a new volume: *Vorlesungen
über die Menschen und Thierseele* (1863) (Lectures on Human and
Animal Psychology. Eng. Ed. 1894). In 1867 he entitled his
lectures 'physiological psychology'. In 1873-74 they culminated
in the first edition of his great book *Gründzuge der physiologischen
psychologie* (Principles of Physiological Psychology. Eng. Ed. 1904).
This first treatise, covering the whole of psychology, is still
profitably read today. It was to go into six editions, each revised
and brought up to date, the sixth dated 1910-11. The second
edition was translated into French in 1876.

After a year as professor at Zürich, Wundt took a chair of
philosophy at Leipzig (1875). This change was important; it

signified Wundt's acceptance of formal entry into the academic framework to which psychology belonged. Was this not similar to the Trojan horse? The answer is no in one sense, because in the following years Wundt was to publish a Logic, an Ethic and a System of philosophy. However, the answer is yes when one remembers that Wundt, by founding in 1879 the first Institute of Psychology—essentially a laboratory—made the first official action instituting psychology as an original discipline. The creation of this first laboratory, where a generation of psychologists were trained and from which came, in the first 20 years, a hundred important experimental works, was a significant historical fact. Even if the official method was still introspection, the fact that the laboratory was judged indispensable meant that the psychologist was not confining himself to introspection and that he felt obliged to control his results against those of other people. It implied thus that the conditions of observation must be standardized in order to be made comparable, exemplary and significant by dint of being analytical. The experimental method was no longer merely a possibility or a requirement, it had become a reality. Apparatus was needed to define the situation and to record reactions, and Wundt invented several techniques, including the tachistoscope. Moreover, at the same time psychology was unwittingly becoming a psychology of conduct. Of course, the experimenter laid down unwieldy introspective procedures, but he also noted what the subject said or did, and these results have resisted the erosion of time although the theories have crumbled away.

The laboratory work was concerned with sight, hearing, touch, taste, the sense of time, perception, reaction time, attention, feeling (studied either by the impression method, involving the technique of paired comparisons (Cohn 1894) or by the expression method, revealed in modifications in breathing, muscular strength and circulation (1895–1903)), and finally with association. To publish his research, Wundt founded in 1881 the *Philosophische Studien* which, in 1903, broke even more completely with the past by becoming the *Psychologische Studien*.

Wundt was not an undoubted genius, but his prodigious output,[9] erudition, efficiency and influence made him the initiator of experimental psychology.

[9] Boring humorously notes that in 68 years of scientific activity he wrote 53,745 pages, about 2·2 pages a day, or one word every 2 minutes!

4 Content psychology and act psychology

At the end of the nineteenth century Germany turned to psychology as passionately as she had to physiology. It is difficult to combine the history of these developments, and we propose simply to indicate the directions which they took. The principal facts are as follows: against an experimental psychology which was empirical, technical and scientific, that is a psychology of content, another psychology appeared, in the philosophical tradition, giving pride of place to mental activity.

Brentano (1838–1917) was the founder of this school. Although he was a philosopher, originally trained in the Aristotelian tradition, we must mention his work here because he claimed to have established an empirical psychology which he opposed to experimental psychology. His *Psychologie vom empirischen Standpunkte*[10] appeared in 1874, the same year as Wundt's treatise. His line of thought was basically that of phenomenology (Husserl was his pupil); this can be seen, too, in several compromises between his psychological theories and Wundt's. Through a complex connection the *Gestalt* school came under his influence to a certain extent.

His psychology was thus a psychology of the act. When one sees a colour, it is not the colour itself that is mental, it is the *seeing*, the act, that is mental. But the act of seeing has no meaning unless *something* is seen. The act refers to an object which it specifically contains. What Wundt and the others studied was only the content, the objectivity of which could create a problem. Psychology is essentially objective insofar as it bears on the acts of the human mind, acts of ideation (sensing, imagining), of judgement (perceiving, acknowledging, recalling), of love and hate (desiring, feeling). Brentano's ideas were to influence Külpe in the second part of his life and the Englishmen James Ward and W. McDougall. But *Stumpf* (1848–1936) was his true disciple in psychology. Although he was a philosopher, his passion for music led him to combine the two in a psychology of music (*Tonpsychologie* 1883–90). He was professor at Würzburg, Prague and Halle (where Husserl was his pupil and then his *Dozent*), and at Munich, and in 1894 he was finally appointed to the chair at Berlin, where he exerted considerable influence.

[10] English translation in preparation. Also *Untersuchungen zur Sinnepsychologie*, 1907 and *Von der Klassifikation der Psychischen Phänomene*, 1911.

Paul Fraisse

Among his most celebrated pupils were Gelb, Koffka, Langfeld and also Köhler, who succeeded him in 1921. Moreover, independently of Brentano, he formulated the distinction between content and act. He distinguished on the one hand phenomena, the facts of the senses or the imagination, and on the other psychic functions such as perceiving, desiring, wishing. Each is independent of the other in the sense that one can vary without the other also changing.

5 Ebbinghaus (1850–1909)

Ebbinghaus undoubtedly owed his originality to his independent training. After first studying in Germany, moving from town to town according to the fashion, he then went to England and to France, where he worked as a tutor. In Paris he bought a second-hand copy of Fechner's *Elemente der Psychophysik*, which made a great impression on him. Illustrating what we have said about the exemplary value of this book, Ebbinghaus followed its suggestions in studying the more complex processes such as memory. His idea was to use repetitions as a measurement of memory; he invented meaningless syllables so as to have material whose associations were not already known. He constructed 2,300 of these and, with this material and some poetry, he devised two classic methods of memory study—the complete mastery method and the savings method. He also solved important problems: the effect of the length of material to be learned, the rate of memorization as a function of the number of repetitions, forgetting and its curve as a function of time, etc. All these experiments formed the contents of his work *Ueber das Gedächtnis* (1885), a model of clarity and precision which proved that experimental psychology could emerge from the realm of sensation provided that it innovated.

It should be remembered that as *Dozent*, professor extraordinary at Berlin, then at Breslau and Halle, Ebbinghaus founded with König the *Zeitschrift für Psychologie und Physiologie der Sinnesorgane*, which became the organ of the independent psychologists as opposed to Wundt's journal. Ebbinghaus' *Traité de psychologie* (1902) and also his *Abrégé* (1908) were later translated into French and were very influential. We should also mention that in 1897 he devised the *completion test* of mental abilities of schoolchildren at the request of the aldermen of Breslau, who were trying to arrange a better use of the children's working hours. The success with which this method has been used in all intelligence tests is well known.

6 The Würzburg School

The Würzburg school stemmed from the reaction of one of Wundt's pupils. *Külpe* (1862–1915) was in fact one of the first great self-trained psychologists, although he had studied history and psychology simultaneously. He worked more or less continuously with Wundt for twelve years, during which time he wrote his *Grundriss der Psychologie* (1893), resolving to write only of scientific facts, no matter what might be omitted as a result. There was no mention of thought in his book at all. It was precisely this omission which determined the direction of his research from 1894, the year in which he became professor at Würzburg. He believed, contrary to Wundt, that it was possible to experiment with the higher mental processes, and he attempted to do for thought what Ebbinghaus had succeeded in doing for memory. In a sense he failed, but from this failure (by a reaction) twentieth-century psychology was born.

His method, introspection, was not original. He started from Wundt's position, namely that psychology is the science of immediate experience, whereas physics is that of mediated experience. He reformulated it in this way: psychology is the science of facts insofar as they depend on the experience of the subject, while physics also springs from experience but is concerned with facts only insofar as they are independent of it. To study thought, one has only to ask the subjects to think and to describe their experience. Unfortunately this attempt, like Binet's about the same time, had disconcerting consequences. In studying the judgement by which a subject decides whether one weight is heavier that another, a mass of images and sensations is found, but nothing which corresponds to the judgement itself. To explain judgement, like the association of ideas, something different from the content of the individual experience is necessary. This was called, successively, by the pupils to whom Külpe entrusted the research: *Bewusssteinlagen*, or conscious attitudes (Mach and Orth), *Aufgabe*, or set, disposition to act (Watt) and lastly, determining tendency (Ach).

Paul Fraisse

To understand better the content of conscious ideas, these psychologists broke down the stages of a mental process, concentrating on only one moment at a time. For example, in a word association, they distinguished four moments: the preparatory period, the appearance of the stimulus word, the search for the response, and the occurrence of the response word. They thus arrived at *systematic experimental introspection*, which unfortunately failed to fulfil its promise, since the most important point was missed. They further established, at the same time as Binet, the existence of imageless thought. This result was to have a great influence on the thinking of Külpe, who was led to associate with thought content something else (borrowed from Brentano, through Husserl)—creative attitudes, which he called functions. His point of view thus came very close to Stumpf's.

But his early death prevented him from reaping the benefits of the revolution he initiated, although he always claimed that he admitted nothing that was not based on experience. If thought is approached from the point of view of content psychology, matter itself disappears. The time for a new psychology was near.[11] It was approaching the more rapidly because systematic experimental introspection was coming to an end through unresolved differences of opinion among its proponents, since each observer was acting as his own control.

One of Wundt's pupils, *Titchener* (1867–1927) during his 35 years at Cornell, was the American exponent of content psychology based systematically on introspection. By the very vacuity of his major work, he emphasized the basic errors of this psychology. Let us give one example of his inconclusive arguments. Titchener explains many perceptive ideas by means of stimulus error. What does this entail? Let us take the experiment with the aesthesiometer. Between instances where one point or two points are felt distinctly, there is an area where perception is indistinct.

---

[11] Besides writing on psychology, Külpe also wrote philosophical works. Among his existing works are: *Grundriss der psychologie* (1895); *Outlines of Psychology* (English edition 1909); *Introduction to Philosophy* (English edition 1897); *Einleitung in die Philosophie*, 1895, reprinted 7 times; *Die Philosophie der Gegenwart in Deutschland*, 1902, reprinted 6 times; *The Philosophy of the Present in Germany* (English edition 1913); *Versuche über Abstraktion*, 1904 (1st Congress of Experimental Psychology, Berlin); *Erkenntnistheorie und Naturwissenschaft*, 1910; *Psychologie und Medizin*, 1912, *Vorlesungen über Psychologie*, 1920 (published posthumously, by K. Bühler).

The person committing stimulus error then replies 'Two points', judging his perception from what he knows of the situation, while the psychologist who is only analysing his impression sees nothing more than a single pattern extending beyond one point. Stimulus error is logical by nature and results from inference, says Titchener, but who can judge?

7 From act psychology to the 'Gestaltqualitäten'

However, if the history of one psychology ended with Külpe, act psychology, which we saw born with Brentano, was to see rich developments with the advent of Gestalt psychology, leading us even further from the age of the pioneers. If we are already writing of 'pioneers', it is because, when the Gestalt psychologists left Germany during the Nazi persecution, the history of the reign of German psychology ended.

Behaviourism was to be a revolution, Gestalt psychology was a reaction against the atomism of the associationists. It was, however, a phenomenal psychology (we avoid the word 'phenomelogical', as it has since been adopted by a school of philosophy).

The origins of Gestalt psychology are to be found in the so-called Austrian school, formed mainly of direct and indirect pupils of Brentano: Meinong, von Ehrenfels, Witasek, Benussi. Of these, it was *von Ehrenfels* (1859 1932) who first distinguished formal qualities (*Gestaltqualitäten*) in perception.

How, then, did the matter stand? Perception was believed to be made up of elementary sensations. This was quite clear where it was a question of the *fusion* of two simultaneous sounds or of the *interaction* of distinct sensations. But what happened to the perception of space and time in this framework? There were many solutions—none satisfactory. For example *Lotze* (1817–81), who must be counted as one of the precursors of psychology, formulated the theory of local signs (1852). Each sensation, besides having its own particular quality, also had characteristics closely derived from its location, space arose from connections created between these local signs by experience and movement. *Mach* (1886) believed time and space to be original sensations and maintained that a 'sense' of time actually existed. *Von Ehrenfels* (1890) thought that time and space were new dimensions, which could not be formed by a mere fusion of elements. The nature of

25

squareness does not depend on the received existence of four separate lines, but from their juxtaposition the nature of the shape emerges. The same reasoning might be applied to melody or rhythm and this argument is confirmed by the fact that the form can remain the same whilst the elements are altered. Von Ehrenfels maintained that these formal qualities resulted not from the relationship between the elements, but from the activity of the mind in combining them. The concept of formal qualities was thus brought into the open by act psychology. The Gestalt psychologists were to retain the idea of *gestalt*, but not its interpretation, at the same time acknowledging their debt to von Ehrenfels, and to the other members of the Austrian school who had extended his influence.

8 The Gestalt psychologists

The first was *Max Wertheimer* (1880–1943). A pupil of Stumpf and Külpe, he also spent many years with the Austrian school, so that it is impossible to assign him to any one master. His earliest experiment on stroboscopic movement was done with *Schumann* at Frankfurt, with Köhler and Koffka (1912) as subjects. If two light stimuli, A and B, are presented consecutively in the order ABABAB, and if the time interval between A and B and B and A is long, two stimuli are seen. If the interval is shortened, at a given moment alternating movement between A and B is perceived. If the interval is shortened further, the two stimuli are seen simultaneously. This movement, which he called the *phi-phenomenon*, depends on the whole situation and not on the separate factors. The experiment was to provide an example for him and for the Gestalt psychologists. The whole is not the sum of the parts. It is something more which cannot be deduced from the parts. Observation was essential.

An outline of the fundamental ideas of form psychology is superfluous here. They hardly belong in a history and since the work of Paul Guillaume (1937) they are an accepted part of psychological knowledge. The principles were worked out by Wertheimer and his followers and colleagues, *Koffka* (1886–1914) and *Köhler* (1887–   ). The destinies of these three were linked. They were all pupils of Stumpf in Berlin, in 1912 they met again in Frankfurt, and later in Berlin, where Köhler succeeded Stumpf in 1922. In 1921 they founded the *Psychologische Forschung*. They were together, too, in America, where they published important works: *Gestalt Psychology* (Köhler, 1929); *Principles of Gestalt Psychology* (Koffka, 1935), and where they continued their research.[12]

Three other important psychologists were attached to the school: two pupils of *G. E. Müller* at Göttingen, *D. Katz* (1884–1953) (A German who finished his career in Stockholm after Hitler's racial laws came into force,) the Dane, *Rubin* (1886–1951), to whom we owe the distinction between figure and ground in perception (1915), and *A. Michotte* (1881–   ) from Louvain. Michotte became connected with this school of thought and its experimental work in 1923. He was particularly interested in the structure of movements and the perception of action, the culmination of his work being his study of phenomenal causality.[13]

To these men we owe the fundamental laws of *Gestalttheorie*: laws of the organization of forms, principles of relativity, and of transposition, isomorphism of physical and physiological forms and, lastly, field dynamics. The concept of field, confined first of all to perceptual field, was gradually extended to field of activity, which comprises the exterior world and objects, to become, with another Gestalt psychologist, *Kurt Lewin* (1890–1947) (also from the Berlin school, also emigrated to the U.S.A.), the life-space field, which comprises both the subject and his temporal and spatial environment. We will refer to Lewin again later, as his work has a contemporary significance (see p. 70).

[12] The works of the Gestalt psychologists include:

Max Wertheimer: Experimentelle Studien über das Sehen von Bewegungen, *Zeits. Psychol.*, 1912, 61, 161–265, refers to the experiment quoted in the text; Untersuchungen zur Lehre von der Gestalt, *Psychol. Forsch.* 1921, 1, 47–58, the first manifesto of the school; *Productive thinking*, 1945.

W. Köhler: *Intelligenzprüfrung die Menschenaffen*, 1917, translated into English by Ella Winter as: *The Mentality of Apes*, 1927; *Die physischen Gestalten in Ruhe und im stationären Zustand*, 1920; *Gestalt Psychology*, 1929; *The place of value in a world of facts*, 1938; *Dynamics in psychology*, 1940.

K. Koffka: Beiträge zur Psychologie der Gestalt, *Zeits. Psychol.*, 1913, 67, 353–449, and in 1915 and 1919 and afterwards in *Psych. Forsch.* until 1932; *Die Grundlagen der Psychischen Entwicklung: eine Einführung der Kinderpsychologie*, 1921 (English Edition, *Growth of the Mind*, 1924); *Principles of Gestalt Psychology*, 1935.

[13] Many works, inspired by Michotte were published by his pupils (Van der Veldt, de Montpellier, Mac Neill, Fraisse, Nuttin). His own principal work, *La perception de la causalité*, was published in 1946, the English edition in 1963.

Paul Fraisse

The doctrine of the Gestalt psychologists betrayed its origins. They brought to light many important facts, but their method of interpretation is outmoded. The idea of form cannot be explained simply by the isomorphism of physical and physiological shapes. Today research is being done into the laws of the composition of forms, and the work of a connectionist such as *Hebb* plays an important part in this (*The organization of behavior*, 1949).

England

Germany knew how to welcome this new science into its chairs of philosophy. In England the university structure resisted for a long time, and it was outside the universities that psychology flourished, being dependent on two great personalities, Darwin and Galton, who gave the English school its particular character.

1 The birth of comparative psychology: Charles Darwin (1809–1882)

Darwin is universally known as a great evolutionary theorist. His fundamental book, *The Origin of Species* was published in 1859. Apart from his main work, his influence in psychology was considerable on account of the way in which he presented certain problems.

Continuity between the species down to man was not only physical but psychological. Although it was no longer accepted that there was on the one hand an animal-machine and on the other man, distinguished by the possession of a soul, at that time a complete field of psychology comparing man and animals started. Darwin himself showed the way in 1872 with his *Expression of the emotions in man and animals*, in which he concluded from a great number of observations, that man's emotional expressions were a survival of animal habits of direct use to them.

In this new avenue of research animal psychology was to develop with *Romanes* (1848–94) and *Lloyd Morgan* (1852–1936), who was well known for his advice never to explain an action by a higher faculty when a lower would suffice. With this canon, Morgan reacted against the anthropomorphism of Romanes (who was, to some extent, the English Fabre), and also Darwin. In fact, as Canguilhem recently pointed out, (1960) Darwin did

28

not lower man to the level of animals, but raised animals towards man by endowing them with attention, curiosity, memory, imagination, language, reasoning ability, and a moral and religious sense. Animals were not objects of study as such until Morgan. But it was in America that this branch of psychology achieved full dignity.

2 Psychological heredity and Galton's work

The evolutionary theories, whether of Lamarck or Darwin, assumed biological and psychological heredity. This gave rise to the careful research into heredity which is the distinguishing feature of the English school even today.

The first of these workers, chronologically, was a cousin of Darwin, *Galton* (1822–1911) who was to be in many ways the pioneer of the new psychology in England.

According to his contemporaries, Galton had an ingenious mind. All his life this rich gentleman was an independent worker, undoubtedly interested in psychology, but also in many other problems, mainly related to his principal interest.

This interest was demonstrated in his first work, *Hereditary Genius* (1869). Using as a basis reputation as a criterion of genius, he showed that eminent men often had eminent parents. Obviously the law has its exceptions, and after this research Galton used statistical methods, an important innovation which we shall discuss later. For the time being, we shall follow the development of his thought on heredity—a subject to which all his published works were devoted. In *English men of science, their nature and nurture* (1874) Galton followed the same investigation, and for the first time used the concept of nature for heredity and of nurture for environment. Confronted with the problem of individual differences between men, he approached them with these two principal variables. It was hardly surprising that, as early as 1876, he had the idea of studying identical twins, which enabled him to carry out an experiment which would be 'referred' to, since they had the same hereditary endowment. Galton sent out questionnaires from which he extracted information, but without basing it on narrow statistics. The method was often used later, notably by Thorndike (1905), Newmann (1937) and Zazzo (1960).

Galton's *Inquiries into human faculty and its development*, which

29

appeared in 1883, is considered to be the origin of the theory and assessment of individual difference. His purpose was to measure human aptitudes as he was deeply convinced that since the Athenian civilization the human race had degenerated and must now be enriched by substituting deliberate selection for natural selection. In 1883 he coined the word 'Eugenics' to describe research into the best conditions for human reproduction. In 1904 he endowed at University College a Laboratory of Eugenics, from which *Pearson* was the first to benefit.

An intelligent selection demanded that one draw up a balance sheet of the possibilities of each factor. Galton launched out into the measurement of human abilities and the establishment of methods and apparatus. From this arose the invention of the test, a rapid means of measuring a large number of subjects, a striking contrast to the German method—an unwieldy procedure aimed at the study of several supposedly typical subjects. Galton, moreover, sought to measure overall differences rather than to analyse the processes. 'It is the total result which interests us'. The test method did not swerve from this path for a long time.

In this connection also he constructed *Galton's whistle*, for measuring the highest audible sound, *Galton's ruler*, for testing the ability to judge distances, and much more apparatus which is no longer used. His tests were already of a behaviouristic type, since evidently one can hardly understand a man's potentialities except through what he does. However, Galton remained an introspectionist; he was one of the first to use the questionnaire method to determine types of imagination.

Thus armed with his methods and his apparatus, (much of which was similar to that used in contemporary German laboratories) he opened in 1884 an Anthropometric Laboratory at an international health exhibition. He hoped to obtain statistical results on the extent of human abilities from different aspects. For threepence visitors could measure their abilities, which an assistant noted down—nearly 10,000 people took part.

If Wundt was the founder of so-called general psychology, then Galton was the originator of the psychology of individual differences. Should they necessarily be put in opposition by calling one experimental psychology and the other applied psychology? Such a mistake would be impossible today when it is obvious that experimental psychology must involve the two great variables of behaviour, heredity and environment, (see Chapter 2). Nevertheless, it is true that a differential psychology is nearer to being directly of use than the psychology of cognitive functions, which explains why applied psychology developed more quickly in England than experimental psychology. However, this fact should not deceive us as to the nature of the researches or the disciplines themselves. Nowadays applied psychology is often called upon to present its problems in terms of the adaptation of the task to the man as much as of the man to the task, and also in general psychological terms. The Soviet reaction to this subject was typical (see Bauer, 1952), like that of Ombredane and Faverge (1955) in quite another context.

3   Statistics and psychology

Galton introduced statistics into psychology and he also initiated important developments within the statistical method. He discovered 'on the job' that measurement in psychology, which has neither a zero nor a true unit (see Chapter 4), can use only comparisons, based on the statistical distribution of measurements. Before Galton, *Quetelet*, (1796–1874) applying the normal Laplace–Gauss curve to the distribution of biological or social data, found that the height of army conscripts was normally distributed. But the conclusion which he drew was completely opposite to Galton's. For Quetelet the important things was the average, and measurements which deviated from this were 'errors' of nature. With statistics it was possible to describe the 'average man'. Galton, on the contrary, in his work *Hereditary Genius*, used the law of normal distribution to convert the frequency of the occurence of genius into a measure of its intensity, a procedure which anticipated the principles of measurement by reduced distances.

It was also Galton who devised in 1877 the correlation method, starting from the principle of 'regression towards mediocrity'. The heights of sons are more closely grouped around the mean than those of the fathers, since the son's height depends, to a certain extent, on the father's. Galton had the idea of expression the ratio between the height of fathers and sons graphically thus revealing the existence of a line of regression, which was the basis of the correlation coefficient, whose symbol is always r (regression).

Paul Fraisse

Pearson, developing the work of the French mathematician *Bravais*, formulated the mathematical theory (1896), the first step in his long-standing collaboration with Galton.

These researches created a new tradition in England, that of statistical work. Pearson, Yule and lastly *Fisher* were prominent in this work. *Fisher* in the 1930s replaced Pearson at University College. He is well known as the originator of the analysis of variance and developed his method of experimental designs from studying agricultural problems (see Chapter 2).

Moreover, the English psychologist Spearman suggested a very fruitful method of correlation analysis: factorial analysis.

Spearman (1863–1945), after an early military career, trained as a psychologist in the German laboratories (Leipzig, Würzburg, Göttingen) and became reader and then professor at University College in a chair of Mind and Logic. His first contribution to the history of psychology was an article entitled 'General intelligence objectively determined and measured', which appeared in 1904 in the *American Journal of Psychology*. Galton had hypothesized that common causes of variation might emerge through psychological measurement. Spearman established experimenally that in several intelligence tests the subjects were positively correlated in such a way that they could be hierarchically ordered. He interpreted these relations as being dependent on a common factor indicating a general ability. This factor he called G. A matrix of correlations was to be explained by the influence of this common factor and of specific factors corresponding to each test. Later Spearman also recognized the existence of group factors. The synthesis of his work did not appear until 1927 under the title *The abilities of man*.

Factorial analysis, developed in Great Britain by *G. H. Thomson* (1881–1955), professor at Edinburgh, by *Garnett* and *C. Burt* (who succeeded Spearman at London in 1931) and then in America by *Thurstone* (1887–1955) was a new instrument for analysing the structure of human potentialities. It made use of individual differences and their correlations to find out what was common in human behaviour, i.e. the real psychological structure of man. Methods were diversified, then reconciled, the field was extended, especially in the realm of personality (*Eysenck*,[14] *R. B. Cattell*). Certainly there were criticisms, aimed at those who transformed

[14] E.g. in his *Dimensions of Personality*, 1947.

32

factors, mathematicial entities, and sources of hypotheses demanding verification, into psychological facts, but the contribution of factor analysis to our knowledge of the human mind is already considerable.

4 The difficult establishment of psychology within the universities

Given the importance of the English associationist school, and the calibre of its nerve physiologists (among others, *Jackson* (1835–1911), *Sherrington* (1857–1952), and *Head* (1861–1940), it might be imagined that an experimental psychology would have no difficulty in establishing itself. Such was not the case.

The philosophical type of psychology was represented in England at the end of the nineteenth century by men like *Ward* (1843–1925) and *Stout* (1860–1925) who had, oddly enough, succumbed to the influence of act psychology. The first experimental psychologist, in the German sense of the term, was a Doctor of Medicine, *McDougall* (1871–1938), who aligned himself with act psychology on the one hand and with W. James on the other. From 1900 to 1920 he was reader in philosophy at London and then at Oxford, before becoming a professor at Harvard, where he was to become famous for his purposive psychology, which had similarities with Tolman's.[15]

Since 1877 Ward had agitated at Cambridge for a psychophysical laboratory, but the proposal was rejected as sacrilegious. In 1891, however, he gained a little ground. The physiologists, for their part, also gained by the creation of a Readership in Experimental Psychology and Physiology of the Senses, a post occupied by *Rivers* (1864–1932), a former pupil of Hering and of Kraepelin. One of the pupils he had in his small laboratory was *Charles S. Myers* (1873–1946), who succeeded him in 1909. After the 1914–1918 war, Myers abandoned the struggle against academic difficulties and founded in London in 1922 the National Institute for Industrial Psychology whose work was, and still is, brilliant. *Bartlett* (1886–   ) took up the fight and in 1931 became the first titular professor of experimental psychology in the University of Cambridge. In 1928 in London, Spearman had

---

[15] McDougall's work was extremely important and influential. It includes: *Physiological psychology*, 1905; *Introduction to social psychology*, 1908; *Body and Mind*, 1911; *Psychology, the study of behaviour*, 1912; *Outline of abnormal psychology*, 1926.

Paul Fraisse

relinquished his chair of Mind and Logic for a chair of Psychology. Oxford held out until 1947. But to be fair, we should emphasize that even before the creation of chairs, laboratories had managed to spring up here and there.

While mentioning important dates, we should add that the British Psychological Society was founded in 1912 and the *British Journal of Psychology* founded by Ward, Rivers and Myers in 1904.

France

Just as German experimental psychology arose from the meeting of philosophical ideas and psychophysiological problems, and English scientific psychology emerged from evolutionary theory and the psychological problems which it created, French psychology was grafted on to psychopathology as interpreted by philosophers. The first chair of psychology, created for Ribot at the College de France in 1889, was designated a chair of Experimental and Comparative Psychology. Moreover, G. Dumas taught for 30 years at the Sorbonne from a chair of so-called 'experimental psychology' which was not changed to a chair of abnormal psychology until 1939; this only emerged as a chair of experimental psychology in the true sense in 1956. So we shall see that Ribot and particularly Dumas were specialists in psychopathology.

1   The philosophical psychology of the nineteenth century

In the eighteenth century the sensationists had made a profound impression on French philosophers and we see the reaction which they provoked in Maine de Biran. Nineteenth-century philosophy, particularly on the psychological side, was dominated by *Victor Cousin* (1792–1867) and his so-called eclectic school: *Royer-Collard, Thomas Jouffroy, Jules Simon, Paul Janet*. All these came very much under the influence not only of Maine de Biran, but also of the eighteenth-century Scottish school (*Reid, Dugald Stewart*) which, in the face of Hume's scepticism and empiricism, had developed mentalistic concepts in which the mind was assumed to be composed of faculties. They did not have the good fortune to experience the Kantian revolution, and so they still believed

34

that psychology, the science of introspection, could reveal the inner 'principle' of man's mind through his own awareness. Psychology is not simply a science of facts of consciousness, but a philosophy of the mind.

This view, which goes back to Cartesian dualism, was also held by *Bergson* (1859–1941) who, like Ravaisson but with more imagination, subscribed to what this latter called spiritual realism. Bergson in fact used psychological investigations to try to prove that 'experienced time' or memories, was evidence of mental activity, of which the brain was merely the organ.

This philosophical orientation, which was perpetuated in the university tradition, could not accommodate scientific psychology, let alone be its medium. However, the impetus came from outside, through Ribot, who belonged to the English and German schools; he attached French psychology to neuropathology, a field in which France led.

2 Charcot: hypnosis and hysteria

Interest in hypnosis is deep-rooted in France. At the end of the eighteenth century, *Mesmer*, calling it magnetism, achieved a great popular success with his famous *baquet;* in the eighteenth century this esoteric tradition was particularly lively in England, where *Baird* snatched what he called hypnosis out of the realm of magic and gave it a psychological interpretation: an artificial sleep, characterized by monoideism.

France tackled the problem again with the Nancy school (*Liébeault*, 1823–1904) and with *Bernheim* (1837–1919) who used hypnotism as a technique of suggestion to cure patients who were not neurotic. The titles of two of their works give a good indication of the orientation of their thinking: *Du sommeil et des états analogues, considerés surtout au point de vue de l'action de la morale sur le physique* (Liébeault, 1866) and *De la suggestion et ses applications à la thérapeutique* (Bernheim, 1886). Here were the seeds of psychosomatic medicine!

Moreover, Freud, after working with Charcot, was to join these masters in 1889.

It was *Charcot* (1825–93), however, who dominated this era. He was a professor of morbid anatomy (1862), and his clinic became world famous under the name of *École de la Salpêtrière*.

Paul Fraisse

It is not our intention to give a complete picture of his work, but we must stress his great influence which drew scientists from all over the world to the Salpêtrière. His pupils included Janet, Freud and Binet. Charcot was particularly concerned with hysteria. He observed the close similarity between the development of hypnotic states—from lethargy to catalepsy and then to somnambulism—and the progress of hysteria. He considered that to be capable of being hypnotized was a symptom of hysteria, whereas the Nancy school saw it, more correctly, as an indication of suggestibility. But his belief led him to treat those who were, in a sense 'tied in knots' by hypnosis, with some success thus providing the new French school with one of its fundamental characteristics.

3 Ribot and the foundation of scientific psychology

During the reign of eclectic philosophy in France, an outside contribution was needed to get the psychological movement started. It was *Ribot* (1839–1916), a pupil of the École Normale Supérieure and *agrégé* in philosophy, who supplied this in his two works: *Psychologie anglaise contemporaine* (1870) and *Psychologie allemande contemporaine* (1879). His preface of 1870 is a superb manifesto:

> The psychology we are concerned with here will be wholly experimental; it will have as its object only phenomena, their laws and their immediate causes; it will be concerned with neither the soul nor its essence, since this question, being unverifiable, belongs to metaphysics.

At the end of his life he was to reiterate this:

> Psychology is neither spiritualistic nor materialistic, and if it assumes either one of these epithets it forfeits all right to the name of science (Preface to the *Traité de Psychologie*, G. Dumas).

However, this being said, Ribot never actually did any experiments either in the line of Wundt or of Galton. He considered that mental pathology supplies us with sufficient experiments, to which we need only refer.

> Pathological methods touch on both pure observation and experiment. Disease is in fact experimentation of a subtle kind, instituted by nature herself, in well defined circumstances and by processes

36

which are not available to human art. (Psychologie, in *De la méthode dans les sciences*, 1909.)

A complete section of his work was devoted to *diseases of memory* (1881), to *free will* (1883), to *personality* (1885) and to *attention* (1888). During the later part of his career he was pre-occupied with the affective life: *Psychologie des sentiments* (1896); *L'imagination créatrice* (1900); *Logique des sentiments* (1905); *La vie inconsciente et les mouvements* (1914).

In 1885 the Sorbonne recognized the existence of the new discipline and entrusted a course in experimental psychology to Ribot, but it was the Collège de France which offered him a chair in experimental and comparative psychology in 1889.

His influence was great, particularly on the young philosophy students who became interested in the new subject. He suggested to them that they take the same path as he had taken, but advised them to study medicine themselves, so as not to work, as he had done, from second-hand reports. He thus initiated a tradition which has persisted up to the present day through *P. Janet, G. Dumas, Charles Blondel, H. Wallon, A. Ombredane, G. Poyer, D. Lagache* and *J. Favez-Boutonier*. This approach had the advantage that man was studied in his entirety. After clinical psychology, neither English associationism nor German atomism sufficed. Psychologists were thus led to become specifically interested in the higher processes and in the personality as such. The work of Ribot, Janet and Binet are illustrations of this.

4   Pierre Janet (1859–1947)

We must mention the man who best accomplished Ribot's design, although his influence has extended far beyond the nineteenth century almost up to the present day.

Like Ribot, Janet passed through the École Normale Supérieure, and graduated in philosophy. While still teaching philosophy in a lycée at le Havre, he began to study medicine, specializing in psychopathology. At the hospital, he made observations on hallucinated and hysterical patients, which led to his thesis in 1889: *L'automatisme psychologique*, which even then went to two editions. Its sub-title is indicative of its approach: *Essai de psychologie expérimentale sur les formes inférieures de l'activité mentale*. It was an extremely successful book. As early as 1890,

Janet obtained a post in a Paris lycée and, in the same year Charcot made him director of the psychological laboratory at the Salpêtrière. There he finished his medical thesis: *L'état mental des hystériques* (1893) (*The Mental State of Hysterials* Eng. Ed. 1901); to which Charcot wrote a preface praising its attempt to unite clinical work with academic psychology. In 1895 Janet was elected professor at the Sorbonne, where he stayed for a very short time. In 1896 he deputized for Ribot at the Collège de France, replacing him permanently in 1902. For some 40 years, until his retirement in 1936, he enlivened this chair with original, brilliant, and witty lectures, many of which have been published from students' notes. His numerous works have been translated into many languages, and his reputation is international—indeed it is greater in America than in his own country.

To remain faithful to our design of only referring to the impact of a man's work on the development of experimental psychology, we shall not discuss Janet's ideas further. We leave him with regret, for few men have possessed such rich and personal ideas.

Janet practised experimental psychology in the sense in which Ribot understood it. For him, as compared with Freud, there were no frontiers between normal and abnormal psychology and his last, most original works, *Les débuts de l'intelligence* (1935) and *L'intelligence avant le langage* (1936) are completely outside the field of his early research.[16]

Moreover, Pierre Janet was not a man of one theory, despite the fertility of his insights and their ultimate unity. This flexibility distinguishes him from Freud in particular. He deviated, it is true, from the concept of psychology as solely concerned with 'data of consciousness' although he never denied it completely, but psychopathology revealed a new approach—in the same way that animal psychology did for Watson:

> Psychology must be objective in the sense that it must be concerned with what one sees, the actions, movements and attitudes of the subject, his ways of speaking and his words and, consequently, all psychological facts, even if one already knows them, must be definable in terms of observable behaviour. (P. Janet, *Bull. Soc. Franç. Philo.* 1929, p. 78.)

[16] Besides works already quoted, we would mention: *Les névroses et les ideés fixes*, 1898; *Les obsessions et la psychasthénie*, 2 vols. 1926; *L'évolution de la memoire et la notion de temps*, 1928; *La force et la faiblesse psychologique*, 1930.

However, he avoided Watson's excesses of behaviourism. He himself defined very precisely the originality of his conception:

> To make psychology of behaviour applicable to man one must not only account for consciousness, but one must also regard it as something over and above the basic elements of behaviour, not forgetting, when describing them, the higher forms they take, such as believing. This psychology can be described as 'psychology of behaviour'. (Autobiographie, *Etudes phil.* 1946, p. 85–6.)

Thus Janet economized on Watson's roundabout method, and his psychology of behaviour anticipated modern psychology (see p. 80) which integrates into a pattern of conduct both the influence of the situation and that of the conscious and unconscious reactions of the individual to this situation, and explains the actions which impinge on the experimenter or the observer.

Janet studied the conduct of patients, but his interests always went beyond the framework of pathology. He was always trying to discover the phylogenesis and the ontogenesis of behaviour, which led him to stress the great importance of language in psychology and how language is born out of the nature of action. He created symbols, which are still famous: the arrangement of the basket in which a child gathers apples is the beginning of classification, and that of the sentinel alerting his camp is the basis of memory. Language is simply a substitute for action.

5 Georges Dumas (1866–1946)

Dumas was a pupil and the true successor of Ribot. He first graduated in philosophy and then after studying medicine his thesis on *La tristesse et la joie* (1900) opened the way in 1905 to a chair in experimental psychology at the Sorbonne. His Sunday morning lectures at Sainte-Anne are famous. Abnormal psychology, which he taught, was destined to become an aspect of general psychology, particularly that part concerned with effective behaviour. He combined anatomo-physiological, psychological and pathological data with the results of his experimental observations concerning, in particular the emotions and their influence on circulation, breathing and expression.

His influence was assured with the publication of his *Traité de psychologie* (1923–24) and his *Nouveau traité de psychologie*

39

Paul Fraisse

(7 vols. from 1931). These representative works of French psychology contributed greatly to the development of the new science and they are still extremely useful today.

6   The creation of experimental psychology: Alfred Binet

We have concentrated on that aspect of French psychology, which rightly regarded as experimental right from the beginning, so that there should be no doubt of its scientific character. But neither Ribot nor Janet did any experiments, and Dumas devoted only a part of his time to experimentation.

It was *Binet* (1857–1911) who created experimental psychology in the strict sense. His training was original compared with others of his generation: *licencié* in law, then *licencié* and doctor of natural sciences. He was on the fringe and was to remain there. The Collège de France rejected him in favour of Janet, and the Sorbonne preferred Dumas. Moreover, on Ribot's advice, he too took the path through the Salpêtrière, and if his first book shows mainly Taine's influence (*La psychologie du raisonnement*, 1886; *The Psychology of Reasoning*, Eng. Ed. 1899), the subsequent ones were more in Charcot's footsteps (*Le magnétisme animal*, 1887; *Les altérations de la personnalité*, 1892; *Alterations of Personality*, Eng. Ed. 1896).

Nevertheless, Binet was not a pupil, but an innovator. The way was opened to him when he was nominated, in 1892, co-director of the new laboratory of physiological psychology, created in 1889 under the directorship of Beaunis, a physiologist.

In 1895 he became the sole director of this laboratory which was attached to the École Pratique des Hautes Études at the Sorbonne.

It was supplied with all Wundt's material, but Binet guarded his independence in relation to the German school. Unlike Wundt, he considered that experimental psychology should study the higher mental processes, particularly thought and intelligence.

A thorough experimentalist, he believed more in facts than in theories. This submissiveness to facts caused him to alter course several times during his career.

Moreover, his method was a new one: comparison. He approached psychology through the study of exceptional subjects,

40

first mental patients and then those with supernormal abilities (great calculators, chess players) and finally children, in whom he became interested towards the end of his life, forsaking even his laboratory at the Sorbonne for that of the school at La Grange-aux-Belles.

The comparative method led him to develop an individual psychology, but his main concern was always to know 'how the mental machine functions'.

From Taine, his studies on intelligence led him to systematic introspection (quite independently of the Würzburg school, from which he was later to claim priority for the Paris School). He made use of what he called the questioning method, culminating in *Étude expérimental de l'intelligence* (1903) a study carried out mainly on his two daughters, Armande and Marguerite. He arrived at the same conclusions as the Würzburg school: that there is an imageless thought which escapes introspection. Despite this result he remained faithful—in theory—to introspection although he did not believe that it can give us direct or infallible knowledge of psychic facts. In practice he abandoned it in creating his *Échelle métrique de l'intelligence* (1905 and 1908). The educational authorities, anxious to improve the teaching of backward children, set up a commission to find means of doing this. Binet devised an ingenious solution to this problem: to measure the intellectual level directly by using a series of tests, knowing the level at which they are passed by normal children. In this way he supplied a means, not only of understanding intelligence, but of classifying individuals, thus providing the foundations of quantitative methods in psychology. In a few months he was able to develop a satisfactory test simply by drawing on his long experimental researches on memory, attention, imagination and children's intelligence. These researches had given him the opportunity to devise many simple but revealing tests. His stroke of genius was to use them to determine a mental age which could be compared with the chronological age.

Others, particularly in England, had tried to measure intelligence, but mainly from tests of a sensory nature. Binet introduced a revolution by measuring intelligence directly from performance. It was his experimental findings which guided him in his practical solutions, but even the success of his scale, especially abroad, set him examining his theories. In 1907, following the lead of Thomas

Simon, whose name is still associated with Binet's in the construction of the test, and bearing in mind English structural psychology based on the association of ideas, he wrote: 'In counterpoint to a structural psychology we propose making actions the object of thought and seeking the essential quality of thought in a system of action' in the same article he concludes: 'Psychology has become the science of action'. (*Année psychol.* 1908, p. 145 and 146).[18]

7 Advances in experimental psychology

From its beginnings in the nineteenth century, the new psychology became more securely entrenched. In 1896 one of Wundt's pupils, *Bourdon* (1860–1943), founded the second French psychological laboratory at Rennes, where he worked mainly on perception. This laboratory, taken over by *Bourloud* is still active today. In 1906 *Foucault* (1865–1947) founded a laboratory at Montpellier which unfortunately no longer exists.[19]

The new psychology also produced its journals: in 1876 Ribot founded the *Revue philosophique* which was, in fact, the first organ of psychology. Since then, however, it has become more faithful to its title than to the intentions of its founder. In 1894 Binte began to publish *L'année psychologique*. In 1904 Janet and Dumas created the *Journal de psychologie normale et pathologique*. In 1901 the Société Française de Psychologie was formed. These victories must not give a false impression, however. If the École Pratique des Hautes Études and the Collège de France welcomed scientific

[18] Binet's principal works are: *La psychologie du raisonnement*, 1886 (*The Psychology of Reasoning*, Eng. Ed. 1899); *Le magnétisme animal* (with Féré), 1887 (*Animal Magnetism*, Eng. Ed. 1887); *Les altérations de la personnalité*, 1892 (*Alterations of Personality*, Eng. Ed, 1896); *Introduction à la psychologie expérimentale*, 1894; *La psychologie des grands calculateurs et joueurs d'échecs*, 1894; *Contribution à l'étude du système nerveux sous-intestinal des insectes* (thesis, 1894); *La suggestibilité*, 1900; *L'étude expérimentale de l'intelligence*, 1903; *L'âme et le corps*, 1906, *The Mind and the Brain*, London 1907; *Les idées modernes sur les enfants*, 1911.

[19] From Bourdon's work, we would particularly mention: *La perception visuelle de l'espace*, 1902; *L'intelligence*, 1926.

From Foucault's: *La psychophysique*, 1901; *Cours de psychologie*, 1926–8, 2 vols.

From the work of Bourloud, (1888–1954), who was mainly in the tradition of the Würzburg school: *La pensée d'après les recherches experimentales de H. J. Watt, de Messer et Bühler*, 1927; *Principe d'une psychologie des tendances*, 1938; *Le caractère*, 1942; *Psychologie*, 1948.

psychology, the University reserved judgement for a long time. In Paris it was through the Institut de Psychologie, founded in 1921 by Henri Piéron that scientific psychology was first taught, and until 1939 there were more foreign students than French ones.

However, the creation in 1948 of a masters' degree in psychology marked the beginning of a new era and after that chairs in psychology multiplied.

Henri Piéron (1881–   ) was the pioneer of modern French psychology and, as we shall see later (see p. 56), of a psychology of behaviour, to which subject all his writing was devoted. Piéron graduated in philosophy and pursued medical and scientific studies which culminated in 1912 in his work on *Le mécanisme du sommeil*. His entire training was in the École des Hautes Études. In 1912 he succeeded Binet as director of the laboratory of physiological psychology, and then went to the Collège de France where a chair of sensory physiology was especially created for him in 1923. He was in the great tradition of French nerve physiologists. As a young man he had been secretary to Janet and later worked in Binet's laboratory. Although the scientific aspects of psychologists interested him, he was first and foremost a psychophysiologist and his best work concerned animals and the study of sensation. He summed up his work in the provocative title which he gave to his recent collection of articles: *De l'actinie à l'homme* (1958 and 1959).

Piéron also left his mark on French psychology through the liveliness which he instilled into institutions and the uses to which he put psychology. In 1911 he returned to Binet's laboratory and *L'année psychologique* appeared under his direction for 50 years, with important contributions from him. He founded the Institut de Psychologie and the Institut d'Orientation Professionelle which he still directs. He enlivened the Société Française de Psychologie and ensured the representation of French psychology at all the international congresses from 1900 onwards. He was the first president of the Union Internationale de Psychologie Scientifique (1951–54).

What is more, Piéron does not belong to past history, but to the present and he has written the chapter on psychophysics for this treatise.[20]

[20] Henri Piéron's works include: *La psychologie du rêve du point de vue médical,* 1902; *Technique de psychologie expérimentale* (with Toulouse) 1904 (*Principles*

Paul Fraisse

America

'American psychology inherited its physical body from the German experimentalists, but got its mind from Darwin' (Boring, p. 506). America is a land of émigrés. Although it has welcomed everything and everyone, it has been able to shape its own traditions and, in its turn, to become both principle and model. Because we have chosen to mention it last, it must not be thought that it is behind Europe in achievement. Often it has led the way. However, the riches of its creative work has been so great and so varied that we shall regretfully have to omit biographies and deal only with the main currents of thought.

The growth of experimental psychology in America is like the growth of its towns and industries. In Europe psychology had to fight for a place among disciplines and institutions, to get itself recognized as a new science and not simply as a branch of philosophy. America is new, its universities do not aim to conserve, but to create. Scarcely had America welcomed psychology than it gave it a new look and helped it to come to terms with its own problems.

1 William James (1842-1910)

James was the first American psychologist and has numerous descendants. His very interesting life is known to the French reader, thanks particularly to the portrait given by Zazzo (1939).

His career was varied. He began as a painter and then studied chemistry. Finally he took up medicine, but made a break in his studies to take part in a naturalist expedition to the Amazon basin and to travel for a year and a half in Germany. From then on his health began to fail, and he often had to interrupt his studies and later his teaching. He now believed that his true vocation was philosophical, but he nevertheless continued his scientific career. In 1872 he was nominated psychology instructor

of Experimental Psychology, Eng. Ed. 1920); *L'évolution de la mémoire,* 1910; *Le problème physiologique du sommeil,* 1913; *Le cerveau et la pensée,* 1923 (*Thought and the Brain,* Eng. Ed. 1927); *Psychologie expérimentale,* 1927; *Psychologie zoologique,* 1941; *La sensation, guide de vie,* 1946; *Psychologie différentielle,* 1949; *Traité de psychologie appliquée,* 1949-1959.

at Harvard and became interested in German physiological psychology. In 1875 two rooms were put at his disposal (some like to consider this as the first psychological laboratory in the world) in which students taking his course in 'the relations between physiology and psychology' were able to carry out experiments.

In 1878 he began his famous *Principles of Psychology*. This work, which he thought he could write in two years in fact took him twelve. It was a masterpiece and had an immediate success and it remains a classic as much for the quality of its presentation as for the author's theories. Moreover, in 1890, when his book was published, he gave up psychology as he had given up painting, chemistry and medicine, and devoted himself to philosophy, becoming a celebrated pragmatist (*Pragmatism*, 1907).

James did not experiment, and even had a personal aversion to the practice; however, he was an initiator: he sent his student *Stanley Hall* to study under Wundt. It was with James that *Thorndike* began his experiments in animal psychology; *Dewey*, *Angell* and *Woodworth* were his pupils. And he directed American psychology along its first path: functionalism. James rejected the elementism of the current German psychology. Of course, he started from the consciousness, but what was important for him were not the data *in* consciousness, but the data *of* consciousness— a personal consciousness whose continuity is the basis of personal identity, an ever-changing consciousness and one which never has the same sensation or the same thought twice: a consciousness which selects what suits it from the world in which it is immersed.

All this anticipated Würzburg and agreed with the expressions used by Brentano and Wundt. But James did not speak of the act. Our states of consciousness were, according to him, a *function*.

> They reveal to us things which are either objects and physical phenomena or other states of consciousness.

He went on:

> Consciousness . . . has in all probability been evolved like all other functions, for a use . . .

This phrase is revealing: Americans had read Darwin and their pioneer way of life gave them a more than academic understanding of his thought.

This would be an appropriate place to recall the quarrel about

Paul Fraisse

emotion which was unleashed by the publication of James in 1884, but we shall mention this in the chapter on emotions. Let us merely record that James considered the organism in its entirety, in striking contrast to theories like Wundt's in which emotion is treated as a reaction stemming from the comprehension of sensory material.

2 Dewey and functionalism

Before dealing with developments in experimental psychology, we shall first finish our consideration of the theoretical position. Psychology became functionalist, not because James took this standpoint, or even because functionalism found its theorist in Dewey. All the Americans at that time were functionalist and Boring, as historian and eye-witness, stresses the fact that the crucial problem for the New World was in fact adaptation to the environment.

Strictly speaking, no-one called it 'functionalism'. James and Dewey spoke simply of function. Titchener, who carried on Wundt's tradition in America, defined his own psychology as structuralist to distinguish himself from what he called the *functionalism* of the Chicago school. What exactly was the Chicago school? In historical terms, it was the coming together in Chicago in 1894 of *J. Dewey* (1859–1952)[21], *J. R. Angell* (1869–1949), *G. H. Mead* and *A. W. Moore*.

The first important contribution this school made was Dewey's article *The reflex arc concept in psychology* (1896). His aim was to write a critique of atomism, which he based not on the elements of consciousness but on the reflex arc. The important thing for him was the co-ordination of the elements of a response and not the elements themselves or even their sum: Even a simple reflex is still a co-ordination: in fact there is not a stimulus *and* a response, a stimulus is only a stimulus insofar as it awakens a response, and a response is a response only because there is a stimulus. The reflex, Dewey maintained, was a means of setting up a useful connection. It is the action of a living organism, adjusting to its environment.

[21] Dewey is best known as a psychologist and philosopher of education, to which he devoted the best part of his career, first at Chicago, but mainly at Teacher's College, Columbia from 1904 to 1930. His works include *Psychology*, 1886; *Human nature and conduct*, 1922.

After this first step, the ideas of the school asserted themselves. Following a statement by Angell, Dewey's successor, it is possible to summarise this in three propositions:

(a) 'psychology of mental operations' as distinct from the psychology of mental elements,
(b) 'psychology of the purposiveness of consciousness' in which the mind is 'primarily engaged in mediating between the environment and the needs of the organism',
(c) 'psychology of the total mind-body organism' reinstating semi-conscious behaviour at an organismic level.

The Chicago school still presented psychological problems in terms of consciousness, but in a new way. In another social context its concept would have culminated in a philosophical theory, like the movements which led to Bergsonism or to phenomenology. We need only remind ourselves of the evolution of Brentano's successors. But in America the outcome was to be quite different. These views harmonized with the approaches of animal psychology, educational psychology and the use of mental tests. We must emphasise that Watson was Angell's pupil and in 1903 had taken his doctorate with him on the neurological and psychological maturation of the white rat. But Watson was to refuse point blank to present the problem of performance in terms of consciousness, while the Americans' loyalty to the functionalist point of view allowed contemporary psychology to reach a compromise by interpreting human activities in terms of Janet's 'conduct' rather than Watsonian 'behaviour'.

3 The champion of experimental psychology: Stanley Hall (1844–1924)

Hall, the son of a farmer, first prepared for the ministry before becoming professor of psychology at Antioch College, Ohio. His early studies had already taken him to Germany for three years. In 1874 when Wundt's *Physiologische Psychologie* appeared, he found his true vocation and wanted to study in Leipzig. However, he had for a time to accept a post of tutor at Harvard, which enabled him, under the direction of James, to take a doctorate in philosophy (the first in the course of scientific psychology) on the muscular perception of space (1878). He then left for

Paul Fraisse

Leipzig where he worked with Wundt and with the physiologist Ludwig. He also worked with Kries in Berlin.

On his return to America he was invited to lecture at Johns Hopkins University, Baltimore, and in 1883 he founded the first psychological laboratory in America. The first of many, for by 1892 there were already 17. *Dewey*, *J. McK. Cattell*, *Sanford*, *Jastrow* all worked in this first laboratory. In 1887 Hall founded the first American psychological journal, the *American Journal of Psychology*, and in 1888 he became the first president of the new Clark University at Worcester, Mass. He taught psychology there and founded a new laboratory which he gave over to his pupil, E. C. Sanford.

In 1892, at his instigation, 31 psychologists created the American Psychological Association of which he was the first president. He founded the *Pedagogical Seminary* (now the *Journal of Genetic Psychology*) and in 1915 the *Journal of Applied Psychology*.

This 'founder', who has himself described his position as an artificial one, was not content to practise laboratory psychology. His interest in developmental stages in animals and man led him towards genetic psychology, in which he made intensive use of the questionnaire method. His main book is devoted to adolescence.

Always open to every advance in psychology, Hall was the first to invite Freud and Jung to America. In 1909 they attended conferences at Clark University. It was with great interest that he discovered Pavlov's work. His last book, *Senescence* (1922) introduced yet another new subject to psychology.

4   The other founders

Among the founders of American psychology in these years 1880–90, besides Stanley Hall, we must mention: *Ladd* 1842–1921 who gave America its first textbook of psychology, *Elements of Physiological Psychology; Scripture* (1864–1945) who developed the Yale laboratory where *C. E. Seashore* (1866–1949) began research into problems of tonal audition and prepared a work on the psychology of music; *Baldwin* (1861–1934) who, like Scripture, was trained in Germany but who also visited the Salpêtrière.

Despite his preference for theoretical work, Baldwin created the Toronto and Princeton laboratories (1893), founded the *Psychological Review* (1894), the *Psychological Index* and, ten years

48

later with Cattell, the *Psychological Bulletin*. Baldwin took up a functionalist position and his thought was to a great extent influenced by Darwin's theories. More a theorist than an experimentalist, he devoted the second half of his life mainly to philosophy. He was a great friend of France, and supported America's decision to enter the war in 1917. After his retirement he chose to live in Paris, and he died there in November, 1934.

James McKeen Cattell (1866–1944) played a particularly important role. Twice he worked with Wundt and obtained his doctorate under him in 1886. On his return to America he founded first the laboratory at Pennsylvania, then that of Columbia University in 1891. He was to remain there for 26 years. His experimental contributions on reaction time, association, perception, reading and psychophysics are numerous. In connection with each of these problems he was particularly concerned with individual differences, following Galton's lead without being deliberately influenced by him. It is well known that he was the first to speak of mental tests (Mental tests and their measurement, *Mind*, 1890, 15, 373–80) and towards the end of his life he became preoccupied with applied psychology, notably in the Psychological Corporation, a large private company.

Cattell was a very active man and editor of several journals. His influence was felt through his pupils, in particular *Thorndike*, whom we will come back to later, and *Woodworth* (1869–   ), who, after working with him for a long time, succeeded him at Columbia University and taught there until 1942. Today Woodworth is still the man who best represents American experimental psychology in his work and through the influence which his writing has had. As a functionalist, he endeavoured to show the agreements rather than the disagreements between psychologists; his work, *Dynamic Psychology* 1917, put into concrete form a twenty-year project which he had called a 'motivology'. Processes responding to internal stimuli could themselves become drives.

5   Structuralism v. functionalism

These pioneers all adhered more or less to functionalism. But *Titchener* (1867–1927) meanwhile managed to carry on another school, faithful to Wundt's teachings. It must be admitted that many of his colleagues came from Germany, but they brought

Paul Fraisse

with them only the basic tenets and methods which they adapted
to the American climate. Their activities included the study of
animals, children and mental patients. They were particularly
concerned with individual differences and the application of
psychology. Titchener withdrew into his laboratory. He built up
an autonomous science of general laws of the mind. His controversy
with Baldwin over reaction time is famous (1895–96). Lange
had demonstrated, in Wundt's laboratory, that reaction time with
a motor predisposition to act quicker was than reaction time with
a sensory predisposition. Baldwin cast doubt on this law and
maintained that there were sensory and motor types of observers.
Titchener opposed this thesis which was not in fact incompatible
with the first. He would not accept that there were different
kinds of minds—a statement of individual difference could not be
a law unless it could be related to specific conditions.

Titchener was a proponent of content psychology, faithful to
introspection right to the end. Furthermore, he was English by
birth and he became increasingly isolated at Cornell University
where he taught from 1892–1926. However his authority and
erudition were to gain him many pupils. *Washburn, Pillsbury,
Bentley, Whipple, Baird, Boring* and *Dallenbach* trained under him.
With them he formed a select group of psychologists calling themselves, in defiance of all the others, 'experimental psychologists'.
This attitude has in no small measure contributed to a persistent
misunderstanding of the nature of experimental psychology,
since it claimed to distinguish it from child psychology, abnormal
psychology and even, in Titchener's time, from animal psychology.
This misconception is still found in some recent French works.[22]

Titchener was not wrong, however, to maintain that individual
differences become objects of science only when they are explic-
able. Science proceeds from the general to the particular. And it is
true that today we are beginning to go beyond the mere ascertainment of the existence of individual differences when establishing laws of differentiation.[23]

[22] France, however, with Ribot and Janet, knew how to take the word 'experimental' in its true sense, as designating a scientific method and not an aim, or a
theory or a place of work.
[23] His principal works include: *An outline of psychology,* 1896; *Experimental
psychology: a manual of laboratory practice,* 1901–05; *Lectures on the elementary psychology of feeling and attention,* 1908; *Lectures on the elementary
psychology of thought processes,* 1909; *A textbook of psychology,* 1909–10.

50

6 The rise of animal psychology

Zoologists have always, unwittingly, practised psychology to some degree. But the psychological significance of studies on animals only became apparent with Darwin. We have already mentioned the work of the Englishmen Romanes and Lloyd Morgan and shown how, in their keenness to establish the continuity between animals and man, they had been tempted to endow animals with qualities which they *wished* to find in them.

It was from Germany that there came another, entirely mechanistic conception of behaviour. *Jacques Loeb* (1859–1924) applied to animals the theory of tropism, taken from botany (1890). From 1891 until his death, Loeb taught in America. His theory was dialectically opposed to functionalist theories. Moreover, he concentrated on the lower organisms, whilst they were concerned with vertebrates.

For the functionalists psychology, even at the end of the nineteenth century, was still based on introspection, and the study of animals presented a major difficulty from this point of view. They tried to solve this by recourse to analogy, inference or empathy. But these means themselves had meaning only when applied to vertebrates. What became of empathy when one was studying the behaviour of the paramecia? In any case, Loeb, who studied only the responses of organisms to physical forces, found it easy to dispense with empathy.

During these same years *Beer, Bethe* and *von Uexküll*, who together constituted a German objectivist school, realized that they could not account for animal behaviour either in physiological terms or in current psychological terms, whose significance was linked with introspection and subjectivism. They put forward a new terminology using, for example 'reception' for sensation, 'phonoreception' for audition, and 'resonance' for memory (1899). However, at the same time biologists, such as *Jennings* (1868–1947) refused to accept the mechanistic position, which seemed to them to be unable to account for the variability of behaviour—even in the protozoa.

Animal psychology received a new impetus with the early works of *Thorndike* (1874–1949). His attention was aroused by W. James's *Principles* and he went to study under him at Harvard, where he became interested in the intelligence of chicks. At first he did not know where he could study them; he kept them in his bedroom, and then in James's cellar. Then Cattell suggested that he should accept the post of tutor at Columbia, and gave him enough space to continue his experiments. So Thorndike set off with two of his chicks in a basket. In 1898 he took his doctorate. His thesis: *Animal intelligence, an experimental study of the associative processes in animals*. Until that time animal psychology had been pursued mainly by more or less systematic observation. Thorndike took from Lloyd Morgan the idea of learning by trial and error and also the law of effect. But he defined them more exactly by demonstrating how success determines the nature of the association which leads to that success. Thus he gave to association—and to learning in general—his second law, the first being the law of frequency. But he went still further and invented new experimental techniques as well, in particular, puzzle-boxes, boxes presenting a problem or secret, whose system must be discovered by the animal. In 1897 he also devised the maze technique, the maze being constructed of books placed on their sides so that the chicks had to discover the way out. However, it was *Small* who really established the maze technique by making a scale model of the Hampton Court maze and using rats, animals admirably adapted to this kind of situation (1900).

Thorndike's thesis was the beginning of an experimental movement in animal psychology, although he himself did not long remain in this sphere. Cattell, in 1899 suggested that he applied his techniques to children. He continued his studies at Teacher's College, Columbia, doing research on the law of effect in children and adults, combining theoretical research and practical work.[24]

We have already mentioned Watson's thesis of 1903, and to this we must add his article on somesthetic sensations of the rat in the maze situation (1907). This was the last time that Watson used inferential methods to interpret his results in terms of consciousness.

The movement towards comparative psychology was by then general. Laboratories existed at Clark, Harvard and Chicago. In 1910 there were eight. In 1911 the *Journal of Animal Behavior*

---

[24] Thorndike's main works are: 'Animal intelligence', *Psychol. Monog.* 1898; *Educational psychology*, 1903; *An introduction to the theory of mental and social measurements*, 1904; *Educational psychology*, 3 vols. 1913–1914; *Fundamentals of learning*, 1932; *Human nature and the social order*, 1940.

was founded. Of all the psychologists attached to it, the greatest was *Yerkes* (1876–1956). From 1900 until his retirement in 1941, he worked on crabs, turtles, frogs, pigeons, crows, doves and monkeys. At first based at Yale, he was later able to create laboratories in Florida for the study of apes. After his retirement they were called the Yerkes Laboratories of Primate Biology.

The progress of comparative psychology in the first half of the twentieth century was often linked with the development of laboratory techniques. *Hamilton* devised the multiple choice apparatus (1911) which Yerkes perfected (1915); *Hunter* devised the technique of delayed responses (1913) and the temporal maze (1920), *Warden* the obstruction apparatus (1926), *Lashley* the jumping box (1930) and *Skinner* his famous box (1938).

Comparative psychology opened the way to behaviourism. It was successful in establishing laws which produced a better understanding, by analogy, of the major human functions, and suggested useful methods in child psychology. It remained faithful, it is true, to the concepts of classical psychology, considered as a science of consciousness, but it became increasingly apparent that this heritage was sterile and even paralysing. Functionalism had already directed the thought of psychologists in another direction by concentrating on the principle of adaptation. Applied psychology, on the other hand, achieved its first successes with mental tests, which owed their effectiveness neither to introspection nor to an interpretation based on analyses of consciousness.[25] The time was ripe for the behaviourist revolution.

Russia

From the outset the development of Russian psychology has been influenced by physiological psychology. *I. M. Sechenov* (1829–1905) was a physiologist trained at St. Petersburg, but from 1836 to 1863 he travelled all over Europe and worked with all the great psychologists and in particular the Germans, Ludwig, Johannes Müller, Helmholtz and the Frenchman Claude Bernard. During his career at St. Petersburg, Odessa and finally Moscow, he was

[25] It is well known that the practice of mental tests received a considerable boost, in America and elsewhere, from the success of the methods used in 1917 to create the American army. It is interesting to recall that it was Yerkes who then directed the army's psychological services.

mainly interested in the nervous system. He discovered that spinal reflexes were inhibited by the action of the cerebral cortex (*The reflexes of the brain*, in Russian, 1863). In 1870 he published an article entitled 'Who must investigate the problems of psychology, and how'? To the question 'Who'? he replied: the physiologist; and to the question 'How'? he replied 'by studying reflexes'. This was an original position for an age when introspection was the only method, and it was to leave a strong impression on Russian psychology.

I. P. Pavlov (1849–1936) was not one of Sechenov's pupils, but he was greatly influenced by his work. He too began his career as a physiologist, and he made a name for himself in physiology by discovering, in particular, the neural connections of the pancreas.

From studies on digestion he formulated a technique which would enable him to collect internal secretions, and thus discovered that a gastric secretion could precede the absorption of food. He discovered conditioned reflexes which he called, at first, psychical reflexes (1903). His stroke of genius was to see immediately the significance of this method for the study of higher nervous activity and for psychology as a whole; his work, until his death, had great singleness of purpose. We shall see later how he supplied Watson with the principle for the objective study of behaviour. Pavlov was one of the creators of modern psychology, and he was awarded a Nobel prize in 1904.[26]

V. M. Bekhterev (1851–1927) was more a psychiatrist than a physiologist. In 1907 he founded the Institute of Psychoneurology at St. Petersburg, where he used the method of conditioned reflexes. In 1910 he published an *Objective Psychology* and in 1917 *General Principles of Human Reflexology*. Bekhterev invented the term *reflexology*, which he defined as 'a scientific discipline which poses the problem of studying the response reaction to external or internal stimuli' (quoted by Bauer, 1952, p. 55).[27]

Thus, before Watson, Pavlov and Bekhterev had founded an objective psychology, without recognizing it as such. Pavlov

[26] English translations of Pavlov's works include: *Conditioned Reflexes*, 1927; *Lectures on Conditioned Reflexes*, 1929; *The Work of the Digestive Glands*, 1910.
[27] French translations of Bekhterev's works include: *L'activité psychique et la vie;* trs. Dr. Keraval, Paris, Boulanger, 1907; *La psychologie objective*, trs. Kostelyeff, Paris, Alcan, 1913; *La réflexologie collective*, trs. Kostelyeff, Neuchatel, Delachaux and Niestlé, 1957.

claimed to be studying higher nervous activity and Bekhterev his new discipline, reflexology.

After the Soviet revolution, *Kornilov*, at the head of the Moscow Institute of Psychology, developed a reactology, based on the recording of the duration, strength and form of reactions, taking into account subjective experience to a certain extent. *Vygotski* deviated slightly from the mechanist position in assigning a role to consciousness, which he regarded as the ability of the organism to provide its own stimulation. This was to mediate such instrumental processes as memory or language. His pupils, *Luria* and *Leontiev* who, together with *Teplov*, dominate present-day psychology, attempted to reconcile the views of their master and Pavlov.

3 The behaviourist revolution

1 Origins

Psychology as the behaviorist views it. When this article by Watson appeared in the Spring 1913 issue of the *Psychological Review* it opened a new era in psychology as a whole, and particularly in experimental psychology.

We call this event a revolution, but only on condition that its impact is precisely defined. Behaviourism modified our conception of psychology and, more particularly of its subject matter. It was not however, the actual beginning. In fact, the practice had for a long time preceded the doctrine. With Fechner's studies of differential thresholds, Wundt's work on reaction times, Ebbinghaus' on the memorisation of meaningless syllables, Dumas' studies on bodily reactions under emotion, and Binet's work on the intellectual levels of children, were we not already well advanced in the study of behaviour?

If Watson's article was of the greatest importance, it is because it marked a ruthless break with established ideas and because for several years the author defended his position in polemical writings and with burning conviction.

The doctrinal argument evolved from the works of many whose principal steps we have already noted. Boring traces the history of behaviourism back to Descartes who, in his conception of 'animal-machines' was in effect an ancestor of behaviourist psychology. The same could be said of La Mettrie, who applied Descartes' concept of animals to man (see p. 4). Among the philosophers, August Comte must also be given a place in the genealogy. His three ages of humanity are well known: theological, metaphysical and positive, or scientific. In this final stage only truths supported by observation or experiment are accepted and so psychology was excluded from his scientific system. A. Comte was the first to demonstrate that introspection, the method then current, was invalid because our mental life cannot continue unaffected while it is observing itself. He maintained that the only possibility was a social science in which man is studied in relation to his fellows.

If Pavlov was the first among psychologists to study the laws of behaviour without recourse to mentalistic concepts, the first person clearly to formulate the programme and the point of view of behaviourist psychology was Henri Piéron in 1908 in his inaugural lecture at the École Pratique des Hautes Études on *L'évolution du psychisme*. In it he maintained that psychology, if it wished to be scientific, could not take the unverifiable facts of consciousness as its object:

> If psychological research is not concerned with consciousness, what else should it be concerned with that is not already studied in physiology? It should be concerned with the *activity* of organisms and their sensori-motor relations with their surroundings, with what the Americans call behavior, the Germans *das Verhalten*, the Italians *il comportamento* and which we [the French] rightly call *le comportement*. While physiology is concerned with the understanding of how systems of communication work, taken in isolation, psychology is concerned with the complex interplay of these systems and their function, which enables life to be continued and perpetuated; (for example) taking the differentiation of the sexes, the pursuit of the female and the acceptance of the male are indispensable preliminaries to the reproductive function; however physiology ignores them. (*Revue du mois*, March 1908, p. 292; *De l'actinie à l'homme*, 1958, vol. I, p. 4).

Piéron's entire work bears out this idea. If the protected himself by creating a school, it was because he preferred the study of facts to doctrinal battles. But he created his own revolution before Watson.

2 Watson (1878–1958)

In 1907 Watson studied the 'sensations' used by the rat to find its way round a maze. We have already mentioned that he took his doctorate in Chicago. He became a professor of animal psychology there. From 1908 to 1920 Watson taught at Johns Hopkins, and it was there—where the first American laboratory had been created—that Watson developed the theory of behaviourism.

After his first article, in 1913, his thought entered a new stage, when he realized that the conditioned reflex presented him with the 'key to its construction', to quote his own words. To this subject he devoted his presidential address to the American Psychological Association (1916). *Psychology from the Standpoint of a Behaviorist* (1919) showing that all psychological problems could be approached from a new point of view. Although Watson was to continue to fight for the cause of behaviourism, he left the university in 1921 and went into business.[28]

Watson's behaviourism can be explained mainly by the failure of 'pure' introspection. Introspection disclosed its limitations with Külpe and Binet, since they had to admit that imageless thought existed. But even this result could not become scientific. It was unverifiable, and Titchener's rigour only served to emphasize its inadequacy. At Würzburg Ach claimed that as far as sensation and image were concerned, there was something impalpable which he called *Bewussheit*, which might be translated into French as '*vigilance*' and into English as 'awareness'. The problem of the number and nature of the components of mental life had always been the object of dispute between schools of psychology. Titchener denounced in Ach what he called stimulus-error. According to him, Ach was confusing a fact of consciousness with his own interpretation, which was a question of logic. Having only this to go on, who could decide between Ach and Titchener?

The problem centred around the accuracy of observation. Science depends on the scientist's perception reading of an outline, a graph, observation of a reaction or of phenomena in general. The criterion of the value of an observation may be sought in conviction or internal evidence; however, these only serve to establish the coherence of a thought not its objectivity.

---

[28] Also: *Behavior: an introduction to comparative psychology*, 1914; *Behaviorism*, 1925; *The behavior of the newborn infant*, 1929.

If this criterion remained the philosophers' keystone, scientists sought to substitute another—*consistency*, the cross-checking of inter-subject observation. Science socialized the approach to phenomena.

Then Watson, as an animal psychologist, maintained that the difficulties encountered by introspection did not exist in animal psychology and that the methods of the latter could be satisfactorily applied to child psychology. Psychology had now only to renounce introspection and to be content with external observation like all the other natural sciences.

But method and material could not be dissociated, and a break with one entailed a new conception of the other. The sort of psychology that Watson practised could not remain a science of the data of consciousness. It became the 'study of what man does, from his birth until his death'—in a word, of his behaviour.

Watson did not deny the existence of consciousness, as is often said of him, but he denied that consciousness could be an object for study or an explanatory principle. Certain spiritualists who more or less lumped together the mind, the soul and the consciousness, objected to this. Admittedly Watson's rebellion went a little too far. He virtually emptied man of all content in order to study him better. But his extreme positivism was useful in that it freed psychology of an extreme egocentricity. Not all psychic life takes place in the consciousness, whether one conceives of it as an active principle or as an area of association of mental elements. Watson went to the limit: the study of behaviour consists in establishing the relations existing between stimulation and response in the organism. More precisely, being given a response, there must be a group of antecedents serving as a cause for this effect. Thus:

> The stimulus being given, psychology must predict the response or, inversely, the response being given, psychology must specify the nature of the stimulus.

Human activity comes down to the stimulus-response pair, symbolized as S-R.

What should be understood by stimulus and by response?

By stimulus, Watson meant the sum of excitation which acts on the organism at a given moment:

> light of different wavelengths, sound waves of different frequencies and amplitude, fine particles affecting the olfactory organs . . . and

lastly muscular movement and glandular secretions which can in turn serve as stimuli by acting on sensitive nerves.

More often, behaviour is determined by a complex collection of stimuli; Watson talked of environment or of situation.

By response, he meant:

the body of changes which is produced in the unstriped muscles, the muscles and the glandular secretions.

These definitions, which seem amusing to us today, emphasize the fact that the revolution overran its objectives. On the one hand there was a description of situations in physical terms and on the other a description of responses in physiological terms. A strict application of this method would have ended in utter confusion, because if there are constants in the situation and in the response, they can be extracted only by a psychological analysis made in terms of objects, persons and relations on the one hand and of acts on the other. This victory was to be established by the work in the following decade, for neither Watson nor any of the other behaviourists were able to apply his programme to the letter.

This is made clear in the case of language. Watson considered it as behaviour. He maintained that language was a verbal response which must be described in terms of lip movements, tongue movements, laryngeal movements, etc. But when Watson turned to verbal responses he did not make use of this psychophysiological aspect, but in fact, used the *content* of verbal responses, that is to say a system of symbols. Moreover, by interpreting these symbols as responses, he gave language its true importance; it is communication of information, and not a direct apprehension of meaning.

There remained, of course the problems of thought and image. Here Watson introduced an important distinction between *explicit*, easily observable, behaviour and *implicit* behaviour. He maintained that what introspection treated as thought or image corresponded to implicit responses—rough outlines of movements, gestures, expressions and, above all, words. But these implicit responses, according to Watson, were a false window rather than an established and studied reality. Admittedly, as both Ribot and the Chicago school emphasized, ideas can induce motor effects, and genetics show a syncretic relationship between

Paul Fraisse

thought and language, but we know that there can be total inhibition of laryngeal response in the adult.

3 Behaviourism and physiology

Behaviourism is often accused of desiring to reduce psychology to physiology and the manner in which Watson definted situation and response would seem to justify this reproach.

It is true to say that in one sense, Watson's outlook, like Piéron's, was reductionist. In 1908 Piéron said:

When the progress of physiology provides an adequate expression for the modalities of behaviour, scientific psychology will lose its individuality, as physiology will one day undoubtedly be entirely swallowed up by chemistry and chemistry itself will find—in physics—the mathematical symbolism which will, by the harmonic unity of its formulae, permit the expression of the apparent diversity of natural forms.

And in this perspective, Piéron did not cease to be on the alert for every advance in physiology which would enable better understanding of psychological processes. It was no accident that his successor at the Collège de France was *A. Fessard*, a nerve physiologist.

Actually, Watson was less clear on this point. In 1914 he wrote:

No-one believes more than I in the entirely psycho-chemical nature of all responses, from the simplest to the most complex.

Basically the type of explanation which he advocated corresponded to an ideal and virtually unattainable stage in science. This *attitude* needs no justification, it is indispensable to the scientist, who must never accept any *a priori* consideration of one of his objects as irreducible. He must go ever further in his analysis of the most complex by the most simple; thus, following the birth of psychophysiology, we have seen that of biophysics and biochemistry. Such an *attitude* implies no metaphysics, no postulate. Science only knows as irreducible that which it has itself established as irreducible, taking into account its methods at any given moment.

Strangely enough, Watson, unlike Pavlov or Piéron, was little concerned with physiological explanation. He maintained that the

60

The evolution of experimental psychology

psychology of behaviour could dispense with knowledge of the nervous processes:

> It is perfectly possible for someone studying behaviour, without knowing anything about the sympathetic nervous system, the glands, the unstriped muscles, and even the central nervous system, to write a complete and accurate study of the emotions. (*Psychology from the standpoint of a behaviorist* p. 195.)

The psychologist looks for the relations between the situation and the responses which he observes. We mentioned earlier that Watson began from an empty man. Not only did he neglect the activity of the consciousness, but he claimed that one need have no knowledge of physiology.

Here we touch on a fundamental principle of the entire behaviourist approach. They did not deny that something occurred between the stimulus situation and the response, but they were not concerned with it. This school grasped what was closest at hand: observable data. Moreover, they thought, as Piéron had already stated, that the difference between the physiological and the psychological was simply that between the part and the whole. Behaviour, as Tolman was to say later, in *molar* as opposed to the segments of behaviour, which may be called *molecular*. This a-physiological attitude was found again in Holt, Hunter and more particularly in Hull, who often referred to neurology, but without going into precise details. Skinner also held a similar position. In a recent text, examining the temptations of the laboratory worker, he included among them preoccupation with the Inner Man. This arises when the experimentalist seeks to explain, instead of describing, or when he proceeds by inference and postulates entities or events of a physical nature; these, says Skinner in the best behaviourist tradition, cannot be causes of behaviour, at the most they can but 'interpret it'. Or, the experimenter may begin to refer to physiology and thus comes up against events of another order. 'Behaviour is an acceptable subject matter in its own right'. This neo-positivist profession of faith is unequivocal:

> We can predict and control behavior, we can modify it, we can construct it according to our criteria, and all this without answering the explanatory questions which have led researchers to the study of the inner man. (Skinner, 1961.)

61

By contrast, another American school endeavoured to explain behaviour by physiological mechanisms. *Weiss* (1879–1931) worked out a form of behaviourism more obviously reductionist than Watson's, going as far as physico-chemistry. Psychology was to be concerned with the physical processes which occur in the nervous system, but it concentrated on the interactions of organism and environment. Weiss stressed the social aspects of the latter, which was why his doctrine was christened 'bio-social'.[29] *Lashley* (1890–1958), a pupil and follower of Watson, was also a reductionist who endeavoured to reinstate the continuity of organic life from the filtering virus, through mammals and to the human mind, this last term embracing an indefinite number of complex structures and relationships.

He was, moreover, a great experimentalist. By neurosurgical techniques he attempted to define accurately the physiological laws of learning, in which organizational factors were especially sought after, and this brought him very close to the approach of the Gestalt school. Today *Hebb* belongs to the same tradition although he opposes Lashley at the level of physiological explanation. He believes, like him, that we must account for the 'organization of behaviour'—the exact phrase which he used for the title of his main work (1949). But he has attempted to understand contemporary neurology, which undoubtedly reveals a great complexity of nerve centres and channels, without ever displaying a mass-action of nervous tissue such as Lashley believed existed. Hebb is still a connectionist, even if he maintains that groups of nerve cells exist which act together as units. Although he looks for the physiological structures underlying behaviour, he is not a reductionist:

> It is impossible to substitute neurophysiological concepts for psychological concepts now or in the furture, but it is possible to maintain a liaison (translatability of terms) . . . between the two universes of discussion. (1960).

4 Behaviourism and learning

Watson's reaction against mentalism could only lead him to a systematic distrust of all pseudo-explanatory terms such as faculties, tendencies, aptitudes or dispositions. He admitted heredity,

---

[29] Weiss's works include: *Theoretical basis of human behavior*, 1925.

but it was specifically physiological. Certainly man was constructed at birth in such a way that he was endowed with simple reactions and reflexes, but in practical terms his behaviour was the result of learning.

Watson believed in the omnipotence of education and Skinner, more recently, has unequivocally defended this oft-quoted affirmation of Watson:

> Give me a dozen healthy, well-made children, and the kind of world I need to bring them up in, and I will undertake, picking them at random, to train them in such a way as to make each one a specialist in a profession of my choice—doctor, businessman, lawyer, even a burglar or a thief—independently of their talents, leanings, tendencies and aptitudes and regardless of the profession and race of their antecedents. (*Behaviorism*, p. 104.)

Such an idea obviously opened the way to deeper research into learning. In fact, Watson was only reflecting in a more extreme form the American tradition by following the footsteps of Dewey and the Chicago school, of which he had been a pupil. Thorndike had already turned from animal psychology to educational psychology, applying his law of effect. Obviously Watson did not follow him on this point: satisfaction and displeasure were categories of subjective experience which Watson had dispensed with; frequency and recency were sufficient laws of association—the basis of learning. Moreover, the theory of conditioned reflexes, which he applied, confined itself to speaking of the reinforcement of the conditioned stimulus by the unconditioned stimulus.

Forty years of study and arguments of great intellectual finesse, sometimes involving excessive detail and a proliferation of ingenious experiments, were centred on this controversy and Guthrie, Hull, Tolman, Razran and Skinner played prominent parts in this (see Chapter 7). The links between Pavlov's reinforcement, the reduction impulses (drive) of Hull and Thorndike's law of effect dominated the scene; however, each of them started from different points of what is undoubtedly a complex process.

Studies in learning overlapped those in motivation. They also formed an chosen territory for the meeting of American and Freudian psychology since Freud was also of the opinion that early education plays a large part in the formation of personality.

We should add one more point: if Watson and the learning

psychologists borrowed a lot from Pavlov, they also stripped Pavlovism of its neuro-physiological aspect. The method of conditioned reflexes was, for Pavlov, and still is for his school, a means of studying higher nervous activity. More often than not, the Americans neglected this aspect, which they sometimes considered as more theoretical than experimental. Admittedly Pavlov's key-concepts, such as those of excitation and inhibition are more explanatory than descriptive, but their heuristic value is undeniable.

More recently the reconciliation of behaviour and the physiological, indeed the physico-chemical, mechanisms of learning is one of the richest subjects for research.

5 The lineage of behaviourism

As Boring says (*op. cit.*, p. 645), in 1920 all the Americans had become behaviourists, except Titchener and his group. However, the quarrels between the different schools were many. Tilquin has given the French an account of these arguments (1942).

Before marking the main stages of neo-behaviourism, we must mention that today all psychologists have adopted the central standpoint common to the works of Piéron, Janet and Watson. Psychology studies the activity of living organisms, as a function of the physical and social situations in which they exist. However, many psychologists do not wish to be called behaviourists, since this label is still more reminiscent of Watson's theoretical excesses than of this positive contribution. If, then, in following the development of behaviourism, we cite only a few eminent names, this should not be taken to mean that other psychologists fell short or reverted to mentalist types of psychology.

Taking into account the diffusion of behaviourist ideas, we shall mention particularly the names of those who have made a theoretical contribution to the understanding of those ideas. It would be difficult to classify these ideas, and equally difficult to draw up a genealogy, since these men were almost all contemporaries. So, like Boring, we shall present them in the order in which they published their views.

Watson brought about a revolution, but his theoretical formulations were far too systematic. All his successors, in one way or another, brought about a deepening of his views and sought ways of taking into account everything of psychological importance without recourse to introspection.

Tolman (1886–1959) came under the influence of *F. B. Holt* (1873–1946) as a student at Harvard.[30] Holt, who was more a theorist than an experimentalist, accepted the principles of behaviourism, but endowed them with more subtlety than had their founder. For Holt, in effect, the response was a whole whose significance must be grasped, this significance being indicated not just be being aware of it, but by the appropriateness of the response in that the situation.

We have stressed the essential weakness of Watson's concepts: a refusal to see situation and response in relation to the organism. Tolman, conscious of this weakness, took up Holt's point and developed it in his magnificent experimental work and his theoretical works, which enlivened the time he spent at Berkeley from 1918 until his death. In 1922 he decided that only a Purposive Behaviourism could account for the behaviour of animals. This was the title he gave to his main work, *Purposive Behavior in Animals and Men* (1932). The rat in the maze is orientated: he is looking for food. Whether or not the rats are conscious of this is not the problem. They act, and their behaviour has an objective. The response, then, can only be seen as a whole and not as the sum or product of partial reactions. Much research has shown that the same end can be attained by different molecular reactions. Behaviour, B is dependent on a great number of independent variables: situation, S, physiological drive, P, heredity, H, age or maturity, A and previous practice, T, etc. Among the behaviour variables, some are directly observable, others can only be inferred from the behaviour itself: these are the intervening variables which are to behaviour what electrons or gravitation are to physics; it is their effect not their presence, which is apparent.[31]

Thus, Tolman introduced, between stimulus and response, a mass of factors, observable or inferential, hereditary or acquired, which gave consistency to both animals and man. His theories

---

[30] Principal works: *The concept of consciousness*, 1914; *The freedom wish and its place in ethics*, 1915, and especially *Animal drive and the learning process*, 1931.

[31] At first the Americans used intervening variables and hypothetical constructs as interchangeable terms, but MacCorquodale and Meehl (1918) proposed that intervening variables should only refer to concepts which classified empirical relations, and hypothetical constructs to concepts designating hypothetical processes or entities.

of learning and motivation, inspired by the same realistic spirit, introduced into behaviour elements from Freudian and Gestalt psychology, although Tolman was attached to neither of these schools. He remained a true behaviourist, able to integrate into his system the most constructive contributions whether from consciousness or from phenomenal description, that psychologists had to offer. His idea of 'intervening variables' which happily took the place of facts of consciousness, played a considerable part in the evolution of psychology. They refer to the subject, but not to subjectivism, since they are studied on the basis of controllable observations.

Hunter (1889–1954), a fairly orthodox behaviourist in the Watsonian tradition, would have like to eliminate the term 'psychology', which admittedly is equivocal if one traces its etymology, and to replace it by *anthroponomy*. But he is less known for this suggestion than for his work on delayed reactions and temporal mazes.[32]

Skinner (1904–   ) is the youngest behaviourist and, accordingly on of the most contemporary. He was far ahead of his time: as early as 1931 he defended the thesis that all correlation between stimulus and response must be considered as a reflex. His work, *The behaviour of organisms* (1938) gave him the opportunity to give it prominence. Skinner is a positivist. The psychologist must describe rather than explain. He considers the phenomena he observes as antecedents and consequences and seeks to discover the relations between the two. Of course, he noted that in these relations the state of the organism plays some part, but he adopted a strictly operational position in the matter (see p. 68). He noted the phenomena of reinforcement, the effects of privation on the activity of the organism, but he spoke of neither pleasure nor drive but of the effect of a certain succession of stimuli or of a certain privation.

His search for the laws of relations between antecedents and consequences led him to distinguish two forms of behaviour: *respondent*, the classic case where the response follows a stimulus and *operant*, the case where the response appears to be spontaneous

[32] Hunter's works include: 'The delayed reaction in animals and children', *Behavior Monog.*, 1913; 'The temporal maze and kinesthetic sensory processes in the white rat', *Psychbiol.* 1920, 2, 1–18; 'Psychology and anthroponomy' in Murchison, *Psychologies of 1925*, 83–107 and *Psychologies of 1930*, 281–300.

and where the appropriate stimulus cannot be found. To the first type of behaviour belongs classic conditioning of the Pavlovian type, where the reinforcement is coupled with the stimulus; to the second type belongs the conditioning, R, also called instrumental conditioning, which is similar to Kornoski's second type of conditioning. Here the reinforcement is coupled with the response.

To study this behaviour, Skinner invented 'the Skinner box', which was simply a rat's cage with a lever which, when manipulated, released a pellet of food. This very simple mechanism was to instrumental conditioning what the gastric fistula was to Pavlovian conditioning—a simple means of defining accurately the laws of behaviour, and particularly those of reinforcement (at fixed intervals or after a certain number of responses).

Faithful as Skinner was to Watson, he was more of a realist, and tried to take all the facts into account. Although he did not speak, as Tolman did, of intervening variables, he postulated them and in remaining faithful to his desire not to proceed from 'private' events, he did not greatly differ from his contemporaries.[33]

C. L. Hull (1884–1952) *and the hypothetico-deductive method.* Hull plays two roles in the history of experimental psychology. On the one hand, without claiming to belong to the behaviourist school in any special way, he was one of its greatest members. His influence at Yale, while somewhat belated, was considerable. Many people today take their bearings from him, and his pupils and followers can be found among the most celebrated modern psychologists (*J. S. Brown, J. Dollard, C. I. Howland, B. E. Miller, O. H. Mowrer, K. W. Spence*, etc).

Moreover, he made an important contribution to the experimental method, in a similar way to Lewin, by showing that experimental psychology could enter a new stage. After occasional observation, systematic observation, inductive drawing up of particular hypotheses, Hull suggested a fourth method called hypothetico-deductive. This was characterized by its attempt at the systematic formalization of knowledge. It started from a series of precise definitions and conceptualized assumptions and

---

[33] Skinner's works include: The concept of the reflex in the description of behavior, *J. gen. psychol.*, 1931, 5, 427–458; *The behavior of organisms: an experimental analysis*, 1938; *Science and human behavior*, 1953; *Verbal behavior* 1957

from them theories were deduced which could be submitted to experimental verification.

This method, which he applied to behaviour, and the results obtained by numerous experimenters including himself—the 'goal-gradient' law is well known—were the basis of his famous works: *Principles of Behavior* (1943) *Essentials of Behavior* (1951) and *A Behavior System* (1952).

Hull maintained that behaviour resulted from the interaction of environment and organism, which he placed in the general framework of biological adaptation, a concept which supplied him with the idea of purposive behaviour. This aim was need reduction, the need having arisen from a modification in the optimal living conditions of the organism.

Hull, who also spoke of intervening variables, introduced drive (D) or impulsion as the common denominator of primary motivations, habit (H) or the tendency of a stimulus to evoke that reaction which has previously been reinforced. This is not the place to describe Hull's system in detail. However, he ensured that of the 178 propositions which he formulated, 121 were experimentally studied; but history will undoubtedly record the extent of his work rather than its content. It was an example of the carefulness which is accrued through strictness. It was also part of a contemporary scientific movement which attempts to obtain mathematical models of great generality, and his *Mathematico-deductive theory of rote learning* (1940) written in collaboration with five other colleagues, gives an indication of this trend.

6   Operationism

Operationism was not a school, but a scientific principle which has been able to find a place in psychology only since the behaviourist revolution. According to Tolman, operationism 'seeks to define its concepts in such a way that they might be established and proven in terms of concrete and repeatable operations by independent observers' (1936).

Operationism is the result of the thinking of physicists such as *Bridgman* (1927), the philosophers of the Vienna circle (*Schlick, Neurath, Carnap, Frank*) and also of the endeavour of psychologists who, through the study of animal psychology and the thought of the behaviourists tried to reduce psychology to the operations of behaviour.

Bridgman took as his starting point the difficulties revealed by the theory of relativity. There was no absolute length or distance, but simply intervals which one could measure; given two distances measured by different means (the length of a table, and the distance from the earth to the moon) one cannot say anything about them until the equivalence of the operations of measurement has been established. When no operation of the type defined by Tolman is possible, one is faced with one of those pseudo-problems. Whether the sensation of blue in a given line of the spectrum is the same for Peter as for Paul is one such a pseudo-problem. We can only know whether Peter and Paul *discriminate* between neighbouring lines of the spectrum, and perception is limited by the operation of discrimination. This is in effect the technique used for animals using movement as a criterion and in man with a verbal criterion.

Operationism was called upon to contest, for epistemological reasons, the private facts of consciousness, that is to say those which are not externalized.

In short operationism supplied a criterion of what is scientific and what is not. This movement of thought has an important place in psychology. Actually, Tolman had been thinking in these terms for many years, but it was at Harvard that his ideas were worked out. *Stevens* and *Boring* were the spokesmen for this group from 1935 onward.[34]

Operationism was, and still is, disputed. It is natural that certain scientists allow themselves to be tempted by exploration, which operationism would seem to forbid. But most psychologists today accept this modern form of empiricism, at least as a yardstick by which they can distinguish what science reveals from what is merely speculation. Operationism supplied behaviourism with its natural climate of expression and with an appropriate language.

[34] The basic references on operationism in psychology are: S. S. Stevens, The operational basis of psychology, *Amer. J. Psychol.*, 1935, 47, 323–30, E. C. Tolman, An operational analysis of demands, *Erkenntnis*, 1936, 6, 383–90; E. G. Boring, Temporal perception and operationism, *Amer. J. Psychol.*, 1936, 48, 509–22, and particularly Symposium on operationism, *Psychol. Rev.*, 1945, 52, 241–94, those taking part were Boring, Bridgman, Feigl, Israel, Pratt and Skinner.

4 Towards the unification of psychology through the diversity of problems

In 1925, C. Murchison published *Psychologies of 1925;* five years later *Psychologies of 1930* appeared. This brilliant series in which great names expounded their own conceptions of psychology, was short-lived. Why?

A concise history can mention only the secondary causes, but History itself records that, through Nazism two worlds of thought and research met—Germany and Austria on the one hand and America on the other, and that this union precipitated the unification of psychology which is taking place before our eyes.

In 1930 Titchener had only just died when the Gestalt school was flourishing in Berlin, Freud was at Vienna, in America the neo-behaviourist school was endeavouring, after Watson's breakthrough, to make a science of psychology without mutilating reality. There was not *a* psychology, but several psychologies. Ten years later, when the Second World War had broken out, the picture was quite different. Koffka, Wertheimer, Lewin and Köhler were in America and had had fundamental works published in English. Freud and many of his followers were in England or America and these currents of thought had, with profit to both sides, encountered Anglo-saxon empiricism.

1 The influence of 'Gestalt' and Lewin's work

America certainly discovered the Gestalt psychologists before 1930, and Koffka was even established in America as early as 1927. But their influence was increased by the publication of two fundamental works: in 1929 Köhler wrote, in English, *Gestalt Psychology* and in 1935 Koffka wrote his *Principles of Gestalt Psychology*.

If America adopted Gestalt psychology one might say that it was Americanized in the process. In fact the initial resistance to the Gestalt theory was great because, starting as it did from a phenomenal approach to perception, it still seemed to be a mentalist psychology. But the Americans realized soon enough that although Gestalt psychologists made great use of the verbal reports of their subjects, this procedure was neither essential to the theory nor foreign to a behaviouristic use of language. The Gestalt psychologists studied animals (Köhler's book on the intelligence of the higher apes was translated into English in 1925), children (Koffka's book was published in 1921 and appeared in English as *The Growth of the Mind* in 1924), and mental patients (A. Gelb and K. Goldstein, 1920).

If the Americans remained fairly insensitive to the hyper-theoretical attractions of isomorphism, they were much attracted to wholism and the criticisms levelled against elementism. In fact functionalism was better adapted to a theory of structures than to artificial syntheses of elements. Koffka presented a field theory of behaviour, extrapolating, as it were, the principles arrived at from studies in perception. Lewin was to go still further with his theory of the psychological field.

The Gestalt psychologists, who were brilliant experimenters, enriched American work not only on perception, but also on memory, learning and thought. Signs of their influence can be found everywhere, even if 'Gestaltism' hardly exists as a school any longer. Moreover, *Köhler* (1959) continues to defend its fundamental concepts while answering the criticisms which they provoke.

We have chosen at this point to present the work of *Kurt Lewin* (1890–1947), since although many people minimize his early attachment to the Gestalt school, it seems to us fundamental. His essential idea was that of field: at each instant the behaviour of an individual is determined by a structured whole comprising the subject and his environment. Together they form the life-space, which includes the totality of the facts, physical or social, conscious or unconscious, which act upon the individual.

This field is dynamic. All behaviour seeks to restore the balance between the individual and his environment, a disturbance of which is the source of tension. Lewin, who was student, *Dozent* and then professor extraordinary at Berlin, clearly applied Gestalt principles, derived from work on perception, to the problems of motivation and personality. Lewin held that psychology could not dispense with a causal concept, which one could call instinct, libido or tendency. In Lewin's field forces not only the orientation of the subject played a role but the forces of other people and even of objects which had a valence—positive if they were attractive and negative if they did not.

These concepts or dynamic constructs possessed, for Lewin, the status of Tolman's intervening variables. They were dynamic elements determined indirectly and defined operationally. The theory had to establish a system of empirically verifiable concepts.

Independently of Hull, but at the same time, Lewin established and used the hypothetico-deductive method, but less strictly than Hull and without the same concern for quantification.

From his field theory he developed a model, which he called topological (after that branch of geometry which is concerned with the spatial relationship of forms which remain basically unchanged throughout their continual modification). This geometric model stemmed from the importance he attached to the movement of the organism, to its space, to the actual or imagined distances between the subject and the persons or objects in the field, and also from the barriers which could arise between elements in the field. The theory is expounded in *Principles of topological psychology* (1936). The psychological field made it possible to present psychological problems according to Galilean optics and no longer to those of Aristotle. The distinction which Lewin drew between these two points of view is well known.[35] Aristotle defined things by their essence that is, their belonging to a class defined by common characteristics, while Galileo established laws, that is relations between things. This point of view is doubly important: it eliminated explanations founded on the vague assignation of a characteristic, and it obliged one to take into account all the factors which determine a course of behaviour.

Thus the unique quality and no longer only the general, or to put it better the common characteristic, earned scientific status.

Lewin's thinking was extremely fertile; admittedly it can be argued against, but we must acknowledge its fertility, as his experimental work and that of his immediate followers bears witness. The effect of tension engendered by the interruption of a task (*Zeigarnik*, 1927; *Lissner*, 1933), the discovery and the experimental study of aspiration level (*Hoppe*, 1931, *Frank*, 1935) and studies on frustration and regression (*Barker, Dembo* and *Lewin*, 1941), are all well known.

[35] This and other important extracts from his works can be found in *Psychologie dynamique*, published by C. Faucheux, Paris, Presses Universitaires de France, 1959.

Europe retained from Lewin's works the dynamic psychology of personality. America enthusiastically received his later work, the study of group dynamics. The first research in this area, by Lewin, Lippitt and White (1939) was famous, and the international climate of the time increased its importance. It demonstrated the superiority of groups directed by several democratic leaders over those which were directed in an autocratic way and over those where the climate was extremely permissive—this superiority was expressed in the atmosphere, the camaraderie, the feeling of belonging to a group, etc.

To study group dynamics, Lewin had only to apply to social psychology his basic concepts of general psychology; the group, while it is not an original entity, is nevertheless a whole whose properties differ from the sum of its parts. If the individual and his environment form a psychological field, the group and its environment form a social field where distinction must be made between groups and sub-groups, members, barriers, channels of communication, etc.

Lewin, carried away by the enthusiasm and zeal of his followers, in fact founded experimental psychology. Admittedly his precursors (see Chapter 30), had developed highly sophisticated methods of observation: measurement of opinion from representative population samples (*Gallup*, 1936); attitude scales (*Thurstone*, 1929; *Likert*, 1932; *Guttman*, 1941); and sociometric measurements (*Moreno*, 1931), but group dynamics did more than just record. It experimented by modifying the conditions of the situation on the scale of a small laboratory group as well as that of an industrial unit or a district. Moreover, Lewin was asked to extend his investigations during the Second World War and to place his talent at the service of his new country. After the war he founded the Research Center of Group Dynamics at the Massachusetts Institute of Technology. After the early death of its founder this important Center moved to Ann Arbor, Michigan where, under the direction of *Lippitt* first and now *Cartwright*, it still continues its work.

2 Freud and his influence on experimental psychology

The reader may be surprised that we have not yet mentioned in detail *Sigmund Freud* (1856–1939) whose work is of considerable importance to psychology. This is simply because the impact of his work was not immediate. We shall not attempt to do more than sketch a biography of Freud and the stages in his thinking, on which there are many excellent studies in French (see among others, D. Lagache, 1955 and D. Anzieu, 1959).

Freud was primarily a doctor and a clinician. He had cared for and cured patients in a new and original way, using age-old techniques such as hypnosis and, later, free association. He was also a great theorist who wanted to construct a theory which was at once explanatory and coherent—a theory which he was to alter several times. Some of the concepts in his system depended more on metapsychology than on psychology (libido, life and death instincts, the three components of personality: the id, ego and super-ego), while others, on the other hand, could easily be given the status of intervening variables and be operationally defined (defence, resistance, regression transference, etc.). Certainly Freud, a man of one school and one theory, took little heed of this, but others have since put it to the test. It is well known, that Freudian ideas were slow to take hold, perhaps because of resistance to their all embracing notion of sexuality and possibly because of his uniqueness and esoteric quality. Psychoanalysis is a faith, and to believe in it one must first 'fall to one's knees' (is not didactic psychoanalysis an 'initiation'?). But the spread of these new, vital ideas was inevitable. We have already remarked how Stanley Hall had invited Freud to America in 1909. Psychoanalysis slowly but surely conquered the U.S.A., and also the puritan countries, to which it explained the consequences of puritanism and suggested a remedy for it. Here again, America, by rallying to a cause, inspired original work. Freud's works, were assimilated but in an empirical manner so that their scientific verification was concentrated upon.

Gradually Freud's ideas have inspired, directly or indirectly, the creation and development of projective methods (*Rorschach*, 1921, *Thematic Aperception Test*, 1935), which are particularly valuable in the investigation of personality; his theories have been tested by appropriate observations (see Farrell's synthesis, 1954); they have also supplied problems and a system of explanation to psycho-sociological studies (*Margaret Mead*, 1942, *Kardiner*, 1939; *Linton*, 1945) and have even inspired laboratory work in human and animal psychology. There is hardly an experimenter who does not use one or other of Freud's concepts, but the most systematic applications were made by *R. R. Sears* who directed more than 150 pieces of research in this connection (*Survey of Objective Studies of Psychoanalytic Concepts*, 1943). This was carried out by a team at the Yale Institute of Human Relations, and culminated in a series of essays, *Frustration and Agression* written by J. Dollard, L. W. Doob, N. E. Miller, O. H. Mowrer and R. R. Sears. Hull's influence is apparent here, as is also that of Tolman, Lewin and J. A. Murray. *Masserman*, for his part, pursued researches in animal psychology on conflict, presenting the problems in psychoanalytical terms and studying them on the behavioural plane.

We shall end this account with following statement by Tolman:

> Freud the clinician and Lewin the experimentalist are the two men who will always be remembered because their different but complementary positions made psychology, for the first time, a science applicable to real individuals and real societies.

3 Developments of the last twenty years

Around the 1940s, psychology was shaping its present outlook, which we shall try to outline in this conclusion. The period 1940–1960 was not unproductive; during this time experimental psychology made notable progress, either because of circumstances or because of developments in allied disciplines. We will detail them briefly, as the reader will find in these chapters a living example of it, which conveys more than any description of its history can possibly do.

A) THE INFLUENCE OF THE SECOND WORLD WAR

The two world wars had profound repercussions on the development of psychology in the U.S.A. The first war sanctioned psychological tests, which proved useful to orientate and select millions of men thrown into war without any real military preparation. In the second, because of its more ideological character (democracy and liberty fighting fascism) the problems of the morale of the combatants, the balance of personality and the social relationships within groups took precedence over the ascertainment of aptitudes. The urgent need for practical solutions and the generous subsidies given by the Army, Navy and Air Force, considerably stimulated research in these directions.

During the war, and more particularly since the war, the problems presented by the handling of modern military and civil machines has led to fertile developments in what the Americans call *Human Engineering*. For example, complex devices were constructed for pilot training so that as far as possible errors of perception were eliminated and the execution of numerous simultaneous movements was made as easy as possible. This problem gave rise in Great Britain to work in the Cambridge Laboratory and in America to that done by *Chapanis, Fitts*, etc. (see Chapter 7).

B) THE PROGRESS OF NERVE PHYSIOLOGY

Nerve physiologists still use the ablation method, experimentally in animals and therapeutically in man, but the progress of surgical techniques and in particular of anaesthetics, have made it possible to perform very delicate operations on the brain, so much so that we speak of psychosurgery. Moreover, thanks to progress in electrophysiology, it is now possible to study in a sufficiently analytical way the electrical activity of the brain as revealed by Berger (1929) and its relation to various psychological states. Lastly, stereotaxic apparatus made it possible to destroy highly localized areas thermo-electrically; specific excitations or receptions could be studied through implanted electrodes, which animals could carry while performing very complex activities. These technical advances revealed the very complex functions of the cerebral cortex, of the diencephalon and the rhinencephalon. Until these last decades, physiologists had studied principally the functions of the medulla and of the sensory and motor cortical areas. These researches established new laws of the relationship between the organism and his environment. Today we know the diverse functions of the hypothalamus in the regulation of drives (hunger, thirst, sex) and more generally of antagonistic behaviour and emotional reactions. Governed by hormonal actions and peripheral stimuli, the hypothalamic nuclei are, moreover, dependent on the deep formations of the cortex or rhinencephalon (hippocampus, fornix, amygdala, septum, cigulum). This was hardly known before except as an olfactory area, but we know that it constitutes an instinctive and affective brain whose activity influences aggression, avoidance, satisfaction and emotional behaviour in general. Experiments, particularly those of Penfield (1959), have shown that this region, and in particular the hippocampus and the temporal regions is important for the recording of experience, that is in the function of memory. The rhinencephalon, in conjunction with the neocortex and the hypothalamus, integrates the interoceptive and exteroceptive aspects of organic life with all their motivational and affective connections.

The thalamus, with its wide innervation is essential for the coordination of sensory impulses and sends projections into the associative areas of the cortex.

Nerve physiology had discovered, in the spinal column the activities of the reticular formation which extends from the bulb to the mesencephalon. This is a non-specific area existing and functioning parallel to the sensori-motor system from which it receives impulses. Its influence extends to almost all the functions of the central nervous system perhaps to link and integrate them, more probably to increase or decrease the level of awareness. About this time, problems of attention were assuming new dimensions (see Chapter 9).

We must refer again to the functions of the frontal lobes, which became better known after Fulton's experiments on monkeys, and after lobotomy operations. This region, which closely connected to the rhinencephalon, is an area which integrates affective life and the personality generally.

In general today, nerve physiology lays greatest stress on the non-associative connection in the central nervous system, that is those between the sensori-motor and cognitive areas and the centres of vegetative and affective life.

At the same time, physiology sees the nerve centres less as a mass of connections between the centripetal and centrifugal impulses than as a very complex system of control and coordination where different elements react on each other. In the same vein psychology no longer considered behaviour in terms of simple reactions to stimuli.

c) INFORMATION THEORY AND CYBERNETICS

The work of Wiener (1948) on cybernetics—the science of control and communication—and that of Shannon and Weaver (1949) on the theory of information, has shed new light on the subject matter of psychology (and physiology).

In a system of communication what is received does not automatically depend on what is sent. Information, in the cybernetic sense, does not depend on the meaning of the message but on its uncertainty—an altogether new point of view. The theory of communication became mathematical, or to be more precise, probabilistic, since the connections between the sender and the receptor are looked at from a stochastic point of view. This theory has not only approached studies of language (Miller, 1956), i.e. inter-personal communications in a completely novel way but it can also be fruitfully applied to the human organism itself, considered as a system of communications between stimuli and responses. Studies in perception (Piaget, Broadbent) and in sensori-motor reactions (Fitts) have benefited from this. We are striving today to understand human behaviour in general, and particularly learning, in terms of probabilistic models.

E. Brunswik (1952) did much to press home this approach and Piaget (1961) made full use of it by his theory of meets and joins in perception. The truly cybernetic view, that is that of servo-systems operating on a feedback principle, has also supplied psychology with models of behaviour, or rather of thought. Ashby's homeostat and Grey Walter's tortoise are modern versions of automata. But in comparing the old with the new, one can see now how far we have progressed in the understanding of human conduct.

D) THE ESTABLISHMENT OF GENETIC PSYCHOLOGY

Comparative psychology, as between animals and man, was one of the sources of the development of psychology. The comparison between child and man came later. Child psychology, at first descriptive and then truly experimental, emerged gradually. It has become, in fact, a genetic psychology, concerned less with knowledge of the child than with providing an explanation of the major psychological functions by studying their origins, that is the stages by which the most elaborate forms of conduct evolve from the most elementary.

Psychoanalysis in its clinical aspect had the effect of stressing the importance of genetic psychology by showing the effects of early experiences and early learning on the adult personality. But experimental research has not yet supplied sufficient proof to satisfy those who seek absolute objectivity. The work of *Wallon* (1879–) on character and personality is an original contribution in which sound thinking combines with rich clinical observation.[36] Binet and *Claparède*, working in genetic and child psychology at Geneva, were pioneers. But it is Piaget who must be acclaimed the creator of an experimentally based genetic psychology.[37] His influence today is world wide. Initially in 1923, Piaget was primarily concerned with showing that the organization of adult intelligence, with its inevitable laws, represented the last stage of gradual process which began with schemata of sensori-motor activity which gradually became internalized and transformed by the intervention of operational schemata, at first concrete, then formal. Since 1943 Piaget felt compelled to complete the early part of his work by developmental studies in perception, because the pre-operative thought of the child is more dependent on perceptual configurations than on thought structures. He has also recorded the creative function of their perceptual processes in relation to intelligence. Twenty-eight pieces of research have already appeared on this theme, and a recent book summarizes them, (*Les mécanismes perceptifs*, 1961).

4 Convergencies

At the risk of seeming to deny the distinctions so dear to those who try to maintain their doctrinal originality, one might say that

[36] H. Wallon's works include: *L'enfant turbulent*, 1925; *Les origines du caractère chez l'enfant*, 1933 and 1949; *L'évolution psychologique de l'enfant*, 1941; *De l'acte à la pensée*, 1942; *Les origines de la pensée chez l'enfant*, 1942.

[37] Piaget's work is most important, particularly: *Le langage et la pensée chez l'enfant*, 1923 (*Language and Thought of the Child*, Eng. Ed. 1926); *La causalité physique chez l'enfant*, 1927 (*The Child's Conception of Physical Causality*, Eng. Ed. 1930); *La naissance de l'intelligence chez l'enfant*, 1935 (*Origin of Intelligence in the Child*, Eng. Ed. 1953); *La construction du réel chez l'enfant*, 1937 (*The Child's Construction of Reality*, Eng. Ed. 1955); *La genèse du nombre chez l'enfant* (with A. Szeminska, 1941) (*The Child's Conception of Number*, Eng. Ed. 1952); *Le développement de la notion de temps chez l'enfant*, 1946; *Les notions de mouvement et de vitesse chez l'enfant*, 1946; *La formation du symbole chez l'enfant*, 1945. (*Play, Dreams and Imitation in Childhood*, Eng. Ed. 1962); *La Psychologie de l'intelligence*, 1947; *Le développement des quantités chez l'enfant* (with B. Inhelder), 1941; *La représentation de l'espace chez l'enfant*, 1948 (*The Child's Conception of Space*, Eng. Ed. 1956); *Introduction à l'épistémologie génétique*, 1950; *La genèse de l'idée de hasard chez l'enfant* (with B. Inhelder) 1951; *De la logique de l'enfant à la logique de l'adolescent* (with B. Inhelder) 1955; *Les Mécanismes perceptifs* 1961.

experimental psychology has become unified. Starting, despite its diverse roots, from the study of facts of consciousness, it has come round to the view common to Piéron, Janet, and Watson: namely that the subject matter of psychology is living man, in *all* his activities. Whereas Watson and the early behaviourists were more concerned with founding a science than constructing a discipline appropriate to its object, they believed it necessary to 'empty' man to begin with before considering him simply as a tangle of situation-response relationships, psychologists today, whatever the different vocabularies, recognize that to account for behaviour one must accept intervening variables besides situation variables. These variables are an hierarchically ordered system of potential modes of response which constitute the personality structure. In accepting this, they remain faithful to their fundamental aim: to study man in his situation, that is in his relations with the physical and social environment. Intervening variables do not, in fact, constitute a return to an inner homunculus who, consciously and unconsciously, pulls the strings. These intervening variables are no longer a ruse to reintroduce data of consciousness into behaviourist psychology. The fundamental step was taken, thanks to Janet and Freud on the one hand and to Binet and the Würzburg school on the other: they established once and for all that the attempt to define the contents of consciousness elude even consciousness itself. More generally, they established that consciousness is neither a mirror nor a glimpse into an inner reality, but rather it is determined by the interpretation of a fact, and accordingly prey to all the weaknesses of its origins. Its mode of operating could be assessed by seeing how far behaviour is modified in situations which impinge on the consciousness or, at the very least, where one expresses being conscious verbally. Language is thus in a favoured position which, as a response, has its own conditions and laws. Which explains, incidentally, the importance now being placed on studies in psycho-linguistics.

There is confirmation of these views in Hebb's presidential address to the American Association of Psychology in 1960, an address entitled *The American Revolution*. According to him this revolution was a behaviouristic one. In its first stage, which ended in about 1938, it had concentrated on behaviour which was sensorily dominated i.e. mainly determined by sensory messages (sense dominated). Now, in a second stage, psychology is concerned more with cognitive behaviour where the preparation of the stimulus is all-important. And this had far-reaching effects. Hebb wrote:

> Mind and consciousness, sensations and perceptions, feelings and emotions, are all intervening variables or constructs and, properly speaking, are part of behaviour psychology. (p. 740).

Here, where Hebb talks of behaviour, Janet would have used 'conduct', and we hope that Janet's terminology will one day be preferred.

If agreement has been achieved as to the purpose of psychology and its basic methods, we can also record that the main systems of interpretation—associationism, Gestalt, functionalism—are no longer in such violent conflict. The history of psychology from now on will be that of its major fields of study, perception, learning, cognitive processes, etc.

There are still, of course, affinities between those who, while dealing with different problems, find themselves giving the same level of interpretation. In fact, in physics, biology, and in the social sciences facts can always be studied at different levels, for example, that of underlying physiological mechanisms or of a description of behaviour or, lastly, of explanatory systems and models. These last can, moreover, be either of a physical (energy) type or biological (adaptation, homeostasis) or even mathematical. The ties between men who work on the same type of studies are considerable and each tends to believe that the plane on which he is working is the fundamental one. There is little to dispute the fact that there are in effect several corresponding levels of explanation. Reductionism, for example, is no longer a problem. Even the Soviet psychologists, whose best research (by their own admission) concerns the *higher nervous activity*, totally accept the specificity of the psychological and the importance of consciousness, whilst aware of the danger of idealism or, if one prefers, dualism which would introduce an ontological factor to explain behaviour. And they are right to defend the specific nature of the scientific plane.

However, there is one problem which remains and will do so for a long time: that of the relations between the physiological mechanisms and the corresponding behaviour. Reductionism and parallelism are no longer satisfactory, but no system of explanation can account for psycho-somatic interactions.

Through these tentative movements, experimental psychology has shown its ability to study increasingly complex human or animal conduct. We are very far from Wundt's physiological psychology, which limited the field of experimental psychology to the narrow horizon of the study of sensations, perceptions and motor reactions. Today the most difficult questions, such as motivation, are the object of thorough and complex studies (see Chapter 15) and Piaget's work has added greatly to our knowledge of the intellectual processes.

Moreover, we have seen the creation of an animal psychology which brought about a reappraisal of methods of human psychology. Evolutionism, which stimulated research on animals was also the origin of early systematic observation of children in the form of monographs (Darwin, 1877; Preyer, 1887). The questionnaire method (Galton, 1876; Stanley Hall, 1891) extended the area of research. Then the time came for systematic, descriptive and interpretative studies of child psychology, which consisted of the works of Binet, Thorndike, Claparède, Gesell, Piaget, Koffka, Wallon, Terman and Charlotte Bühler.

The age of reliance simply on single direct or equipped observation is past. Experimentation, in order to discover the determining factors of child development, is now quite common and its only limitations are those imposed by respect for the child. We have also seen how genetic psychology developed out of studies on children.

Abnormal psychology was called experimental very early on, at least in France, but studies of neurological and psychiatric disturbances remained for a long time at the level of systematic observation. Psychopathology is today increasingly experimental insofar as techniques are applied to patients which have been perfected on normal people (Eysenck) and insofar as psychiatry develops effective means of intervention on the therapeutic plane (psycho-surgery, pharmacology, etc.).

Finally, as we have already indicated, the experimental method was introduced even into social psychology, and Chapters 30 to 34 of this treatise might be the best illustration of this achievement.

For a long time individual differences seemed to be the object of recording rather than of experimentation. Factorial analysis has made it possible to analyse and to synthesize these records by supplying structural hypothese. But, since Galton, psychologists have also been concerned with explaining the origin of individual differences and with calculating the parts played by nature and education respectively. This delicate problem has been approached by different methods, (twins, comparative racial psychology, etc.) and it is still with us.

5 ... and tensions

We shall only refer here to the tensions inside experimental psychology, in fact inside psychology as a whole.

We shall simply remind the reader of the extreme tension which exists between psychology and phenomenology, serving only to renew the old conflict between psychology and philosophy. Obviously there is a philosophical psychology, just as there is cosmology and metaphysics. In its rational guise, its aim is ontological. Phenomenology today, supported by the experience of the philosopher, of the clinician and even the results of experiments, seeks to extract the essential significance from behaviour. This step engenders tension only when the phenomenologists present it as exhaustive, or when the scientists refuse to accept anything but scientific knowledge.

We shall now return to the internal tensions in psychology itself. It is not a question of actual splits, but simply differences in emphasis. According to the type of problem approached, according to the temperament of the workers and, lastly, according to the level of explanation at which they aim, one or another aspect of the experimental method predominates, but without undermining unity and fundamental characteristics.

A) QUALITATIVE V. QUANTITATIVE

The psychologist seeks to discover the significant fact. All science is descriptive, that is to say qualitative.

But psychologists quickly saw that the 'fact' which they regarded as significant was not necessarily the same if the experiment was repeated. Often, in the beginning, the results obtained on one or on several subjects were presented indiscriminately, whether expressed in quantitative or qualitative form. Very soon, though, the habit of calculating averages was adopted, which had to represent the true value, the average man according to Quetelet's view.

The habit of treating results statistically with calculations of averages, variability, significant differences between averages, did not appear until towards 1900 in the work of Thorndike and Woodworth on transference. About the same time came the introduction of statistics into psychology, the purpose of which was to take account of all the collected data. Gradually the idea spread that responses which deviated from the average were not 'errors' but merely less *probable* values than others. At the present time this point of view is gaining ground. E. Brunswik (1952) maintained that the probabilistic character of results was due not to the imperfection of the psychologist's methods or to a lack of control of the independent variables, but to the very nature of the characteristically variable adaptations of the organism, as several functionally equivalent responses,[38] are possible in the same situation.

This probabilistic view sometimes preceded, sometimes followed the progress made by the statistical method. It flourished with Fisher and the technique of experimental designs, treated by analysis of variance (*The design of experiments*, 1935). When several variables produce results which are simultaneous we no longer seek to neutralize some so as to vary only one, but we consider several situations with several different values or variables (from the qualitative or quantitative point of view) and statistical calculation determines the probability of any one of them producing a significant effect.

In spite of this attitude, which it must be admitted increased the risk that psychological facts would be hidden by mathematical procedure, others continued the basic research for psychologically significant facts. Pavlov, Binet, the Gestalt psychologists, Piaget, were in this vein—all Europeans, incidentally. They merit the name of 'pioneers' because they started their research in unknown territory and in unknown relationships between the environment, personality and reactions. Should their method be condemned

---

[38] E. Brunswik goes even further. In his ecological theory, the situation itself varies, and psychology must be more concerned with methods than with correlations between situations and variable responses.

because they disregarded statistical laws? Undoubtedly their scorn of these laws could sometimes lead them to take particular cases as a general law. But on the other hand, a new intuition should not be rejected because of its lack of statistical verification.

After the pioneers, other psychologists had to systematize the areas which had been laid bare and to decide how much could be regarded as 'certain' how much 'probable' according to the canons of statistical calculation. Moreover, the great authors who we have quoted were aware of the problem. Binet himself said:

> To a man who believes he has worked a miracle and brings it to us with hasty enthusiasm, we would say: do it again twenty times and calculate the percentage for us.

Similarly, in cases where he himself did not verify his hypotheses, Piaget was satisfied with the work of his pupils and followers whose results were based on statistics.

But the tension between quantity and quality sometimes has another source, closer to the opposition between the experimental method and the clinical or case method.

One is devoted to a segmentary approach, the other to a global approach to the personality. But as we have explained elsewhere (Fraisse 1956) the clinical method, when it is directed towards research (and not towards diagnosis or advice) is a necessary stage corresponding to the observation stage in Claude Bernard's schema. This phase is especially necessary when the problems are more complex and when behaviour results from more numerous and interdependent variables. Science always progresses by analysis, but on the condition that the important relations have previously been discovered. Sometimes this is better achieved by qualitative observation and sometimes by complex calculation and quantified observation (simple and multiple correlations, analysis of variance, factorial analysis, etc.). We shall conclude this section by quoting from the Gospel 'One sows the seed and another gathers the harvest'. Are not both necessary?

B) LABORATORY V. FIELD RESEARCH

The laboratory is attractive because of its rigour, and this is necessary to control and analyse the variables. But, at the same

85

Paul Fraisse

time, the psychologist is always wary of becoming too distant from normal life and of studying merely an artificial man.

This concern is justified. Each person is more receptive to one person than to another. Also, it may be that the same psychologist switches dialectically from laboratory work to field studies. This is apparent in Lewin's work, for example. The social psychologist is especially liable to do this.

A rather different source of conflict, but one which has much in common with analagous preoccupations, exists between fundamental research and its applications. The latter often follow on from the former: the Binet–Simon test, the result of ten years of study on intelligence, is a good example of this. But the demand for practicability often imposes temporary empirical solutions which, in their turn, raise theoretical problems. The part played in the history of experimental psychology by the problem of the personal equation is well known. Seguin invented the 'form-board' for the education of oligophrenics as early as 1842. We have shown the after-effects of the wide applications of psychological methods in the American army in the two world wars. Projection tests and attitude scales were practical methods before they became ways to study the personality. This list would be very long if it were to be exhaustive.

To return to our first point, the laboratory must undoubtedly draw its problems from everyday life. Even in animal psychology this is essential. The objectivist school of *Lorenz* acknowledged this. The ecological point of view of *E. Brunswik*, although entirely different in character, followed the same line of thought, without contradicting the demands of experimental psychology; he demanded that experiments be increasingly *representative*, that is to say that they should take into account all the ccological variables. He supplied a good example of this method by studying size-constancy in a child in numerous situations of his usual environment, a constancy which was seen, in these conditions to be even more absolute than in the laboratory.

To be productive, psychology must proceed from the simple to the complex. The psychology of remembering has progressed very rapidly, thanks to the invention of meaningless syllables. Once the basic principles were understood more complex situations could be tackled, like those involving the use of work with known characteristics (frequency, associative value, etc.). Similarly,

86

perception can go from the study of geometric *gestalt* to that of empirical *gestalt* (Brunswik). Once known, the main principles of emotional reaction, of standardized complex situations can be made use of in the same way that films are used. Examples are legion.

Because of this desire for simplification experimental psychology had to neglect individual differences at first. Then it began to integrate them, at first using groups as homogeneous as possible as to age, sex, culture, etc. Gradually individual differences became a fundamental fact. Having learned, thanks to Fisher, how to treat multifactorial experiments, psychology integrated situation variables and personality variables.

Our conclusion is resolutely optimistic. Experimental psychology has mastered its method. It is equipped today to take account of all the complexities of life. Its conquered territory becomes ever wider, but the surface has only been scratched.

The modern history of psychology has scarcely begun.

Bibliography

A history of psychology in autobiography, ed. C. Murchison and Boring, Clark University Press, 4 vols., 1930–52

Centenaire de Th. Ribot, Jubilé de la psychologie scientifique française (1839–89–1939), Agen, Imprimerie Moderne, 1939.

Current trends in information theory, University of Pittsburgh Press, 1953

La psychologie du XXᵉ siècle, special number of *Journal de Psychol. norm. path.*, 1954, 47–51, 1–228

ANZIEU, D., *L'auto-analyse*, Paris, Presses Univ. de France, 1959

BAUER, R. A., *The new man in Soviet Psychology*, Cambridge, Harvard Univ. Press, 1952

BERTRAND, F. L., *Alfred Binet et son œuvre*, Paris, Alcan, 1930

BORING, E. G., *A history of experimental psychology*, New York, Appleton Century Crofts, 1929 and 1950
—*Sensation and perception in the history of experimental psychology*, Appleton Century, 1942

BRUNSWIK, E., 'The conceptual framework of psychology,' *International Encyclopedia of unified science*, vol. 1, no 10, University of Chicago Press, 1952

CANGUILHEM, G., 'Qu'est-ce que la psychologie?' *Rev. Metaph. Mor.*, 1958, 12–25
—'L'homme et l'animal du point de vue psychologique selon Ch. Darwin,' *Rev. d'hist. des sciences*, 1960, XIII, 81–94
—'Physiologie animale' in *Histoire générale des Sciences*, Bk. III, 1, 469–84, Paris, Presses Univ. de France, 1961

CHAPLIN, I. P. and KRAWIER, I. S., *Systems and theories of psychology*, New York, Holt, Rhinehart and Wilson, 1960

CRONBACH, L. J., 'The two disciplines of scientific psychology,' *Amer. Psychologist*, 1957, 12, 671–84

DONDERS, F. C., 'Die Schnelligkeit psychischer Processe,' *Arch. Anat Physiol.*, 1868, 675–81

FARRELL, B. A., 'The scientific testing of psychoanalytic finds and theory,' in BRAND, H., *The study of personality: a book of readings*, Wiley 1954

FLUGEL, J. C. *A Hundred years of psychology*, London, Duckworth, 2nd edition, 1951

FOUCAULT, M., *La psychophysique*, Paris, Alcan, 1901

FOULQUIÉ, P., *La psychologie contemporaine*, Paris, Presses Univ. de France, 1951

FRAISSE, P., *Manuel pratique de psychologie expérimentale*, Paris, Presses Universitaires de France, 1956

GUILLAUME, P., *Introduction à la psychologie*, Paris, Vrin, 1943
—*Psychologie de la forme*, Paris, Flammarion, 1937, 1938

The evolution of experimental psychology

HEBB, D. O., 'The American revolution,' *Amer. Psychologist*, 1960, 15, 735–45

HEIDBREDER, E., *Seven psychologies*, New York, Century, 1933

KOHLER, W., 'Gestalt Psychology today,' *Amer. Psychologist*, 1959, 14, 727–34

LAGACHE, D., *L'unité de la psychologie*, Paris, Presses Universitaires de France, 1949

—*La psychanalyse*, Paris, Presses Univ. de France, 1955

LEWIN, K., *Dynamic Theory of Personality*, New York, McGraw-Hill, 1945.

MAC CORQUODALE, K. and MEEHL, P. E., 'On a distinction between hypothetical constructs and intervening variables,' *Psychol. Rev.*, 1948, 55, 95–107

MARK, M. H. (Ed.), *Psychological theory: contemporary readings*, New York, Macmillan Co. 1951

MAYER, J., 'Illusions de la philosophie expérimentale au XVII siècle,' *Rev. gén. des Sciences*, 1956, LXIII, 353–62

MILLER, G. A., *Language and communication*, New York, McGraw-Hill, 1951

MURCHISON, C., *Psychologies of 1925*, Worcester, 1925

—*Psychologies of 1930*, Worcester, 1930

MURPHY, P., *Historical Introduction to modern psychology*, London, Routledge & Kegan Paul (revised edition) 1949

NAVILLE, P., *La psychologie, science du comportement: le behaviorisme de Watson*, Paris, Gallimard, 1942

OMBREDANE, A. and FAVERGE, J. M., *L'analyse de travail*, Paris, Presses Universitaires de France, 1955

PENFIELD, W. and ROBERT, L., *Speech and brain mechanisms*, Princeton Univ. Press, 1959

PIAGET, J., *Les mécanismes perceptifs*, Paris, Press. Univ. de France, 1961

PICHOT, P., 'L'origine française des tests "form-boards" et leurs applications cliniques', *Egypt. J. Psychol*, 1947, 3, 1–14

PIÉRON, H., 'Histoire succincte des congrès internationaux de psychologie', *Année psychol.*, 1954, 54, 397–405

RAMUL, K., 'The problem of measurement in the psychology of the eighteenth century', *Amer. Psychologist*, 1960, 15, 256–65

REUCHLIN, M., *Historie de la psychologie*, Paris, Presses Univ. de France in the series 'Que sais-je?' no. 732, 1957

RIBOT, TH., *La psychologie anglaise contemporaine*, Paris, 1870

—*La psychologie allemande contemporaine*, Paris 1879

SHANNON, C. and WEAVER, W., *The mathematical theory of communication*, Univ. of Illinois Press, 1961

SKINNER, B. F., 'The flight from the laboratory', in *Current trends in psychological theory*, Univ. Pittsburgh Press, 1961

89

Paul Fraisse

TILQUIN, A., *Le behaviorisme*, Paris, Vrin, 1942

TITCHENER, E. B., *A Text Book of Psychology*, New York, 1909

WIENER, N., *Cybernetics or control and communication in the animal and the machine*, Cambridge, M.I.T. Press, 1948

WOLMAN, B. B., *Contemporary theories and systems in psychology*, New York, Harper and Brothers, 1960

WOODWORTH, R. S., *Contemporary schools of psychology*, New York, Ronald, 1931 and 1948

WUNDT, W., *Principles of Physiological Psychology*, 2 vols. Translated from the 2nd edition by E. B. TITCHENER. London, 1904.

ZAZZO, R., *Psychologues et psychologie d'Amérique*, Paris, Presses Univ. de France, 1941

Chapter 2

The experimental method

Paul Fraisse

1 The nature of the experimental method

Experimental psychology represents that body of knowledge acquired in psychology by the use of the experimental method. After a century of productiveness in the physical, natural and human sciences, this method no longer needs introduction. Moreover, it would be difficult to add anything to the work of Claude Bernard except that in each science the experimental method has its own procedures and rules, which are the outcome of difficulties encountered and overcome by past workers. We propose to try and explain the specific problems of the experimental approach in psychology.

Whatever the actual subject matter of each experimental procedure may be the method remains the same in principle. Although the experimenter's first move must be guided by the fact, he will not be satisfied with that. His aim is to discover new facts,[1] and he cannot do this unless he knows all the conditions governing their appearance. At that particular moment he is capable of foresight. But to achieve this end, the experimenter had had to connect together the intricate relationships between the essential facts, and the more complex his object the longer and more difficult the task will have been.

It is a matter of disentangling a thread and of proceeding by stages in order to succeed. Each stage is characterized by the

---

[1] An ideal which is far from being achieved, even in the most advanced sciences. But it is in this perspective that one should understand the enthusiasm of scientists when they were able to transform matter, to create an artificial satellite, or to carry out test-tube fertilization.

establishment of *a relation between two or more facts*. The graduated network of these relations constitutes the body of a science.

The experimental method is really only a way of acquiring knowledge. Its essential feature is to maintain the coherence of a system of relations *controlled* by the experiment. This mode of knowledge is essentially distinct from that of philosophy, which is based on the evidence of propositions and the demands of reflexive thought, and culminates in a system of knowledge as coherent as possible. Its reasoning is directed by the laws of thought, while in science, this control is ensured by empirical verification. It is nevertheless true that the experimenter's task does not consist merely of recording facts or even relations. Scientific activity is also the work of thought and, as Claude Bernard showed, we must be concerned less with method than with experimental reasoning. The fact is invoked or elicited essentially to verify the hypothesis set up by the experimenter. 'A fact is nothing by itself, it has value only through the idea to which it is attached or through the proof it furnishes'. (Claude Bernard, p. 93.) But what is a fact in psychology? Even the history of psychology is in a sense the history of answers to this question (see Chapter 1). Let us begin with what is a matter of common agreement, even if the formulation varies slightly.

The object of psychology is human psychism, or rather, to avoid the term 'psychism' which has a somewhat mysterious and esoteric ring, human personality envisaged as a unified combination of all its processes.

The real difficulty in psychology arises from the duality of ways in which this personality is perceived. Each man is capable of two types of knowledge, one by which he understands his own sensations, impressions or thoughts, the other by which he sees himself live and act as he sees others live and act, and under this guise, he knows himself knowing his fellows.

The philosopher attaches fundamental importance to this inner grasp of the subject by himself; either he harbours the secret hope of thus attaining the principle of all psychological activity, or he thinks he will thereby discover essential meanings. The psychologist's attitude is different. Since this inner grasp has an inexpressible character, he knows that this aspect cannot be a scientific fact. In our perception of nature, of the actions of others, or of works of art, the ineffable escapes science. It must be understood, however, that certain people attach more importance to these original impressions than to science.

Moreover, this inner grasp of the subject by himself does not introduce a discontinuity between psychology and the other natural sciences. In fact, despite its inexpressible character, it can be expressed in language in the same way that language serves to communicate information received about our environment. This verbal behaviour should be considered as action on the part of the subject just like other action. And this is true not only of their nature, but of their *scope*. Through a tenacious, but understandable, prejudice, each man thinks he knows himself better than others know him, thanks to his own intuition, but popular wisdom has already shown that we more readily see the mote in our neighbour's eye than the beam in our own. Psychoanalysis has demonstrated abundantly that the so-called immediate facts of consciousness are constructs, defence mechanisms, that is to say reactional systems and not the possession of something which springs directly from the self. These points have considerable importance, which as we shall see come within the scope of experiment.

Briefly, a personality is understood through its conduct, to use Pierre Janet's expression. And this is as true of knowledge of others as of ourselves. We know ourselves by our reactions to the situations confronting us, these reactions being not only gestures or words, but even our manner of interpreting situations and the responses we make to them.

If man is known from observation of his conduct, the experimental approach, which necessarily concerns the conduct of others, is justified, since these activities also include the expression of inner reactions and the interpretation, by the subject, of his own acts.

2 Conduct as a relationship

A psychological fact is, conduct and as such it implies the schema of relations which the psychologist studies. In effect, an action is the expression of a personality in a given situation. If we call the action R (to stick to Anglo-saxon tradition where R is the initial letter of response or of reaction), this depends on the nature of the personality (P) confronted by a given situation (S). We can then write $R = f(P, S)$. This way of considering a conduct evidently involves taking up a position with regard to historical arguments (See Chapter 1). Consciousness has long been considered, by certain people, the creative source of human conduct. The revolution against this untenable position ended in regarding all conduct as reaction to stimulation. Loeb's concept of tropisms was the extreme position which was found on a more general plane in Watson and with rather more subtlety in Hull. For them, for example, $R = f(S)$. Woodworth in 1929 showed that this schema required further elaboration so the proper role of the organism was introduced, and he proposed the sequence S—— O——R. But the idea of organism only emphasized the biological determination of behaviour. Admittedly it had the advantage of using the same frame of reference for animal and human psychology, but it introduced an unacceptable limitation. Moreover, the idea of organism was even insufficient in animal psychology. We would prefer to believe, along with several others including Lewin and Cattell, that it is personality which intervenes in a reaction to a situation.

To avoid ambiguity, we must add immediately that each term of the fundamental relation must be seen according to particular cases at different levels. Conduct is the act of the subject. This act, if it is always a reaction to a situation, is more or less elaborate in different personalities. The greater the elaboration, the greater also is the part played by the personality and the more the individual aspect of the action predominates over stereotyped reactions. Reflex and automatism are one thing, and the ideo-motor act another.

Conduct (*R*). The same conduct can be seen at different levels. It has its physiological components (endocrine, neuro-vegetative, motor) but it also has its total structure and, in short, its result. For example, a verbal response, which in our view is an act, can be analysed by electro-physiological techniques at the level of the emission of phonemes, or the nature of the phonemes, or the grammatical structure, or the significance or simply the effect produced on the questioner.

Situation (*S*). Situation can also be analysed at different levels. It is made up primarily of physical stimulations which act on our sensory receptors. Light, noise and smells have their own effects. But situation is also the perception of objects and the relations between objects or individuals, and these perceptions are determined both by the objective data and by the significance which the perceiver assigns to them.[2]

This last point of view draws attention to the fact that a situation in its most complex aspects is always relative to the individual who is 'in the situation'. In experimentation, the situation is set up by the experimenter, but he cannot simply describe it by using measuring instruments, or even his own perception of it. Although this approach may be acceptable in simple cases where the situation is unequivocal, as soon as the complexity increases, the experimenter must be concerned with knowing how the subject 'sees' the situation. This research can sometimes be the very aim of the experiment, as in certain studies on perception. The study of size-constancy is no more than the search for the connection between the physical description of the object and the phenomenal perception of the subject. When the structure of the situation is ambiguous, as in the Rorschach ink-blots, the vision of the subject reveals his personality. The response depends more on the perceiver than on the stimulation.

Even in experiments which do not have perception as their specific study, the subject's 'own vision' remains an important variable. The subject always interprets the situation and particularly the intentions of the experimenter; it is, then, important that the experimenter should take great care to construct the situation not from his point of view but from the subject's. To be practical, it is always important to complete an experimental procedure with an interview with the subject or through a questionnaire, in which his answers will show up possible differences of interpretation.

In short, what is most important, in explaining an action, is the way in which the subject relates himself to the situation and understands it in terms of his personality (of his organism, his experience, his temperament, his need, etc.). This point being reached,

[2] Taking into account these levels of response and situation, E. Brunswik (1952, p. 5), established a schema which shows the possible analytical approaches. He distinguished the distal stimuli from the proximal stimuli, the first corresponding to objects of the environment, and to what we call 'situation', the second to specific excitations which is called 'stimulation', The same sort of distinction is made between proximal responses (muscle activity, for example) and distal responses which is action properly speaking. These distinctions also correspond to the molecular or molar description of situation and response (Tolman).

Paul Fraisse

we must define our basic formula in more detail, and no longer be satisfied to write R $= f$ (S, P), but rather R $= f$ (S $\rightleftarrows$ P), the double arrow indicating that the conduct depends on interaction between the situation and the personality of the subject.

However, we must stress the fact that this interaction does not mean simply the point of view felt and verbally expressed by the subject. His conduct can depend on aspects of the situation of which he is unaware, or which can influence him without his knowledge. The experimenter who is studying the influence of a situation must always take into account the levels at which he makes his analysis, the way in which the subject evaluates the situation and the deep significance which the reactions lead one to assume.

The explanation of conduct can arise from one or another aspect, sometimes from all of them. This point must not be overlooked. Of equal importance is the fact that a situation is made up of a physical environment, of the presence of natural or manufactured objects, of animals, and finally of other people. When this latter condition predominates, the situation is called social and the psychologist studies interpersonal relations, or those of an individual with the group.

Personality (P). Personality is obviously characterized by the existence of difference levels of integration. Let us, from the outset, adopt Sheldon's definition: personality is the 'dynamic organization of the cognitive, affective, conative, physiological and morphological aspects of the individual'.

Depending on the particular case, one or other (or several) of the levels must be brought to bear. Let us take an example to clarify this. Faced with a child who has difficulty in learning to read, the psychologist can ask himself whether it is a question of bad eyesight, mental fatigue or bad habits, the result of inadequate teaching, absence of incentive, or character or family difficulties. The good clinician thinks of all these possible causes: the good experimenter must know to determine the relevant instances of the personality involved and to take them into account in his plan and in the analysis of his results.

It may seem paradoxical to consider the personality as a simple variable in a relation. If all psychological research is centred on knowledge of the personality, we must not forget that it can be understood only by considering the personality as a mass of relations between situations and actions.

96

3   S-P-R type relations

A) There are three classical methods of approach to these relations: The study of psychological functions, or how the same personality reacts to systematic variations (qualitative or quantitative) in the situation. The diagram is as follows (Fig. 1):

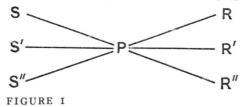

FIGURE I

where S, S' and S" are the different situations to which the various responses R, R' and R" correspond.

Examples: the gradual adaptation to darkness (R) as a function of time (S); the degree of learning (R) as a function of the number of repetitions (S); the defence reactions (R) to varying degrees of frustration (S).

B) The structural study where one seeks to discover the relations between the responses obtained to different situations. The different responses R_1, R_2 and R_3 correspond to the different situations S_1, S_2 and S_3.

The study here concerns the relations between R_1, R_2, R_3 etc., which are indications of the structure of the personality.

Examples: the relations between the reactions to different emotional situations; the relations between levels of efficiency in different tasks, etc. The best techniques to use for this study are correlations and factor analysis.

C) The differential study in which one considers the reactions of different personalities to the same situation S:

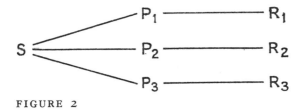

FIGURE 2

The differences between R_1, R_2, R_3 ... are indicative of the differences which exist between P_1, P_2, P_3 (Fig. 2).

97

Sometimes it is the differences between the individuals which are studied and sometimes the reactions of groups, differing in one or other characteristic (age, sex, race, cultural level, etc.) are compared. In this case one discovers an aspect of personality which is common in varying degrees to all the individuals in a group.

Examples: variations in efficiency (in one sphere or another) as a function of age and sex; the resemblances and dissimilarities in the emotional expressions of different nationalities.

Each of these three methods of approach gains in clarity from the others[3] even if university tradition and practical necessity often entrust these researches to different specialists.

1   Observation

1   The stages in experimental research

While chance or genius sometimes upset the most carefully codified procedures, it is still true that the pattern of experimental progress generally comprises four phases:

A) Observation to discover noteworthy facts and to gain precise knowledge of them.

B) The establishment of hypotheses on the relations which may exist between the facts.

C) Experimentation, in the strict sense, having as its object the verification of these hypotheses.

D) The working out of results and their interpretation.

We shall study each of these stages of experimental reasoning in turn, but first let us make it clear that their importance varies according to the particular stage of scientific development. Observation plays an important part in new sciences and in new problems. In psychology much research still consists simply of systematic observation. In the more established sciences, a first experiment leads on to a second, which supplies a more precise verification or a generalization of results.

[3] In approach C, the differences between the subjects (or the groups of individuals) are studied, but in approaches A and B several subjects are usually used. In A, this is done in order to isolate a relation functionally dependent on characteristics of the individuals and to establish its generality. In B several subjects are required also because the structures are only found by establishing the co-variance of $R_1R_2R_3$ in all the subjects.

2 *Observation and experiment*

Is there a difference in nature between these two stages of research? Like Claude Bernard, we would answer no, while making it quite clear what it is that distinguishes them.

Roger Bacon, as early as the thirteenth century, differentiated between passive, everyday observation and active, informed observation. In all observation, as in all experimentation, the worker is ascertaining a fact. This fact is always in some way the answer to a question. A truism, perhaps, but forgotten by many researchers, is that one finds only what one seeks. Consulting rooms and laboratories have cupboards full of observation files, with which nothing is done and nothing can be done because the observations have been accumulated without precise questions having been asked. So, the difference between observation and experiment is in the nature of the question asked. In observation the question is in some way an open one. The researcher does not know the answer, or he has only a vague idea of it. In experiment, on the contrary, the question becomes an hypothesis, that is it supposes the existence of a relation between facts, and it is the object of the experiment to verify this hypothesis.

But there are also what are called 'seeing experiments' where the experimenter has no answer to his question and where he decides to observe the conduct of the subject in response to situations created by him. In this case the minute difference which can be seen between observation and experiment amounts only to a difference of degree between the two procedures. In observation the situations are less rigorously defined than in experiment, but as we shall see, this may include all the gradations between naturalistic and contrived observation.

A third difference, also one of degree, between observation and experiment no longer concerns the control of situations, but rather the precision with which one can record the conduct of the subject. Observation must always be satisfied with less strict procedures than experiment, and our remarks on observational method will be mainly devoted to the way in which one can ensure strictness of observation without using standardized experimental situations where the number of predictable responses can be limited.

But obviously all that we say about observation could equally

Paul Fraisse

apply to experiment, especially when it becomes somewhat complex.

3 The circumstances of observation

We may distinguish between occasional observation and systematic observation:

a) *Occasional observation* obeys no rules. It is what any psychologist can do in everyday life on himself or on those around him. Its role in the general development of a science diminishes as the science builds up a body of knowledge, but it undoubtedly continues to influence the psychologist in his thinking and his attitudes.

After this observation, arising out of everyday life, come those which occur incidentally in the course of professional activity, like that of a teacher, a publicist, an engineer. The precise nature of these activities, and their repetitive character enables more important and more original observations to be made. The results are even more interesting when such observation arises in the course of the psychologist's practical work or experimental research. We refer here to cases where the psychologist is led to make an observation outside his actual work. Great discoveries have been made in this way: in 1888, Féré, a neuropsychiatric doctor at Bicêtre, attached some importance to the remark of a patient with abnormally dry skin who claimed that he felt a prickling of the hair and skin, particularly in cold dry weather. Thus Féré had the idea of measuring the static charge of the skin after friction and established that this charge disappeared under the effect of certain stimulations. The discovery of the psychogalvanic reflex was thus made. Similarly, Pavlov discovered conditioned reflexes in the course of experiments on the physiology of digestion, by observing secretions which could not be explained by biochemical actions.

b) *Systematic observation* occurs within a defined scheme which, by its very precision, reduces the area of study.

This observation can be called *naturalistic* if it studies the behaviour of individuals in the circumstances of their daily life. Occupational and social psychology mainly employ this technique. Observation of shoppers, factory workers, all kinds of investigations. Sometimes the observer endeavours to 'see without being

100

seen'. We shall mention later some of the techniques currently employed in this type of study. Sometimes the observer intrudes into the life of people, but tries to see their conduct and their conversations in the context of their daily professional or family activity, seeking as far as possible to diminish the social distance between the researcher and the subjects.

Observation can be called *clinical* in the sense that Lagache (1949) used the term. In this case the conditions of the environment are fixed by the researcher. The clinical interview, such as is practised in consulting rooms or hospitals is observation of this kind; it has its framework, its rituals, its objective, even if the conversation is supposedly free and non-directional. Many observations on the dynamics of small groups belong in this category. The participants are placed in a situation where they are observed either without or, more often, with their knowledge.

As well as the environment, the observer sometimes defines the task which the subjects must undertake; Lagache called this the structured clinic. Here we are coming a great deal closer to the conditions of experimentation and this observation can be confused with the 'seeing experiment'. The difference lies essentially in the greater or lesser freedom allowed to the subject. Observation, to justify its name, must not alter the spontaneity of conduct.

4 Difficulties of observation

In all sciences observation has its difficulties and pitfalls. In psychology they are considerable, but the main problems which arise have been defined. Observation is always the perception of conduct, a record. Now, nothing is as deceptive as the word 'perception' which, by its etymology, would appear to allow us an adequate grasp of the object. Actually, it has its laws and its limitations. Among the mass of excitations which bombard our receptor organs at any given moment, we seize on only a few, either because they impinge by their intensity or because we are sensitized to them by the interests of our current activity. Thus, from all the available information, we select according to our current orientation and, furthermore, when a stimulation is not very well defined, we interpret it in terms of our anticipation and more especially of our personality (Fraisse 1951 and 1961).

Insofar as scientific observation is the search for the answer to a question, it engenders a favourable attitude, an opportunity not to let the significant fact escape. But an over-orientated approach makes one blinkered, and we are in danger of interpreting results in the hoped for direction when in fact their significance is ambiguous.

Reuchlin (1950) made a study of the possibilities of observation in a very standardized situation. The subjects performed, before two observers, two manual tests. During a pilot study, a list had been drawn up of all the possible ways of behaviour during these tests. (Thus, in Kohs' cube test: change cubes, drop a cube, ask questions, etc.). This list comprised 24 actions, and the observers had to note them down as and when they appeared. Comparison of the two records showed that on 6 of the 24 actions the observed frequencies differed significantly, and it appeared that these differences were mainly due to the fact that one of the observers had ignored many of the verbal reactions of the subjects. In other words, one of them had *selected* his observations, and paid more attention to motor behaviour than to verbal expressions.

Besides this selection, our perception also remains limited by our ability to comprehend. At a given moment it is very difficult to grasp facts proceeding from different sensory channels. Moreover, in the same sphere, it is impossible for us to perceive numerous facts simultaneously because our range of perception includes only five to seven separate types of event.

The poverty of our simultaneous observations cannot be compensated for except by using methods of recording other than human perception. Films, photographs, tape-recorders all afford today the means of catching the fleeting observation and referring to it as often and for as long as necessary. Every psychologist knows this, and yet too many still carelessly trust to their eyes and ears. These mechanical means of recording, which can be used today in such a way that they have no disturbing effects, have the added advantage of modifying the transient nature of psychological conduct by making it possible to fix it.

In some cases, it is true, it is not the fleeting nature of the conduct which is an obstacle to observation, but rather the over-long duration of the phenomenon to be observed. Botanists have overcome this inconvenience—a more considerable one in their subject—by using film and the technique of frame-by-frame recording. Speeding these films up makes it possible for them to reconstruct the event. This method has sometimes been used in psychology; for example, the degree of agitation of an individual or of a group can be studied by taking shots every second. This cinematographic technique is only another application of time-sampling. When it is impossible to retain the whole of a length chain of action, the observer notes down from moment to moment (every 5 seconds, for example) what the subject or the group is doing. The extent of the observations depends, obviously, on the nature of the activity being studied.

5 Recording of observations

Observation can only validly grasp externalized conducts with a verbal or motor basis. One does not observe intelligence, but how a person solves his problems; not sociability, but how many times and to how many people a subject speaks in a given situation.

To be productive observation must be analytical. Certainly the analysis must be able to select the significant segments of behaviour, but in this direction—with rare exceptions—psychologists are more often tempted by syncretism than by pointillism.

To guard against inference and premature generalizations is also the only means of assuring maximum objectivity in observation, this being clearly defined by the virtual or actual agreement of several observers. If this criterion is not respected, the observation loses all meaning and becomes only the more or less subjective impressions of an individual.

But, in ensuring the precision and objectivity of observations, the problem of language is fundamental. It is not enough to observe the facts. So that agreement between several observers is possible, or so that at least the notes on the observations can be understood by the reader as well as by the person who took them down, the terms employed must be operationally defined, that is, they should be as fully descriptive and as little interpretative as possible. One does not observe an 'oral' behaviour, but rather sucking of the thumb, clothes, etc.

All this constitutes the preamble to notation. What should be noted down? This important operation is done in two stages. A preliminary investigation will make it possible to define the field of observation and to draw up a list of conduct to be noted. In the actual observation, two main techniques are possible. Either one

notes at each moment only the presence or absence of a particular
form of conduct, and the final record will indicate the observed
frequencies. Or in a more detailed analysis one attempts to assess
the intensity or the duration of a conduct. For noting intensity,
the technique of estimation scales is used: there are several kinds,
which we will simply enumerate:

A) For each conduct one can note, on a three-, five- and sometimes seven-point scale, the intensity, defined by an adjective or
adverb. For example the intensity of an emotional reaction like
the trembling of the hand could comprise three degrees: much,
moderately, not at all. A five-point scale would introduce finer
degrees. Everything depends on the action which is being observed and the degree of exactness which is possible in making
judgements.

B) The same technique can be still further refined by marking
on a vector the position which seems to characterize the intensity
of the conduct. In the example below, the mark put on the segment
indicates an intensity coming somewhere between 'moderately' and
'not at all', but tending towards the latter.

much   moderately   not at all

FIGURE 3

C) When the actions do not differ intensively, but qualitatively,
each manifest form the action takes can be characterized by a
more complete description. The simplest case is that of dichotomy.

6 The presence of the observer

The presence of the observer introduces a new variable into
the subject's environment and to a certain extent modifies his
behaviour. This is true even in microphysics, where observation
introduces a source of indeterminacy; even more so in animal or
human psychology, when the subject can see the observer.

The solution to this difficulty is to see without being seen
whenever possible. To this end, one-way screens have been
devised. A well-lit room, where the subjects are, is separated by a
sheet of plate glass from the darkened room where the observer

sits. In this situation the subject sees only a mirror, while the observer can see without being seen. What is more, systems of microphones and telephones allow him to hear the noises and the words. Gesell made great use of this method for studying young children. Social psychology often uses this technique.

Another procedure consists of replacing the observer by recording apparatus, cine-camera, tape recorder, etc. If they are visible they often intimidate the subjects less than a human presence. Current television techniques combine the advantages of one-way screens and filmed recording. A cine-camera records behaviour, which is transmitted to a television receiver, allowing observation from a distance and of several groups or individuals at once. This is often useful in research, and also in teaching it is used at the Clinical Psychology Laboratory of the Hôpital Henri-Rousselle.

But these techniques are only practicable in certain cases. More often the observer is present, and he must realize that he introduces a new factor into the observation itself. His discretion, his tact, the fact of being as close as possible to the subject will, as we have said, diminish the inevitable effect of his presence.

7 *The personality of the observer*

Thus, the observer is a factor in the observation situation. We have already mentioned that what he observes in this privileged situation dpeneds on his attitudes. But this problem becomes more difficult when the observation concerns complex aspects of character or personality. In this case, not only can the presence of the observer influence the subject, but—whether seen or not—the observer is more or less qualified to judge the behaviour of other people.

Thus, Estes (quoted by Allport, p. 501) after asking 20 different psychologists to study eight people during one academic year, obtained their most objective evaluations on the personality traits of his subjects. He then filmed the behaviour of the subjects in precise, expressive situations (taking off their coats, putting on their ties, playing, or even fighting with each other). These brief sequences were presented twice to 35 judge-observers who were all psychiatrists or clinical psychologists of at least two years' experience. They had to guess the personality traits which had been the object of the prolonged study. The results of this research, where the observations of the judges could be compared to relatively objective facts, showed that the value of the observations depended on the particular judge who made them.[4] The ten best judges were shown to be best for all the observed traits, and their results were 33 per cent higher than those of the ten worst judges. Neither age nor the length of time they had practised their profession, nor the fact of having undergone instructive psychoanalysis had any systematic influence on the results.

However, we must not conclude from this research that the ability for observation is an innate gift or a general aptitude. From his research, Vernon (1933) classed observers into three groups:

  a) those who are good judges of themselves; they are characterized by high intelligence and a sense of humanity,
  b) those who are good judges of their friends and acquaintances; they are less sociable than the former, but have a more artistic temperament,
  c) those who are better judges of strangers; they are very intelligent, gifted from the artistic point of view, but asocial in certain respects.

Generally speaking, it seems that an essential determinant of the usefulness and accuracy of observation concerning personality is the existence of a similarity between the observer and the subject. Men are better judges of men, and womon of women. It is the same with people of the same race or the same social level.

It is immediately obvious that this rule has its limitations. The observer tends to judge the subject through his own prejudices as to the subject's person, milieu and race. But is he more objective when he sees the other through the haze of stereotypes? Thus we come back to one of our previous conclusions. Observation, to be objective, must note precise conduct and not venture carelessly into sweeping judgements of complex personality traits.

Despite all precautions, observation remains marked by a certain subjectivity. The solution, when 'the game is worth the

---

[4] It also depends on other factors: a) the personality of the subject. On the whole extraverts are easier to observe than introverts, and those who have more definite personalities easier than those whose personalities are less well defined; b) the nature of traits. On average, the manifest traits, such as inhibition-excitation or dominance-submission are more accurately assessed than latent qualities such as objectivity-subjectivity.

candle', is to use several observers who make independent notes. The multiplication of observers does not necessarily increase the validity of the notes, because all might contain the same systematic error (for example: Whites judging Blacks, or vice versa), but it does increase the accuracy, that is to say the probability that another group of observers would arrive at the same conclusions. For example, to obtain a coefficient of reliability of 0·90, it needed four judges to establish academic knowledge and 18 to estimate impulsiveness, (Symonds, 1931).

8 Self-observation

The problems of self-observation are legion, and we shall mention one aspect of them here. Very often in work on personality or inter-personal relations, the observer uses records which the subject has based on himself, i.e. autobiographies, letters, and self-analysis. But more often, in more systematic work, self-observation takes the form of answers given to a questionnaire prepared by the observer. In this case one does not observe the conduct of the subject, but calls on his experience. Thus, to ask a subject to answer the question 'Do you get angry when anyone teases you?' replaces a possible, but difficult, observation by provoking information furnished by the subject himself and based on a mass of observations.

The questionnaire method is very interesting. Besides the fact that it substitutes very brief facts for hypothetical observations, it enables one to collect information on conduct which would never lend itself to direct observation. For instance, there are questions such as: 'Have you ever dreamed that your father was dead?' or 'Do you look underneath your bed before you go to sleep?'

Finally, the questionnaire is indispensable when one wishes to know the effective reactions of the subjects, their interests, their attitudes and their opinions. Thus: 'Do you think you are misunderstood?' or 'Would you rather be an architect or a chemist than a shopkeeper or factory manager?'

We cannot go into the theory and practice of the questionnaire method here. Let us simply stress the fact that in our opinion the replies to questionnaires must be considered by the observer as conduct and not as facts with an objective content. We have emphasized the difficulties of observations on others, and hence *a fortiori* on oneself. Psychologists, particularly for practical reasons, have studied all the possible distortions of replies to questionnaires; insincerity, the influence of judgements of the value of the conduct being investigated, that is the influence of what one estimates to be good or socially acceptable and what one considers to be bad or socially condemned. When self-observation concerns the intensity of a trait each of us has a very personal scale of values which, in the professional observer, is balanced by the weight of his total experience.

In the clinical use of questionnaires, psychologists have thus learned to distinguish the manifest content from the latent content of replies, and they have developed systems of interpretation, as, for example, the MMPI. Psychologists who use inventories or questionnaires must remember that self-observation does not supply an immediate fact with an indisputable value, but a reply which must be interpreted.

2 The establishment of hypotheses

This phase of research is not only the most important, but also the most difficult to explain, and even more to state the norms of. Hypothesization is the creative phase of experimental reasoning, in which the worker imagines the relation which could exist between two facts. The setting up of the hypotheses is the work of thought. It differs from the phases of active observation or of experimentation in that the worker is apparently doing nothing, but it is this moment which gives his work its original value.

One can apply to the setting up of hypotheses all the systems usually associated with invention: intuition and tentative trial and error. Each discovery, great or small, has its particular history. Invention is the work of the imagination, but the imagination would be powerless if it did not have the support of an excellent scientific culture. This last, always useful, is indispensable in developed sciences, into which category psychology henceforth falls. It is only this culture which leads to the perception of fertile relationships and the avoidance of retracing old paths.

Let us try and pinpoint some of the main features and indicate several universally valid principles. We will distinguish two main categories: inductive hypotheses and deductive hypotheses.

1 Inductive hypotheses

These arise from the observation of facts, which can occur in all the circumstances previously described. The hypothesis is in the form of a possible reply to the question which the experimenter has asked himself and consists of assuming the existence of a relating between facts, such that the presence or the modification of one will imply the presence or modification of the other and in some way explain it.

Let us take an example, to which we shall refer several times. Through numerous observations, in many circumstances, we have seen that the actions of men in a state of anticipation are very varied. Why? This question lies at the root of our systematic observations. Obviously this anticipatory behaviour depends a great deal on circumstances, conditions, the object of the anticipation, that is to say the situation (S), but we are concerned here with the links which can exist between these actions and the personality characteristics (P).

Obviously it is not enough to say that the diversity of these actions (ranging from placidity to aggression, from calm to anger) depends on personal variation of personalities. An hypothesis exists only from the point when one explains a relation between observable facts. Thus, in a programme of research, (Fraisse and Orsini, 1955–57) we tried to relate anticipatory behaviour and emotional stability. From our observations, we set up the following hypothesis; the greater the emotional stability of the subject, the more likely is it that anticipation will produce reactions suitable to the situation.

2 Deductive hypotheses

At a more advanced stage of research, the hypothesis can be deduced from the relations already known or from the theories which generalize about them. Let us again take an example from our own research. The establishment of a theoretical synthesis concerning the role of attitudes in perception led us to the two following laws:

a) the threshold of recognition of a word (or the minimum exposure time necessary for identification) is smaller when the frequency of the word in the language is greater,

Paul Fraisse

b) the threshold of recognition for any stimulus is shorter if the subject has an adequate pre-perceptive attitude, that is if he has some information on the nature of what is to be shown to him.

In considering these two laws, we could deduce the following hypothesis:

The threshold of recognition of a word, occuring at a normal frequency, is lowered by an adequate pre-perceptive attitude, that is to say that added to the effect of the frequency is that of the attitude (Fraisse and Blancheteau, unpublished research). It will be seen that this hypothesis owes nothing to observation, but is deduced from a body of information previously acquired.

It is possible to go further in deduction. At a sufficiently advanced stage in a science it is possible to set up a series of postulates from which one can draw verifiable consequences, the body of doctrine being validated by successive approximation. Hull (1951) employed this method with some success in the sphere of learning, and called it the hypothetico-deductive method (see Chapter 1, p. 67).

3 The features of a good hypothesis

A good hypothesis is one which will be fruitful and enable a new step (however small) to be taken in science. This said, and with beginners especially in mind, we can detail several formal features of all good hypotheses:

A) the hypothesis must be an *adequate reply* to the question asked. A truism, but one which it is difficult to make explicit. However, 'adequate' does not mean exhaustive. Usually an hypothesis will only explain a part of the facts and in science one must not be afraid of long thought processes. We shall return to this later.

B) the hypothesis must take into account information already acquired and must, from this point of view, be probable. Admittedly the best hypotheses open new channels, but they never contradict scientifically acquired results.

C) the hypothesis must be *verifiable*. This criterion is the most important and creates the most work.

a) the operational character of hypotheses: an hypothesis formulates the relationship between two classes of facts. In other

110

words, the hypothesis is a conceptualization and, as such, has a general bearing. Hence the relation which we have assumed between adaptation to anticipation and amotional stability. But such a relation cannot be verified at this level of generality. The experiment studied particular situations and responses. It related the observed behaviour of the subject in one or more anticipatory situations to the performances in one or more tests enabling us to obtain an approximate determination of his emotional stability. Thus, in one of our experiments we studied: α) the lesser or greater deterioration which anticipation introduced into the speed of reaction and β) the results of tests of a projective nature where the subject had to interpret pictures and complete a story involving anticipatory situations. For emotional stability, we also used two different criteria: one, the differences which were introduced by age, since it is known that on average emotional stability increases as the child develops; the other, a criterion taken from a performance test, to assess the deterioration occurring in a motor task when errors are punished by a loud noise.

The hypothesis which has a *general* bearing is only verified in particular exemplary cases. Only new experiments enable us to prove that the bases are valid and the relationship generally applicable. We shall encounter this problem again at the stage of analysis of results. In practice, the repetition of experiments and the varying of situations makes it possible to verify the generality of a law more and more closely: this is why science only progresses by many workers carrying out numerous, often similar, experiments.

In each experiment one only verifies one relationship between particular situations, even if the hypothesis began by being more ambitious. There is then a dialectic movement between thought and experiment which goes from the general to the particular. An hypothesis is never entirely verified, but the approximation becomes closer and closer. This is more true in the social sciences than in the biological or physical sciences where it is easier to determine the validating instance.

b) Verification may be direct or indirect: verification is direct when either of the two terms of the hypothetical relation can be directly observed. For instance in the example above the effect of the attitude was superimposed on that of the frequency in the determination of the threshold of recognition. But very often the hypothesis is more complex and assumes the existence of an intervening variable which cannot be directly verified.

Thus, hypotheses on the nature of the cones which enable us to see colours can only be indirectly verified. The most likely hypothesis must in effect take account of all the known facts. As our knowledge develops, or margin of choice is gradually reduced. In the example of colour vision, direct verification will be possible when the progress of histology and chemistry makes it so.

Other hypotheses, in particular those which involve factors such as personality traits, motivation, general behaviour characteristics like habit strength (Hull), will only ever be susceptible, theoretically, to indirect verification, that is to say that one can deduce them from the consequences themselves. The theoretical hypothesis becomes increasingly likely as the number of predicted facts increases.

c) Verification is almost always partial. We have already twice stressed this aspect, but we must mention it again. In physiology it is possible to prove. Ablations, sections, organic lesions all enable one to establish the exact functional role of a specific part of the organism. In animal psycho-physiology, one can come near to this ideal. In psychology it is unattainable. An action depends, as we have seen, on two types of variable: situation and personality. But in each type the number of variables involved is very great and, despite all precautions (which we deal with in the following paragraph) the observed behaviour depends only in part on *the* variable envisaged. The likelihood of verification is most often expressed by a statistical criterion: the hypothesis is verified for example at the 0·05 level of significance which means that there are 5 chances out of 100 that the difference (or correlation) found will not be attributable to the particular characteristics of the sample of observations used. This means that the manipulated variable plays a part, but in relation to others which strengthen or weaken its effect.

Partial verification of an hypothesis excludes inverse hypotheses, but not the role of other variables which can be complementary. Thus, in learning theory, authors have been able to verify the importance of associations established between different signs of a situation and have built up a body of hypotheses called S–S. Other workers have proved the importance of the relations established between the signs of the situation and the response by the process callled reinforcement. These hypotheses, called S–R, certainly do not exclude the first. In our opinion, the processes of learning integrate these complex aspects, each system playing a predominant role according to the situation.

It is often as a result of hypotheses and attempts at synthesis that science makes its more noticeable advances. Physical theory, like psychological theory, bears witness to this fact.

3 Experimentation

1 Independent and dependent variables

The object of experimentation is to verify the existence of a relation between two orders of facts. The general principle is always the same. To vary one fact and to observe the consequence of this variation on an action. The factor manipulated by the experimenter is called the independent variable; the factor which it modifies is called the dependent variable. We will employ this terminology throughout.

2 Provoked and invoked experiments

This distinction, introduced by Claude Bernard, is extremely useful in psychology. Provoked experiments are more frequent and more classical. The experimenter manipulates the independent variable and observes the results. The experiment is called invoked when the manipulation of an independent variable has been achieved without the intervention of the experimenter. Cerebral lesions brought about by wounds or illness, differences in cultural levels arising from unequal opportunities in life, or the biological identity of homozygotes would fall into this category. From these cases we must go on to all those where a variation exists in one form or another in the personality which can be used as an independent variable. These cases are precious, because the experimenter does not have the time to introduce variables whose action is slow (an educational system) and he has no right to experiment on man when this experimentation involves grave or irreversible physiological or psychological harm. An experiment can at the same time be invoked as to one variable and provoked as to the other.

3 Experiments and the laboratory

Experiment aims to establish the hypothesis. It is also concerned to verify the greatest possible number of variables and to record behavioural responses as precisely as possible. Evidently it is easier to achieve this ideal in a laboratory where the material and the physical environment are especially arranged for this purpose. By 'laboratory' we do not necessarily mean a vast network of individual rooms. A quiet room can often play this part in a school, a hospital or a barracks. There are even mobile laboratories in vans.

In any case, the laboratory creates an artificial environment. Moreover, its object is not—save in exceptional cases—to create or recreate natural conditions and situations in miniature. The experimenter proceeds analytically and endeavours to create situations which show up the influence of the selected variable as much as possible. He proceeds in the same spirit as the physicist or the biologist. If at the observation stage he often has to resort to naturalistic observation, he must balance this in the experiment. The relationship must be established by endeavouring to eliminate any influences which would mask it. The laboratory is only useful when it uses means which isolate a phenomenon.

There is no danger in this analytical approach at this stage of scientific work. It would be dangerous only if the experimenter rashly wanted to transpose his laboratory results into everyday life, where the variables which he had neutralized would come back into play. We must not forget that the primary object of experimentation is the constitution of a science and that its applications should not be mechanically deduced.

However, not all exeriments can be done in the laboratory, especially in social or applied psychology. In these cases the experimenter may well alter one variable, but he must keep the other normal conditions of people's lives. Thus, it is possible to introduce new teaching methods in one or more classes and to measure their effectiveness after a certain time by comparing these classes with the others where the change has not been introduced. It is also possible to modify the attitude of the management towards the staff in some offices and not others and to estimate the results comparatively.

But it is immediately apparent that such experiments—and they are worthy of the name—leave a great number of variables un-controlled. Let us mention some of them, in reference to the preceding examples: the personality of the teachers or bosses, the nature of the classes or groups, the attitude which prolonged experiment elicits in the groups being studied. We are reminded of the adventures and misadventures of the experiment at the Hawthorne factory. However, the multiplication of experiments from the same hypothesis can increase the value of the verification obtained.

4 Experiment and equipment

The psychological laboratory has the classical characteristic of being weighed down with apparatus. What part does it play? The equipment is simply a means of controlling the variation of independent variables, and of judging accurately the value or the qualities of the dependent variable, i.e. the responses of the subject.

Material can be very complex, but it can also be very simple. In the sphere of language, particularly, much research can be done with paper and pencil and a chronometer. Let us take again the three variables of the psychological relationship to indicate briefly the nature and role of material in human psychology.

A) *The situation.* The aim is to define as accurately as possible the situation and its variations. Into this category come all the instruments designed to measure or to produce in a controlled manner the physical variables of the environment. Light-meter, decibelmeter, audiometer and also olfactometer, gravimeter, etc.

Researchers in perception use presentation apparatus of various types. For example, the tachistocope for controlling the duration of exposure time.

For memory, apparatus is also necessary to control presentation time and succession intervals: cylinders carrying the stimuli which pass in front of a window, projectors, etc.

Sensori-motor studies and those on learning use apparatus to define the task.

We have already mentioned that studies on language and symbolic intelligence reduce material to a minimum. Sometimes the laboratory is furnished to create artificial living conditions: Witkin's tilted rooms, Kleitmann's sleep-study laboratories and, today, cells which reproduce the living conditions of astronauts in which psychological studies are carried out together with the physiological research.

B) *Personality*. Where it is necessary to control the personality variables, the most up-to-date material consists of tests of all kinds (Pichot, 1949).

To provoke physiological change, the laboratory is transformed into a clinic, as in pharmacodynamic research.

C) *Response*. The essential role of the material here is to record the responses.

If physiological signs are to be utilized (see Chapter 8) then recording techniques such as the EEG, the EDG and the EMG are used. The cine-camera captures facial expressions and complex actions, the tape recorder captures verbal responses. A whole series of apparatus is available for the measurement of the duration of phenomena—ordinary chronometers, chronoscopes (Hipp, Arsonval), which are electronic nowadays. Often polygraphs with synchronized motors are used, making it possible to record the moment of stimulus or stimuli and that of the response or responses, etc.

Often a simple sheet of notepaper filled in by the subject or the experimenter suffices.

The value of the experiment does not depend on that of the material used but on the richness of the hypothesis and the accurate definition of the necessary controls. Nevertheless, the fact remains that many of these controls are impossible without apparatus, and in some cases the progress of experimentation depends on technical progress.

5 Isolation and control of independent variables

Up until now we have discoursed without mentioning the classical principle of experimentation: to alter a single variable while keeping the others constant. Such a rule presents numerous problems and we shall slowly see how these are resolved in practice. The planning of the experiment and preparation of results should aim at the closest observation of this rule.

Its very principle can be questioned. *Can* one isolate a variable? Theoretically the question is insoluble, but a century of experimentation has shown it to be possible if precautions are taken and if the results are cross-checked with others obtained under similar conditions. It is often the case that what was assumed to be an independent variable was not in fact one and that the conduct of the subject is explained by other variables, but this is only a classical difficulty of all experimental work and the physico-chemical and biological sciences have suffered the same mishaps.

If in practice it is feasible, it is still not always easy to isolate a variable. There are two possible techniques. One is to neutralize the variable or variables which cannot be maintained constant, and we shall look at actual methods of doing this. The other, more recent, is to construct experimental designs with several variables, the analysis of their variance making it possible to distinguish the relative weight of the results (see p. 129). And what about the control of the other variables? When it is a question of situation variables this could be considered as a possibility, but a personality is not a robot performing stereotyped actions from day to day, or for years at a time. Attention, motivation, and the availability of the subjects are all changeable. These fluctuations explain why his responses vary from one minute to the next within certain limits. We shall see how statistics enable us to dissociate the essential from the secondary in a well-constructed experiment.

Now we shall analyse the problems created by variations of the independent variable (whether of situation or personality) and the dependent variable (responses).

6 Situation variables

A situation has two main aspects, environment, that is the conditions in which the subject is called upon to do something, and the task, defined by the material on which the subject must act when carrying out instructions he receives.

A) *The environment.* Two aspects must be distinguished:

a) The physical environment. This is made up of all the sensory and spatio-temporal conditions, i.e. the framework in which the subject is called upon to perform a task. These conditions must be carefully controlled since they can have a direct or indirect influence on the conduct of the subject.

The influence is direct when the conditions of the environment interfere with the stimuli appropriate to the task. For example, in experiments on audition in which noise in the locality modifies the conditions of the experiment. In many experiments on visual perception, the lighting and visual background in which the actual stimuli appear are variables which must not be neglected. This is why laboratories have sound-proof, darkened and light-controlled rooms.

In a completely different sphere, the disposition of the subjects within the space can also have direct consequences on the behaviour of individuals or groups. Group dynamicists have devised tables and table arrangements which reduce certain objections to a minimum.

The influence is indirect when the environment does not modify the conditions of the task, but acts on the subject by modifying, to a greater or lesser degree, his feelings towards the task (the general atmosphere, his motivations, his fatigue etc.).[5]

Industry has become very much aware of these factors in the last few decades. It is certain that the environment becomes increasingly important the more artificial it is, the prime example being that of the present-day cosmonauts in their capsule. But even in the laboratory these problems must not be underestimated.

b) The social environment. The presence of the experimenter, *de socii* is a very important situation variable. We will not go into this in detail, and what we have said on p. 104 applies equally to experimental work. This heading covers a whole new series of problems peculiar to social psychology. Admittedly it is often necessary to neutralize these environmental variables, but it is only possible if their effects are understood; many experiments have no other aim than to study that independent variable whose effects cannot be known *a priori*. The principle in these experiments is to maintain all the other conditions constant and to vary only the nature of the environment. But it is not possible to be absolutely certain which influence operates in a particular situation, it depends on the task and sometimes on the personality of the subject. To take an example from current university life: there are students who work very well in the library, and others who do not. In this sphere, as in others, we cannot make broad generalizations at present.

    [5] I remember how astonished I was when, as a young man in charge of practical work, having organized an experiment on the influence of distraction on efficiency, (reading during a barrage of signals) I noticed that in many subjects this increased instead of diminished the number of signals blocked per unit of time.

B) *The task.* This is defined by the points to which the activity of the subject is applied the *material*, in other words (which can be important or can be reduced to almost nothing) and by the *instructions* which are an essential part of the experiment. By the instructions the experimenter determines the situation in the way he has decided to define it. Moreover, he defines accurately the nature of the expected response (a rapid reaction, learning, the solving of a problem) which can be determined or indeterminate according to the problems studied. The instructions also fix a certain level of motivation, indicating the importance which the experimenter attaches to eventual successes or failures, i.e. to the responses.

Briefly, instructions aim to make all the subjects come to the task in as similar conditions as possible.

The drawing up of instructions is not always easy. From this point of view experiments on form-constancy are particularly enlightening in the difficulties which they present, telling the subject to reproduce what he sees is ambiguous, since depending on his attitude, he will see the object in its physical substance or the projection of that object if he concerns himself with the phenomenal data. It is wise to try out the instructions in pilot experiments until their significance leaves no room for misinterpretation.

C) *Qualitative and quantitative variations.* Different types of situation can be varied in several ways. The variation is quantitative when the variable takes several values which can be ordered in a continuum. This form of variation, classical in the physicochemical sciences, is the richest, but it is not always possible in psychology; however, it is becoming increasingly applicable. The physical variations of the environment are simple and special cases.

But quantitative does not imply intensive. Quantity is also introduced by the length of the material to be learned (for example: the time (t) to learn a list of works of length l is equal to $t = kl^2$, k being a constant), the number of repetitions necessary to arrive at a particular result, or the time allowed to the subject for a task, or distance, for example that separating an animal from the desired object or from a punishment to be avoided (cf. the approach and avoidance gradients of J. S. Brown), or the frequency of the words in the language, or the rate of information, etc. The techniques of quantification from ordinal or interval scales established in preliminary experiments constantly increases the number of quantifiable variables (see Chapter IV).

Paul Fraisse

But there are still many cases where the environmental variation is of a qualitative kind. Situations differ according to a known criterion. Thus, one can compare reaction times to light and to sound, the subject being warned by a signal, or not being warned by a signal, etc. How are verbal associations influenced by the grammatical functions of the words (nouns, adjectives, verbs, etc.)? What repercussions on memorization has the fact that the material is significant or not?

In social psychology qualitative variations are more frequent; the presence or absence of leader or guide, variations of context, etc.

D) *Organization of the variations.* Whether the differences are qualitative or quantitative, we begin with several situations, S_1, S_2, etc. The order of their presentation is very important. In fact, the subject, after having reacted to S_1 is no longer exactly the same. There can be processes of facilitation (learning, for example) but also inhibition (in the case of a failure, for example), etc. The order of presentation of the situations is thus of great importance. There are three possible solutions available to the experimenter:

a) He can consider the order of variations as a variable in itself and in his case he will find himself with at least two independent variables. He must therefore plan the order of presentation as part of experimental design. We shall study this general technique in a later section (see p. 128).

b) He can seek to neutralize the effect resulting from the order of presentation of the variables. This is frequently done. If the changes induced by the order of the variables are minimal, temporary and reversible (habituation, or temporary lassitude, for example) he can act in three different ways:

α) Disregard this variable. This attitude is hardly justifiable except in preliminary experiments or when the qualitative variations allow the prediction of the minor effects of the order (for example, order of words in a free association test).

β) Neutralize the effect of the order by using the counterbalance or rotation method. Its principle is to make the inverse order correspond to a given order. Let us suppose that we have stimuli S_1 and S_2. They can presented several consecutive times in an alternated order S_1S_2 and S_2S_1, etc. Let us take a further example from psychophysics, through which psychological methodology began to be aware of its problems. A threshold determined by an

120

increasing series of stimuli is followed by one determined in a decreasing series to counterbalance the serial effects. Similarly, an adjustment starting from a greater stimulus value is followed by one starting from a lower value.

Rotation by alternation is justified when the same measurements are taken several consecutive times. If the number of alternations is limited, one can simply use a mirror variation of the type $S_1S_2S_2S_1$, in which it is assumed that the effect of the order S_1———S_2 is counterbalanced by that of the order S_2———S_1. This assumption can be avoided by previous use of a counterbalance which involves not only one but two subjects. For example, the first undergoes the tests in the order $S_1S_2S_2S_1$ and the second in the order $S_2S_1S_1S_2$. In a recent experiment (Fraisse, 1961) where we had four variations paired two by two (S_1S_2, s_1s_2) we used the following counterbalance, equilibrated on four subjects:

$$s_1s_2S_1S_2S_2S_1s_2s_1$$
$$s_2s_1S_2S_1S_1S_2s_1s_2$$
$$S_1S_2s_1s_2s_2s_1S_1S_2$$
$$S_2S_1s_2s_1s_1s_2S_2S_1$$

It is sufficient then, to employ four subjects or a multiple of four to have an equilibrated plan, in which one can sum the values obtained and assume that the serial effect has been adequately counterbalanced.

γ) Neutralize the effect of the order by presenting the stimulations in a random order and varying this order from one series to another. This is the principle of the constant method in psychophysics. If several series cannot be given to the same subject, the order can be varied from one subject to another. With this method it can be expected that the transient effects of the order will neutralize one another. Experimentalists are trusting less and less to blind chance and are organizing chance in advance by the drawing of lots or by using random number tables (Fisher and Yates, 1957).

(c) When the changes introduced by the order of variations are important, durable and more or less irreversible, the preceding methods do not apply.

In principle the solution is to use two or more groups of subjects. One, for example, does the test in situation S_1, the other in situation S_2, etc. This technique was profitably used by Woodrow

(1934) to determine the value of the interval of indifference in the perception of time, that is to say the interval which is neither over- nor underestimated. This value depends so much on the series used that all other forms of experiment give uncertain results. Woodrow overcame this difficulty by using groups of different subjects for each interval (see Chapter 19). Generally speaking, several groups could be used to avoid the counterbalance and rotation methods, but this is a long procedure. This technique is called for when the same subjects have to undergo several successive tests which produce lasting effects. It can become even more complex, as in learning. To take a classic example: does a variation in the type of activity occurring between learning and performance modify the latter? In principle, two methods are possible: α) the same subjects do the experiment several times, each time learning material which is different, but considered as equivalent, only the activity between the learning and its demonstration being modified. In this case, one should beware of adaptation to the situation, rehearsal during the intervening period and interference between over-similar materials. β) two groups of subjects learn the same material, but their activity between learning and performance is not the same. The difference in performance can be attributed to this difference in activity or to a condition already postulated by our preceding example, in order to know whether the *groups are equivalent*. The next section deals with this important problem. We must add here that in this type of experiment one of the groups is often considered as the control.[6]

Let us take the example of studies in transfer of learning: does prior learning facilitate later learning of a different kind? Is there, for example, transfer of intensive training in learning language I by heart to the learning by heart of language II? Two equivalent groups are necessary, and the general design of the experiment is as follows:

Experimental group:

Pre-test in language II—training in language I—post-test in language II

---

[6] In 1901 Thorndike and Woodworth first used the comparison of two groups to study the effects of two learning sequences, ABC and ADC. It was Winch, in 1908, who first used a control group in an experiment on transfer of training and the practice became common after 1920 (Solomon, 1949).

Control group:

Pre-test in language II—no training—post-test in language II

The proof is as follows:

a) the control group is necessary because during the training in language I, especially if this is fairly long and if it is inserted into a curriculum, the subjects may have progressed in learning language II by heart for various reasons. Is progress due to the specific training or to more general factors? The control group, undergoing the post-test after a time lapse equal to the training can provide the answer to this question:

b) the pre-test has two functions: to ensure the equivalent of the two groups as to the function studied and to assess the progress between pre-test and post-test.

The control group method is classically employed each time one studies important effects of situations behaviour (effects of specific learning, pharmacodynamic effects, changes occurring in the environment or the task in workshops, offices, etc.).

7   Forming comparable groups

This is a delicate and fundamental problem. Two groups are never absolutely equivalent, but how can one achieve adequate comparability?

A basic rule: two groups should be equivalent at least in those aspects which are relevant to the problems studied: a group of children of the same age, sex or mental level, similar pathological cases, etc.

The first problem to be solved, and one which often needs a pilot experiment, is knowing which are the important variables whose equivalence must be controlled. Is it the intellectual level? the socio-economic level? the personality?

The first question being answered, good criteria (sometimes in the form of tests) of the equivalence must be found, and the problem is even more delicate when one proceeds from biological variables to social or personality variables.

In practice this is often done in the following manner. To form comparable groups, one starts with a population which is already homogeneous from many points of view. Children of a given age, from the same district, students of a particular subject at a particular level, people in similar work, etc. However, the advantage gained at the beginning will eventually be lost. The results obtained will be relative to the population studied. But researchers can rarely allow themselves to use *two* equivalent and representative samples of the population of a given country. And even in this case, the results obtained could not be extrapolated, from France to China, for example.

Starting from this population, several procedures are possible according to the degree of equivalence desired.

A) Subjects are chosen at random from a given section of the population. If it is fairly homogeneous considering the variables studied, it can be taken for granted that the inevitable individual differences will compensate each other. This method is even more valuable when the groups are more numerous and the population more homogeneous. In fact, we ourselves almost made a gross error by putting questions concerning a measurement of optico-geometric illusions to the residents of a students' hostel who belonged to different faculties. It was argued that this population could not be considered homogeneous; the science and the arts students in fact gave completely different results (Fraisse and Vautrey, 1956).

B) If the variables which *must* be controlled are known, the equivalence of the groups can be established in this respect. The simplest case is the one mentioned above (p. 123), a case where there is homogeneity or resemblance between the test which establishes the equivalence and that which constitutes the experiment.

But in this case the degrees of comparability can vary:

a) one can be satisfied by the comparability of the norms of the two groups, absolute equivalence or absence of significant difference between them;

b) one can ask that the performances of the subjects in the pilot study be comparable in their norms and range of variation;

c) lastly, one can form paired or matched groups. From one or more preliminary tests, the subjects having obtained similar scores are assigned two by two respectively to each of the groups. The most perfect equivalence possible is that of identical twins, each member of a pair being assigned to each group.

8 *Personality variations*

Since personality is a combination of very different facts and forces, only some of them can be modified by some action of E,[7] and for others one can only draw on the variety offered by nature and by society.

A) *Manipulated variations.* a) *Biological variations:* it is often possible to act on the physiological or psychophysiological components of an action. To quote some examples:

α) Pharmacodynamic influences on normal or sick people: drugs can act on the intelligence (glutamic acid), the emotions (neuroleptics) efficiency (amphetamine), etc.

β) Through the effect of deprivation or satiety, by pharmacodynamic action or social situations, one can act on the basic forms of motivation (hunger, thirst, sex).

γ) Modifications of stimuli can act indirectly through their general action on the organism. For instance in the effects of prolonged sensory deprivation (Bexton, Heron and Scott, 1954).

The distinction between direct and indirect action is sometimes fine.

b) *Psychological variations:* E has within a certain margin the possibility of acting on the way in which S approaches the situation. To quote two clear instances:

α) Influence on attitudes. We have mentioned (see p. 101) that S must make a choice from all the factors of a situation. The instructions have the effect of directing this choice. By varying the instructions and thus the attitudes, one can study the effect of that variable. The pioneers of experimental psychology discovered the differences which the motor or sensory dominance of a attitude played in the speed of reaction time. More modern researches have studied the effects of attempts to influence attitudes on perception, memory and the solving of problems.

β) Influence on motivation. Here we take up a question already touched upon earlier, but this time the motivation is varied directly by instructions which may or may not use classical reinforcement to place a value on the results to be obtained social motivation ('people of your level succeed to this or that degree'); academic or business interests ('your result will count for the exam' or 'you will receive a particular reward for a particular result'); personal

---

[7] For the rest of this chapter we shall refer to the experimenter as E and to the subject as S.

reactions (S knows his results or simply where he succeeded or failed. The results announced can be truthful, but are sometimes 'faked' to produce reactions to success or failure at will).

In this way one studies not only the influence of the degree of motivation on conduct, but also the influence of motivational conflict, etc.

(B) *Elicited variations.* It is impossible to change the age, sex, temperament and character, past experience, social status, self-estimation, etc., of S. However, all these variables have a great influence on his conduct. To discover them, one need only use the differences resulting from nature or from society. It is sufficient then to form two or more groups possessing a particular trait in varying degrees. This method is classical in the psychology of individual differences, but when it goes beyond establishing and measuring differences, it becomes part of experimental psychology and it involves the study of relationships between different aspects of the personality. The subject matter of psychology is the personality but it is not enough to study, for example, the laws of memory, one must also seek to discover how these laws are affected by the intelligence, character or interests of S. In an earlier age, experimental psychology did not take account of individual differences, which it glossed over in research on the main characteristics of responsiveness, but in its later stages it was these very differences which became the object of study. They were reproduced by manipulating those personality variables which could be controlled, in an attempt to explain them.

The problem remains to form comparable groups, but there is an additional difficulty: these groups, equivalent in all 'essential' points must differ in that aspect which one wishes to vary.

Here again experiment only progresses by successive approximations by bringing to light these 'essential' variables by means of trial and error.

To take a single example: it seems that genetic studies present few problems in countries where there is strong civil administration. Even so it is very difficult to find groups which are comparable only in their intellectual capacity at each age level. Classes of seven-year-olds contain very different individuals in a given geographical area, yet all educational systems introduce some form of selection. How can we find at 14 years and *a fortiori* in adults, groups comparable to those of 7 years?

9   Variations in responses

Each of the subject's responses is significant. However, experimental work cannot confine itself to merely two responses, corresponding to two categories of independent variable, those in which variation in the response can be attributed to that of the variable and those in which it cannot. Such a deduction is possible in physics, and sometimes in physiology, but it is unthinkable in psychology because one can *never* control all the S and P variables adequately.

Let us take the simplest response: to respond as rapidly as possible to the appearance of a stimulus. The time varies considerably from one reaction to another and psychologists faced with these variations have even thought of making this into a test of attention. If we wish to study the effect of the intensity of the stimulation on the length of reaction time (see Chapter 6) it is obvious that we must cancel out these transient fluctuations, and thereby obtain in each situation a large number of responses whose central tendencies we compared in relation to their variance, with a test of significance like Student's t or χ^2. The consequence of this procedure is that our result will have a probabilistic character because, in our example, one or more reaction times to the least strong intensity might be longer than the reaction time to a stronger intensity, while on average the reaction time is shorter for stronger intensity.

In the above case, the experiment could be carried out on a single subject. But one question immediately arises. Will the result obtained depend on a peculiarity of the subject, or has it general validity? This last aspect is critical when one is building up a science.[8] Several subjects must be used, and this is all the more necessary when the situation is more complex. In extreme circumstances elementary sensory laws can be established with one or two subjects, but in the course of very long experiments.

Moreover, the number of subjects must be multiplied each time it is necessary to balance the experimental design, and *a fortiori* when one studies the P variables in a case where the different degrees of the variable require different subjects.

---

[8] The requirements of applicability obviously vary, although an action only achieves its full significance when considered in relation to others and more generally to a norm as expressed in a standardized form.

Paul Fraisse

The greater the number of measurements or of subjects, the nearer the average obtained is to that which one would obtain if the number were infinite.

The reliance which one can place on an average or central tendency depends, than, on the number of measurements carried out. It must be remembered, however, that the possible error on an obtained average is not inversely proportional to the number of measurements, but to its square root $\left(E = \dfrac{\sigma}{\sqrt{N}} \right)$. In other words, if one extends the number of measurements from 25 to 49, one only diminishes the possible error in the proportion of 5 to 7.

We have argued, in this section, as if there was a 'true' value of a response which could be approached through the multiplication of measurements or of subjects by neutralizing extraneous factors. But we are less and less inclined to present problems in these terms. Each response depends on a multiplicity of variables, thus it can only be more or less probable as a result of the variation of the independent variables. Each response is stochastic, and the statistical treatment of data is not a device to extract pure metal from its source, but the instrument by which we can approximate to a description of actual behaviour.

10 Experimental designs[9]

To vary *one* variable, and only one, is not always possible, and we have already come up against this difficulty several times. We would now add that this type of experiment is not ideal since, in general, diverse variables act simultaneously to determine our conduct. This consideration, allied to the facilities offered by the analysis of variance, has led psychologists (following the example of agronomists and biologists) to use increasingly complex experimental designs. Actually each experiment is planned according to a design, which is simply the logical schema determining the nature and order of the different phases of the experiment. The simplest design comes down to comparing the results which match two degrees of the independent variable. These two degrees could correspond to a quantitative difference (e.g. two sets of duration, or intensity) or to a qualitative difference (reaction time to a sound or light). The test case of a qualitative difference

[9] For a development of this question see Reuchlin, 1953 and Fraisse, 1963.

is the presence of absence of a variable. For each degree of the variable a mass of measurements is obtained on one or more subjects. The comparison is made by means of a statistical test (Student's *t*, or χ^2) enabling one to say whether the results obtained in one or other situation justify the rejection of the null hypothesis, i.e. whether to consider the two populations of measurements as not belonging to a homogeneous whole. In this case the difference in the results of the two collections of measurements is explained, at a given threshold of probability, by the difference in the degrees of the independent variable. When there are more than two degrees of the independent variable, the comparison of the groups of results two by two is very long and can lead to errors.

Obviously in functional experiments, where the variations of the independent variable are quantitative, hardly any problems arise. The most important thing is to know the way the independent variable works; as in the case of the curves of learning and forgetting. But it is not the same in factorial experiments,[10] when the differences of the degrees of the independent variable are qualitative, which is often the case. One must then be able to discover the relative role of one of them. Analysis of variance, which we owe to Fisher (1925) enables us to decide, in cases where there are several collections of measurements of the same independent variable expressing different conditions, the significant role of one or another. Its principle is similar to that of Student's *t*. One begins by considering all the collections of measurements as belonging to the same whole, that is to say one admits the null hypothesis.[11] One then calculates the total variance of the whole, which is simply the sum of the variances of the different populations that have been measured. One is comparing two estimates of the variance of the measurements. One of them is calculated in such a way as not to introduce the possible differences between the averages of the sample measurements which have been obtained on account of their different values of the independent variable. The other estimate introduces these differences of averages besides the variations affecting the first estimation ('error').

---

[10] Factorial experiment must not be confused with factor analysis.

[11] This point of departure is valid only if the variances of the different populations are almost homogeneous and the results distributed according to the Laplace–Gauss law.

Paul Fraisse

The two estimations should be equal (their relation, or Snédécor's F relation then taking the value 1·00), if the differences of averages are nil. That is to say if this independent variable has no effect on the phenomenon. In fact, one can only ask that the F relation is not significantly higher than 1·00, and the Snédécor table enables one to know whether this is so.

To sum up, analysis of variance makes it possible to say whether the independent variable has a particular effect, without directly measuring that effect. Thus, it corresponds to a method of detecting the important variables.

Analysis of variance has opened up new perspectives of experimentation in the conjectural sciences. Until now it has been difficult to construct designs treating more than one independent variable. As we have seen the problem was to neutralize the effect of a second variable, usually that of the order, to avoid the sequential effects of the situation which made it easier or more difficult to respond; in brief, to avoid distortion of results.

A step forward was made when it was decided to use different, but comparable groups of subjects to test the effect of an independent variable, some being subjected to one variable and the others not. Why, then, not measure the effect of several independent variables simultaneously if the equivalence of the groups is assured? It was in this way that Fisher worked out his experimental designs, which were devised, in the first place, for agriculture. To be useful in this, experiment must take into account soils, fertilizers and seeds at least. It was costly and often vain to vary only a single one of these variables. Experimental designs were introduced into psychology around 1940, and today they form part of current methodology.[12]

We will mention briefly the principal types of designs used, beginning with the most complex.

A) *Factorial design*. A design is factorial when it uses all the possible combinations of degree of different independent variables which have been selected. Let us take the simplest case. It is decided to study the two values of two independent variables A_1 and A_2 and B_1 and B_2; four combinations are possible, as in the following table:

[12] Though the analysis of variance is the best instrument to study the possible role of several variables, experimental designs are not necessarily subordinated to this method.

130

	A_1	A_2
B_1	I	II
B_2	III	IV

A_1B_1 which group I will undergo; A_1B_2 which group III will undergo; A_2B_1 which group II will undergo; A_2B_2 which group IV will undergo.

Groups I, II, II and IV must be equivalent. Moreover, one could imagine the same subjects in all four situations if the order in which they undergo them is of no importance.

Let us take a concrete example. Suppose that one wishes to study the effect of anticipation on reaction time with two different lengths of anticipatory period, 20 seconds (A_1) and 60 seconds (A_2) and two conditions, which we shall call indifferent anticipation (B_1) (ordinary simple reaction time) and fearful anticipation (B_2) (in reacting the subject administers an electric shock to himself).

Such designs have three advantages (Reuchlin, 1953):

a) Each measurement or group of measurements contributes to the solving of the two problems presented— the effect of the duration of the anticipatory period and the effect of its particular characteristic. To study all the problems while varying only one variable at a time would have needed not 4 but 8 groups of subjects (A_1 and A_2 in the condition B_1 and then condition B_2; then B_1 and B_2 in the case A_1 and then A_2).

b) The grounds on which the inductive argument is based are broader. In our example one studies the effects of two lengths of anticipatory period on two different anticipation situations. In effect the results can be regrouped and one can test separately:

——— the effect of the short anticipatory period A_1, group I+ group III

——— the effect of the long anticipatory period A_2, group II+ group IV then:

——— the effect of the neutral anticipatory period B_1, group I+ group II and:

———— the effect of the fearful anticipatory B_2 group III+ group IV and compare the overall effect of the nature of these anticipatory periods.

c) The possibility occurs of estimating possible *interactions* between the studied variables. We say that there is an interaction between two independent variables when the effect of one of them *on the dependent variable* depends on the value of the other. In our case this could mean that the effect of the nature of the anticipation depends on its duration, that for example the fearful anticipatory period in relation to the indifferent anticipatory period had a different effect on the reaction time depending on whether it is long or short. To discover this it is simply a matter of comparing the difference between groups II and I with that between groups IV and III. If the differences are not of the same order in the two cases, there is interaction; if they are of the same order, there is no interaction.

Analysis of variance enables us to answer this question and also the two questions relating to the actual effect of each variable. However, interaction can only be tested in the case of factorial designs of the type we are studying, that is to say complete designs.

This factorial design can only culminate in an analysis of variance, presented according to this schema:

Source of variation: between the lengths of anticipatory periods (A_1 and A_2)

between the nature of the anticipatory periods (B_1 and B_2)

interaction A and B;

within the groups (experimental error).

A factorial design can obviously be applied to more than two factors and to more than two values of each factor, but then the number of cells in the design and consequently the unwieldiness of the experiment is increased. For two variables with three different degrees, one has $3 \times 3 = 9$ cells, for three variables each with two degrees, $2 \times 2 \times 2 = 8$ cells for three variables with three values $3 \times 3 \times 3 = 27$ cells. Let us use a general formula: for 2 factors having respectively K and L values, one has a design with K × L cells; for three factors with K, L and M values, one has a design with K × L × M cells, etc. In our example we have taken two independent variables related to the situation, but a factorial design with two variables also offers the possibility of studying the interaction between situation and personality. Thus, one can discover the effect of the two lengths of anticipatory period (short and long, with neutral anticipation) on the reaction time as a function of two categories of subjects: those with greater or less emotional stability. These two categories may be distinguished by a preliminary test allowing for the measurement of emotional stability. Here, then is the design:

		Emotional stability	
		Weak	Strong
Waiting time (neutral)	Short	I	II
	Long	III	IV

Groups I and III are equivalent in that they are composed of subjects of less emotional stability; similarly groups II and IV are made up of subjects with great emotional stability. It would be possible, furthermore, to combine the two proposed designs consecutively. One would then have 3 variables each with 2 degrees, which would give a design of $2 \times 2 \times 2 = 8$ cells necessitating 8 groups of subjects:

Nature of anticipation	Waiting time	Emotional stability	
		Weak	Strong
Neutral anticipation	Short	I	II
	Long	III	IV
Fearful anticipation	Short	V	VI
	Long	VII	VIII

Paul Fraisse

B) *Latin squares.* A factorial design is the only one which permits the testing of the interaction of two or more variables, but we have seen that the total combination of several variables of varying degrees rapidly leads to unwieldy experiments. One could, however retain the other advantages of the factorial design whilst simplifying the procedure. The Latin square fulfils this need. Its principle is that each pair of possible conditions must be made use of once and once only. It is used when one wishes to study three variables simultaneously, each having several degrees of variation.

In practice the experiments are arranged in such a way that the rows and columns correspond to a constant variable and each row and each column contains all the possible conditions of the third variable. For instance, in an experiment with three variables, each having three possible conditions.[13] The corresponding factorial design would have 27 cells. The Latin square would only have 3 × 3 and would be set out in the following way:
——— K_1 K_2 K_3 being the possible conditions of the first variable
——— L_1 L_2 L_3 being the possible conditions of the second variable
——— ABC[14] being the possible conditions of the third variable

	K_1	K_2	K_2
L_1	A	B	C
L_2	B	C	A
L_3	C	A	B

A, B and C are found in each row and in each column.[15]

This design is basically an improvement on designs where one of the variables is varied at random in order to neutralize its

[13] We have given an example with 3 possible types, but there can be designs with 4, 5, 6, etc.
[14] Following the style which has given its name to the Latin square.
[15] There is obviously a great number of possible combinations of letters. Table 15 (Fisher and Yates) offers the means of taking (at random) one from all the possible Latin squares.

134

effects. The fact that the rows and the columns are homogeneous makes it possible to regroup the results three times according to the rows, the columns and the letters, permitting the testing of the effect of the three variables.

To refer again to our example on page 133, if A and B are respectively the short and the long anticipatory period, the Latin square will have only 4 cells (instead of the 8 in the case of the factorial design).

| | | Emotional stability | |
		Weak	Strong
Anticipation	Neutral	A	B
	Fearful	B	A

Although the interaction cannot be assessed in this case, its possible effect can be neutralized by multiplying the possible varieties of Latin squares. Thus, the order AB can become BA and the order BA can become AB (for more details see Reuchlin, 1953, p. 71).

Again, the variables could all be related to the situation or, conversely, could bring into play the S variables and the P variables simultaneously. In each case, one can use the same subjects (and even a single one) if the repetition and the arrangement of related experiments does not create complications. In the opposite case, one uses groups of subjects which are treated as equivalent.

C) *Graeco-Latin squares.* A Latin square permits the simultaneous treatment of three variables. A Graeco-Latin square permits the treatment of four. Its principle is to associate each Latin letter of the design of three variables with a Greek letter, corresponding to the values of a fourth independent variable. The distribution of the Greek letters obeys the same law as that of the Latin letters, that is, it must be present in each row and in each column so that each treatment of the third variable (Latin letter) is produced once and once only in conjunction with the treatment of the fourth (Greek letter). For, example, with the three values of each of 4 variables, one could establish the following design:

Aα	Bβ	Cγ
Bγ	Cα	Aβ
Cβ	Aγ	Bα

There are even more complex designs, all based on the same principle: regrouping partial results and comparing them with the total of other results; analysis of variance is not the only statistical instrument, but simply the best adapted.

But we must be very clear on the use of these designs. They enable us to show whether an independent variable has a discernible influence, but they do not enable us to assess how it acts on the dependent variable, i.e. to establish a law. Designs with several variables are properly used then they lead to a practical decision, as in agriculture, or applied psychology. In fundamental science, they are a small part of the research, and tests of the significance of the action or interaction of variables must always be interpreted in the light of our general psychological knowledge.

11 Experimental work in practice

There is a gap between theory and practice which even the most thorough expositions cannot bridge. Experiment in all sciences is learned in sessions of purposeful practical work. Some general advice, however, should not be ignored.

A) *The control of variables.* If the experiment aims to discover the action of one or more independent variables on a dependent variable, all the care of the experimenter must be brought to bear to control all the variables.

a) The S variables: the arrangement of laboratories (sound-proof, darkened, or light-controlled rooms) aims to control the nature of the environment, the various material which is used aims to define the task. E must not trust to his good intentions or his imagination; the prepared material must be practical and appropriate to the problem. Although judgment, imaginative foresight and practice save time and money, and thus forewarned E and his co-workers must be the first subjects of the experiment so as to uncover the possible presence of unwanted variables.

Moreover, when subjects are not familiar with psychological

practice, environment and material may have a disquieting effect. Finally, E must never forget that he is a factor in the overall situation. We have already explained this point (see p. 104).

b) The P variables: these are more delicate and more complex than the preceding ones.

E must warn the subject of the task which he is to perform. This information is given by instructions. Their preparation is very important. They are common to all the subjects, and must be set out in writing and be invariable from the moment the experiment begins. On the instructions depends not only the understanding of the task, but also the intention of E, both of which contribute to establishing a constant and uniform attitude in the subjects. Should E be replaced by a tape-recorder? This is possible but rarely desirable, because the subjects then feel themselves to be less involved.

The instructions must be 'run in', i.e. tried out on several people before the actual event. It is not always easy to express oneself clearly and unambiguously. Instructions can be repeated, but one should avoid having to comment on them. When they are just right, the best thing is to learn them by heart and to present them slowly and persuasively.

The instructions help to define the whole experimental situation and they must ensure the *co-operation* of the subject. The recruitment of subjects is itself an important stage. If it is not done directly by E, but by the leaders of groups or institutions, the way in which these third parties present the experiment to the potential subjects must be supervised. In particular E must have decided whether or not the subjects shall be told the true aim of the experiment. There is no general rule in this matter. Everything depends on which variables are selected for use. Let us add further that verbal explanations are not always enough. As in certain tests, it is useful to arrange if possible for several preliminary trials to allow subjects to become familiar with the task and E to ensure that the instructions are understood correctly.

To *co-operate*, that is to bring to bear a willingness sufficient to achieve the proposed aim is one thing: to be involved in the experiment is another. In certain experiments one seeks to vary either the motivation of the subject from one moment to another, or the motivation of one group in relation to that of another group. One of the classical means of doing this, especially in scholastic or university situations, is to present one of the tasks as being without consequence and the other as designed to measure an ability considered of value (speed, intelligence, memory, or general efficiency). Another means consists of using systems of rewards, even incentives. But this method can be tricky. If there is to be motivation, the reward must depend on the result, which is incompatible with the principle of fixed remuneration, which is also sometimes useful (paid subjects). It is true that one can, in this case, use supplementary variable bonuses.

If motivation is strong, another difficulty arises: the fear of failure can overcome the hope of success, so it appears that the relation between apparent and real motivation is not straightforward.

To this problem of instructions we must add that of the subjects' knowledge of their partial results as the experiment progresses. Sometimes the subject cannot fail to know his results (as in problem solving); more often, he is not directly informed of the quality or quantity of his responses. E, who transmits the results, must know that he is modifying the attitude of the subject by supplying him with guide-marks. Besides he is engendering conflict within the subject who sees his responses as successful or not in terms of his own levels of aspiration. On the other hand, it is possible, and sometimes of interest, to manipulate these responses by communicating prefabricated results, either of success or failure, in those cases where the subject has not sufficient criteria to assess his own performance.

c) The dependent variable: we have stressed the advantage of recording an organic response, muscular or verbal, in as permanent a way as possible and with a high degree of accuracy, taking into account the variability of behaviour studied. The difficulty here for E is to be able to control simultaneously the conditions of the task and the recording of the responses. It is sometimes necessary for there to be two or more experimenters when the experiment is rather complex. When E himself notes down the responses in writing, it is useful to have fairly clear response sheets prepared in advance, so that the risk of error (for example, writing a figure in the wrong column) is reduced to a minimum.

B) *Economy and efficiency*. The material cost of an experiment is often great, the human cost even greater. The preparation, execution and analysis of an experiment is slow work; it is difficult to obtain subjects, and one cannot expect unlimited numbers. For all these reasons, it is desirable to think before embarking on an experiment, to take precautions throughout and particularly to carry out pilot experiments on several subjects at different stages of the preparation of the material and in drawing up the experimental design.

Moreover, an experiment worthy of the name should not be begun before the procedure for the analysis of the results has been fixed. It is too late to discover a difficulty when the results are already collected. It is this constraint which led Fisher to work out his experimental designs.

12 *Methodological errors*

The errors which can occur in any experiment are of different kinds and this is yet another point where nothing can replace practical experience.

Errors of reasoning can arise in the inductive stage of setting up the hypothesis, in its definition, in passing from the general hypothesis to the representative variables, and even in the conceptual analysis of the results.

Statistical errors—not to mention errors of calculation—also lie in wait for the experimenter who is not sufficiently competent; for example: using inappropriate statistical tests in the wrong circumstances (because the representativeness of the results is inadequate or because one has not taken the paired samples into account, etc. . . .).

We would emphasize here another type of error which crops up in the very planning of the experiment, in particular the distortions which inevitably arise from the order in which situations are presented to the subjects. These are so-called systematic errors. Their exact nature obviously depends on the problem which is being studied, and a lengthy enumeration would be of little interest. We have therefore decided to select several of the more frequent statistical errors which are met with in research on perception. These errors are good examples because they show up here better than in other fields: it is, in fact, possible to know the stimulus in two ways, one by physical measurement and the other through the perceptual estimate of the subject. Even when physical measurement is impossible, the very fact that one records different

Paul Fraisse

responses for several subjects is an indication of their 'subjectivity'.

Perceptual errors have, moreover, played a great part in the development of our psychological knowledge: the individual element at the beginning of the nineteenth century; optico-geometric illusions from the second half of the nineteenth century to the present day. Piaget founds a number of his genetic laws on the study of illusions (1961). These systematic errors have also enabled us to affirm and refine experimental methodology, particularly through psychophysical research. Let us mention some of the main general errors:

A) *Time error*. If two stimuli are compared successively, the estimate of the second stimulus is influenced by the presentation of the first. If the first stimulus is considered as the standard and the second as the comparison stimulus, it can be said that the point of subjective equalization (PSE) is not the same as the actual value of the standard. There is a constant error, usually *negative*, that is to say that the PSE is smaller than the standard. For example, to take a series of weights, in estimating which seems equal to the first it turns out that this second weight is actually lighter (see Woodworth, *Experimental Psychology*, Chapter 18).

This error depends on the intensity level of the stimuli, on the interval between them and, of course, on the stimuli which can be interpolated between the standard and the stimulus of comparison. The error also depends on the possible range of the comparison stimuli, since Lambercier (1946) showed that the subject had a tendency to choose a median value (serial effect).

In addition to time error in its strictest sense there are the effects associated with the order in which the comparison stimuli themselves are presented. If the variation goes systematically from greatest to smallest, or vice versa, one tends to perceive the characteristic presented first for longer than that which follows (greatest or smallest). The same effect is to be found when the comparison is spatio-temporal. Thus, if one compares the size of two parts of a straight line presented simultaneously, the fact that one begins with one section which is smaller or larger than the standard gives rise to systematic error in the same way as already mentioned.

B) *Errors by assimilation or contrast*. When the stimuli to be

140

compared are similar, one tends to assimilate them even more; on the other hand minimal but marked differences tend to be exaggerated. These laws apply to time errors, but they have a more general bearing which goes beyond even the framework of perception. The fact is obvious in Delbœuf's illusion: the inner circle is judged greater than the standard, though the outer circle is, in fact only a fraction larger. When the difference between the two circles in increased, the error reverses, the small circle is then estimated as smaller than the standard.

The phenomenon of assimilation is very important; it has often been described as an attempt to restore the mean when making estimates. It was already manifest in the serial effect. In general we tend to underestimate greater values and overestimate smaller ones. Helson (1947) explained this phenomenon by using the concept of adaptation level. Taking into account the context and the stimuli used the subject constructs a level of adaptation, in relation to which he judges all the other stimuli.

This concept of adaptation level enables one to account, in particular, for the phenomenon of *anchorage*. Extrinsic sensory experiences modify the perception of the stimuli used in other respects. Thus, if one puts weights ranging from 200 to 400 grammes into 9 categories, from lightest to heaviest, the 'average' category will correspond, roughly speaking, to the geometric mean of the whole range of stimuli, i.e. 248 grammes. But if, before classing each stimulus a weight of 90 grammes is held in the hand, the average category will then correspond to 186 grammes. If, on the contrary, a weight of 900 grammes is held, the average category will be about 387 grammes. It is, therefore, the tendency to assimilate phenomena which predominates. However, in certain cases, with greater differences between values, the tendency to distinguish between them may predominate.

In anchorage experiments like the above, the context is explicit. But one must never forget that there is always a more or less implicit context which makes up what is termed one's *frame of reference*. Its importance increases as the stimuli become more ambiguous and the norms more subjective. In social or aesthetic perception, the frame of reference is fundamental.

C) *The effects of the activity and attitudes of the subjects.* Besides the errors engendered by the arrangement of the stimuli, there are those which arise from the manner in which the subject acts upon the data. In 1895, Binet showed that there were perceptual illusions which increased with the age and one might say the experience, of subjects.

Charpentier's weight illusion, also called Demoor's, is the best example of this: of two equal weights, in appearance the same type the one with the smaller volume appears to be the heaviest. But other illusions such as the Müller–Lyer illusion also lose their effect in similar conditions. Fraisse (1956) and Piaget (1958) using the tachistoscopic method, found that these developmental laws were more complex than Binet has supposed. The importance of perceptual behaviour can, in fact, be modified solely by manipulating the presentation time with the tachistoscope. The subjects' action may also involve what Piaget calls *centering* error. The stimulus which one fixates, or more usually the one on which is concentrating (Fraisse, Erlich and Vurpillot, 1956), is overestimated in relation to the others. Pre-perceptual attitudes also have a great influence (see Fraisse 1961). They sensitize the subject to expected stimuli (lowering of threshold). They can distort perception in the direction of the pre-perceptual schema. The affective significance of the stimuli influences the perception of their shape or size (e.g.: Bruner and Goodman's experiment (1948) demonstrating overestimation of the size of coins by poor children).

We do not claim to have given an exhaustive list of the systematic errors which can arise in perception, but simply an example of the distortions which the context, attitude of the subjects and order of the experiment can produce. The more ambiguous the stimulus, the more important these phenomena are. Thus, it is predictable that there will be distortions and errors in all experiments, but more often than not we lack objective standards by which they may be uncovered. One cannot be too careful when organizing an experiment or in drawing up the conclusions.

4 The analysis of results and their conclusions

The most fascinating part of experimental work is undoubtedly transforming crude data into significant results by procedures in which imagination and scientific knowledge play an important part. This phase comprises three essential stages: the analysis of results, explanation and generalization.

1 Analysis of results

Starting from multiple and sometimes disparate data, the first task is to establish some form of order, i.e. to *classify* the results obtained and to regroup them in such a way that the experimenter can take them in at a glance. These classifications must obviously be drawn up in relation to the independent variables, remembering that there may be several of these. To extract meaning from the results it is necessary to elucidate again and again.

Three principal means enable these regroupings to be made:

A) *Tables*. Their use is well known. To be valuable, they must be clear. The results can be regrouped in their crude values in frequency or percentage tables. In each case, the most representative and the most useful classification must be found.

B) *Graphs*. We will not dwell on this procedure, which has become familiar in modern techniques. However, we would emphasize that graphs have the advantage of being able to relate two or more variables and by transforming figures into rows or blocks they allow an overall understanding of a mass of results better than tables, which often contain too much information.

This method has one disadvantage, however. Although it symbolizes a great number of results, its representation is relative to the scale adopted. A difference of 1 mm. on a scale of 1 cm. by 1 metre passes unnoticed. However, it becomes considerable (generally involving a change of origin) if the scale is 1 cm. by 1 mm.

However, scales need not necessarily be arithmetical. Many phenomena (in psychophysics—from the point of view of information theory) seem more *simple* if a logarithmic scale of values of the independent variable is adopted. When E makes this transformation, he is guided by a principle which applies generally in scientific methodology: to work towards the simplification of relations between variables and, if it is not immediately apparent, to postulate it and regroup the results accordingly. This principle is fruitful more often than not.

C) *Statistical analysis*. This is often allied to the previous procedure. Regrouping numerical results usually consists of seeking the basic parameters of their distribution which are generally an indication of the central tendency and the dispersion of values around the central tendency. If the distribution of scores is

143

almost normal, the arithmetical mean and the standard deviation are called for. If irregular, the median and semi-interquartile deviation. If the distribution falls within 'i' or 'j' curves for example, it is better to use a graph.

Perhaps we should stress that a distribution which does not follow the Laplace–Gauss curve is no less true, or rather no less representative of the phenomenon than a normal distribution. Not all collections of measurements follow the binominal law. However, if the distribution is nearly normal, one might justifiably wonder whether the irregularities, and asymmetries recorded are perhaps due to procedural error (an insufficient number of measurements, range of values of the independent variable).

These regroupings are only a first step. Statistical analysis must go further.

a) In experiments concerning functions E must find out, over and above the graphic representation, the theoretical law $y = f(x)$ which could link the independent variable and the dependent variable and, sometimes, must make use of statistical tests to enable him to say whether the empirical results correspond to the probable theoretical law.

b) In factorial experiments, which are designed to discover the influence of one or more factors, the general principle of statistical analysis consists of asking oneself whether the null hypothesis can be accepted or not. To reject it means that the different groups of results cannot belong (at a given level of probability) to the same whole. Student's t, χ^2, Snédécor's F, analysis of variance all fulfil this task with varying degrees of complexity. Non-parametric tests today permit the treatment of distributions which are not normal (see Faverge, 1962, Chapter 14).

Moreover, analysis of covariance, which is not widely enough used, enables one to decide whether variations between individuals or groups are significant, and even whether the level of their initial performances is significantly different (see Faverge, 1962, Chapter 12).

These analyses are aimed at detecting the possible action of an independent variable. But it is the object of other analyses to look for the existence and the intensity of a relation between two dependent variables. The correlation technique is therefore relevant. Some psychologists believe that correlations are useful only in applied psychology. This is a serious error. Simple correlation reveals the link between two variables (intelligence levels of father and children, for example); multiple correlation makes it possible to calculate the relation of two variables while maintaining a third constant.

Not all the possibilities offered by the correlation technique are equally used. Of the three techniques which exist at present, the *R correlation*, or correlation between the results obtained in different tests by the same group of individuals is the most frequently used. The *Q technique* which establishes the correlation between two series of measurements made on two individuals or on two groups of individuals is an extension which is too little used. Moreover, it allows one to compare the structure of psychological profiles, a useful way of approaching personality. It consists of finding the correlation between two types of responses given by the same subject at different moments. It is a method of research into reactional *patterns*.

If E finds himself faced with a matrix of correlations he can, like Spearman and Thurstone, ask himself if the sum of intercorrelations cannot be explained in terms of only a few factors. In other words, he is trying, by factor analysis, to discover a number of determinants simpler than the multiplicity of independent variables described in each test.

Like the correlations method from which it is derived, factor analysis permits the discovery or determination of hypothesis. We must admit, however, that for the psychologist factor analysis in its different forms (mono-or multifactorial) can supply only a rough approximation to the nature of psychological variables, since it postulates an additive structure of the way they operate and does not describe a hierarchical relationship as suggested by all other methodological approaches. But science can often progress by using semi-adequate methods, provided that scientists are aware of the relativity of their analyses.

2 Explanations

Analysis establishes; science, if it is to advance, must seek to explain. Factor analysis is in fact an attempt to by-pass the first stage. It postulates the probable functioning of entities which are expressed mathematically though they could equally be expressed in physiological or psychological terms.

Paul Fraisse

Explanation consists in finding out in each case whether or not the type of relationship established is a particular case of a more general, already known and more or less verified law. But obviously types of explanation can differ greatly. Questions can be asked at the level of physiological mechanisms or at that of situation variables. One can also try to discover whether a series of results is explained in terms of intervening variables, whose existence one assumes (factors are of this type) and whose status depends on their ability to provide a fruitful explanation and their congruence with other intervening variables. It would be erroneous in fact to believe that only one kind of explanation can correspond to a given result. In every case one can use different 'reading grids'. For anyone who seeks to explain, the fundamental error is to take a partial cause for *the* cause. This is true if one relies on a single plane, but *a fortiori* if one admits different levels of explanation for one phenomenon. To get away from generalities, let us use the simple example of the emotional reaction of aggression after a need has been frustrated. It can be explained:

a) by the relation between the antecedents and the reaction (the connection between the barrier and the aggression)

b) by physiological mechanisms (discharge of adrenalin, excitation of the intra-cortical centres, movements against the obstacle)

c) by reference to intervening variables, such as frustration.

All three systems of explanation are adequate, no *one* is sufficient. They are complementary (see Chapter 3).

3 Generalization

One must be aware of the paradoxical situation of experimental work. According to classical design, one starts with a number of observations and E formulates an hypothesis which, since it relates two concepts, is necessarily of a general kind. But the moment E sets up an experiment to verify it he abandons this general character and defines a concrete situation in which he observes a particular response. By passing from the general to the particular E hopes to choose a representative sample and not an exceptional case. But once the relationship under study is verified in the particular example selected, has he the right to go from the particular to the general and say that the hypothesis

146

is universally valid? Can he extend what he has observed in a single case to a category? To answer yes is to ignore the uncertainty implicit in every situation; to say no is to render science absolutely impossible and to be satisfied with establishing a catalogue of facts. This tension is the dilemma of every epistemology. On one side the rationalists believe that a concept contains an essence and each definition corresponds to a fundamental property of the phenomenon, formal rigour enabling one to determine its extent; on the other side, strict empiricists do not accept that one can establish a general or a theory on a sum of experimental evidence.

This age-old debate is crystallized today in the conflict between two approaches to psychology: *phenomenology* and *operationism* (see Chapter 1, p. 68).

Phenomenology seeks the very essence of the phenomenon in actual experiences. By giving free rein to the philosopher's imagination, it believes it is possible to isolate a permanent characteristic which gives the phenomenon its significance; Sartre proceeds in this way in his *Esquisses d'une théorie des émotions*, where he is scarcely concerned with relating antecedents and consequences, but rather with discovering the significance of emotion as indicating the relation the subject has to wards his actual universe. The solution is well known: emotion is a magic act which transforms the nature of the situation. This solution owes nothing, or nearly nothing, to empirical data, it is the fruit of mental experience, of the activity of the mind, as Brentano the ancestor of phenomenology would have said, and not an inductive argument derived experimentally.

Operationism is positivist. It seeks to affirm nothing which goes beyond the operation which establishes a relation. This position is wise, and the scientist always feels himself nearer to the empiricist than to the rationalist. However, the scientist himself cannot do without concepts; the operationist takes refuge in those which enjoy general acceptance or a common meaning. This is a distortion of their basic principles and is not even an effective solution, since a science can only progress by forging concepts appropriate to the scientific facts.

The solution to the dilemma, the *via media*, is to abandon a generalization based on the essence of the phenomenon, which Lewin has qualified as Aristotelian (see Chapter 1, p. 76), and to accept only a generalization arrived at inductively from one or more facts and to accord them only one probable value. Although a relation can thus be *provisionally* accepted to have general value, this does not depend on a well-made conceptual analysis of *determinants*, but on repeated confirmation of a relationship by different, but similar experiments; this explains why a science is not made up simply of several 'key' experiments—those which litter the textbooks—but of innumerable researches whose findings gradually increase the value of each generalization.

We should like to describe the process of generalization in more detail, and we must mention that it extends to four different aspects of the experimental process: situation, response, the personality of the subject and the relations between these three aspects.

A) *Generalization of the situation.* I study a single instance of anticipatory behaviour, can I, in my experimental conclusion speak of anticipation as a whole? Analysis based on numerous observations has already enabled me to limit a conjectural generalization to certain types of anticipation but even there one must have studied the same reactions in anticipatory periods of different duration and in a certain variety of situations in order to increase the value of the generalization.

B) *Generalization of the response.* I study a reaction of impatience during the anticipatory period. To generalize by affirming that anticipation engenders reactions of impatience is legitimate only if I note step by step various manifestations which could be subsumed under the name 'impatience concept'. It is impossible scientifically to pass from a particular act of impatience to impatience in general. Science is prudent, and it is from this prudence that the certainty of its views is derived.

C) *Generalization on a personal level.* It is not legitimate to draw conclusions for the whole of humanity from the impatience of a few people in anticipatory situations. The value of the conclusion depends on the representativeness of the population studied. Several well-chosen students might perhaps represent all students, but they certainly do not represent all young people and *a fortiori* men or Man. Here also science proceeds by successive approximations, increasing the area to which a relation applies as and when it is confirmed on more numerous and varied populations. In holding to these three aspects, it would be easy to

148

imagine that at the end of the research whose variety we have outlined the relation between anticipation and emotional stability would doubtless be confirmed, but with very many variations depending on the existence of sub-classes, determined as much by the nature of the anticipatory period as to the type of emotional reaction and to the relative susceptibility of the various subjects according to their age, sex, temperament or race.

D) *Generalization of relations.* The meeting of two variables can occur at several levels of generality. At the most particular level the relation is descriptive, but once such relations are established it becomes possible to combine them and discover a more general type of relation which would be regarded as explanatory in convection with single actions. Thus conditioning was at first a particular relation—the dog salivating at the sound of the bell—but then it became more general when a similar relation was found concerning very varied reactions and stimulati. It acquired an even greater generality when analysis established that this process applied to the relation between two hitherto independent stimuli, etc. But the value of these successive generalizations depends entirely on the fruitfulness of the discovered hypotheses and their experimental confirmation. All we have said about the prudence necessary in generalization applies equally to attempts to generalize results obtained in the laboratory and to extend their practical application. Here again, enthusiasm and scepticism are not scientific attitudes. All psychologists know that the conditions of everyday life have a complexity which is minimized in the laboratory situation. Some also know that essential relations are discovered only at the cost of this. Science and practice will gradually draw together as a result of such daring caution.

4 Conclusion

The experimental method is a form of spiritual advance, a way of reasoning which has a logic of its own but also technical requirements to be met. Its progresses slowly, but to the man who can accept its slowness it offers the pleasure of certainties which, although perhaps partial, are nevertheless definitive.

Bibliography

ALLPORT, G., *Personality; a psychological interpretation*, New York, Henry Holt, 1937

ANDREWS, F. G., *Méthodes de la psychologie.*, Trs. P. FRAISSE, 2 vols. Paris, Presses Universitaires de France, 1952

BENEZÉ, G., *La méthode expérimentale*, Paris, Presses Univ. de France, 1954

BEXON, W. H., HERON, W. and SCOTT, T. H., 'Effects of decreased variation in the sensory environment', *Canad. J. Psychol.*, 1954, 8, 70–6

BROWN, C. W. and GHISELLI, E. E., *Scientific method in psychology*, New York, McGraw-Hill, 1955

BRUNER, J. S. and GOODMAN, C. D., 'Symbolic value as organizing factors in perception', *J. Soc. Psychol.*, 1948, 27, 203–8

BRUNSWIK, E., 'The conceptual framework of psychology', *International Encylopedia of verified science*, The Univ. Chicago Press, 1952

CLAUDE, B., *Introduction à l'étude de la méthode expérimentale*, Paris Flammarion, 1952

DUGUÉ, D. and GIRAULT, M., *Analyse de variance et plans d'expérience*, Paris, Dunod, 1959

ESTES, S. G., *The judgement of personality on the basis of brief records of behavior*, Cambridge, Harvard College Library, 1937

FAVERGE, J. M., 'L'analyse de variance en psychologie', *Ann. Psychol.*, 1950, 49, 341–58
—*Méthodes statistiques en psychologie appliquée*, 2 vols. Paris, Presses Universitaires de France, 3rd ed. 1960–2

FESTINGER, L. and KATZ, D., *La méthode de recherche dans les sciences sociales*, Trs. by H. LESAGE, 2 vols. Paris, Presses Universitaires de France, 1959

FISHER, R. A., *Statistical methods for research workers*, Oliver and Boyd, Edinburgh and London 1925.
—*The design of experiments*, Edinburgh, Oliver and Boyd, 1935
—and YATES, F., *Statistical tables for biological, agricultural and medical research*, London, Oliver and Boyd, 1957

FRAISSE, P., 'L'influence des attitudes et de la personnalité sur la perception', *Ann. psychol.*, 1951, 51, 237–248

FRAISSE, P., 'The influence of age, sex and specialized training on the vertical-horizontal illusion', *Quart. J. Psychol.*, 1956, 8, 114–20
—*Le rôle des attitudes dans la perceptions*, in *Les attitudes*, Paris, Presses Universitaires de France, 1961
—and ORSINI, F., 'Étude expérimentale des conduites temporelles. I. L'attente', *Ann. psychol.*, 1957, 57, 359–65
—*Manuel pratique de Psychologie expérimentale*, Paris, Presses Univ. de France, 2nd edition 1963

GUILFORD, J. P., *Psychometric methods*, New York, McGraw-Hill, 2nd edition, 1954

HELSON, H., 'Adaptation level as frame of reference for prediction of psychophysical data', *Amer. J. Psychol.*, 1947, 60, 1–29

HULL, C. L., *The hypothetico-deductive method* in MARX, M. H. (see below)

LAGACHE, D., 'Psychologie clinique et méthode clinique', *Evol. psychiat.*, 1949, 1–19

LAMBERCIER, M., 'La constance des grandeurs en comparaisons sériales, *Archives de Psychol.*, 1946, 31, 78–282

MAC CORQUODALE, K. and MEEHL, P. E., 'On a distinction between hypothetical constructs and intervening variables', *Psychol. Rev.*, 1948, 55, 95–107

MARX, M. H., *Psychological theory: contemporary readings*, New York, The Macmillan Co. 1951

MCGUIGAN, F. J., *Experimental psychology. A Methodological approach*, Englewood Cliffs Prentice Hall, 1960

PIAGET, J., *Les mécanismes perceptifs*, Paris, Presses Univ. de France, 1961

—VINH-BANG, A. and MATALON, B., 'Note on the law of the temporal maximum of some optico-geometric illusions', *Amer. J. Psychol.*, 1958 71, 277–82

PICHOT, P., *Les tests mentaux en psychiatrie*, Paris, Presses Univ. de France, 1949

REUCHLIN, M., 'Contribution aux méthodes d'observation du comportement', *Ann. psychol.*, 1950, 49, 119–57

—'Utilisation en psychologie de certains plans d'expérience', *Ann. psychol.*, 1953, 53, 59–81

SOLOMON, R. L., 'An extension of control group design', *Psychol. Bull.*, 1949, 46, 59–81

SYMONDS, P. M., *Diagnosing personality and conduct*, New York, Appleton Century, 1931

UNDERWOOD, B. J., *Psychological research*, New York, Appleton, Century Crofts, 1957

VERNON, P. E., 'Some characteristics of the good judge of personality', *J. Soc. Psychol.*, 1933, 4, 42–58

WOODWORTH, R. S., *Psychology*, New York, Holt 1929

—*Psychologie expérimentale*, Trs. I. LEZINE and A. OMBREDANE, Paris, Presses Universitaires de France, 1949

Chapter 3

Explanation in psychology and psychophysiological parallelism

Jean Piaget

1 Introduction

A treatise on experimental psychology must tackle the two questions of explanation and parallelism because the experimentalist necessarily comes up against both. We should point out that each of these problems is implicit in the other; therefore, it is sufficient to recognize the pertinence of one for the other.

1 The need for explanation

The experimentalist is faced with the question of explanation not by virtue of *a priori* principles embodying definition of psychology or rules of experimental method, but because the spontaneous and independent stages of experimental research reach a certain level eventually corresponding to what is commonly called in science the verification of an explanatory hypothesis.

Let us take as an example an 'optico-geometric' illusion such as Müller-Lyer's. Observation first revealed the fact that a horizontal of length L seemed subjectively longer if it had outward-pointing lines at its ends than if it had inward-pointing lines or even no lines (Fig. 1). The first task for the experimenter is to verify

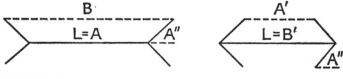

FIGURE 1

whether this fact is general, i.e. whether it is a *law*. The following stages (but not necessarily in this order, because some workers will always tend to miss out steps and seek explanations or causes without having established laws properly) attempt to define the law to be set up as exactly as possible: one would, for example, vary the figures in such a way as to determine in what form or proportions the illusion is greater; or again, one might verify whether the illusion is equally strong, quantitatively, at every age, or whether it increases or diminishes with age; one would study, similarly, the effect of repetition or exercise, etc. But these experiments, which aim at establishing general facts or laws of varying strength will overlap, sooner or later, with other experiments which are concerned with the verification of explanatory hypotheses. This new approach may arise in two ways; discontinuously or more or less continuously with what has gone before.

The discontinuous manner is a feature of explanatory hypotheses which are not closely connected with the establishment of the initial laws. It was supposed, for example, that the Müller-Lyer illusion was due to eye movements along the line L whose size was to be judged. Because of the outward-pointing lines, these movements led to an overestimation of the length of the surveyed line, whereas the inward-pointing lines impeded the movement of the eye and resulted in underestimation. But such explanatory hypotheses, even arising on the edge of fundamental research, do not hinder experimental work and in fact sometimes help it, almost regardless of their accuracy. The particular hypothesis specified gave place, in fact, to two sorts of fruitful controls, which falsified the hypothesis, but which led to the establishment of new laws. One of the controls consisted of measuring the illusion by using a tachistoscope with too brief a presentation period for eye movements to intervene: the illusion remained, thus invalidating the hypothesis, but it led to the establishment of a law of the distribution of errors as a function of the duration of presentation.[1] The other control consisted of recording the eye movements. This also contradicted the hypothesis but led to new general facts being noted. If, on the other hand, the hypothesis had been confirmed, other laws would obviously have been obtained, but this would have been the beginning of an explana-

[1] See Chap. 18 (The development of perceptions) Section 3.

tion, the problem would then be to establish what constituted an explanation and what was its relation to the laws.

2 The continuity between the search for laws and explanatory hypotheses

But the search for explanation can arise in complete continuity with the establishment of the initial laws. For example, by varying the properties of the figure to establish the conditions in which the *maximum* illusion is obtained, one is led quite naturally to modify the angle between the oblique lines or (resulting from this) the angle which they form with the horizontal L. The question would then inevitably arise as to whether it was the angle which was responsible for the illusion, and this would then be another explanatory hypothesis. Controls would show, on the contrary that the angle was not the principal factor, although it played a part, and that the fundamental relation was that between the large and small parallel sides (B and A or B' and A' on Fig. 1) of the trapeziums implicit in the illusion (which, in fact, consists of two trapeziums, one with a large and one with a small common side, the other remaining constant). So, to reduce this classical illusion to trapeziums constitutes the beginning of explanation, but a modest one, since the problem thus shifts on to the reasons for the underestimation of the large base and the overestimation of the small base.[2]

Auguste Comte's positivism proscribed attempts at causal explanation and claimed that science should restrict itself to the establishment of laws. An experimentalist imbued with precepts taken *a priori* from the positivist methodology could thus maintain that he is not looking for reasons but is satisfied with verifying the perceptual laws of the trapezium. But this example demonstrates admirably that he cannot stop there. In fact, as a general rule when two unequal lengths A and B are perceptually compared and when their difference (A < B) goes appreciably beyond their liminal values, A is underestimated and B is overestimated. Surely, then, even the most positivist experimenter begins to wonder whether it is not the same with the base of the trapeziums. To reply that there are cases where, if A < B the difference is reinforced (contrast) and others where, it cancels itself out (assimilation)

[2] See Chap. 18, beginning of section 2.

would not suffice for long, because one must then establish in what conditions or under the influence of what factors contrast or assimilation takes precedence. So, the search for conditions or factors is obviously of an explanatory nature. Another possible reply (which is ours) is that in one trapezium the difference A'' between the lengths of the sides A and B (which is also perceived in the two extensions of the smaller side A or A', Fig. 1) is figural (as opposed to a rectangle, where the difference between the large and small sides does not depend on any particular element of the figure) and that the relations between the sides A or B and the difference A'' are contrasted so that they counteract each other thereby reducing the difference A''. This accounts for the underestimation of B (or B') without using assimilation. One arrives thus at new 'laws' or law-like relations (which are both verifiable and calculable) between B and A'' etc.; but whatever language is used to express them, these partial laws 'explain' the overall relation between B and A and supply at least an approximate explanation. This first approximation obviously introduces new questions which stimulate the search for new laws and new explanations, and so on.[3]

Admittedly, all experimental analysis touches on general facts or laws and on explanatory hypotheses which a certain number of experiments set out to verify. It therefore remains for us, in introducing this chapter, to discover what characterises the 'explanatory' nature of an hypothesis or a system of verified relations as opposed to the purely 'law-like' or 'declaratory' character of relations established solely to determine their generality. We shall of course try to discover this difference with no regard to *a priori* ideas on the law and the cause, and without even starting from the examination of the corresponding problem in sciences such as physics and biology; it is simply in the field of psychological experimentation that we shall endeavour to find out whether there are several criteria of differentiation between explanation (causes) and pure description (general facts or laws).

2 Laws and causes

In the above example we saw how a search for explanation spontaneously includes the establishment of laws and even in some

[3] See Chap. 18, 2 to 4.

cases guides it. We must first point out that the explanatory hypotheses set up to account for laws also draw upon existing laws (whether or not they are subsequently verified by the experiment): it is the eye movements, the angles, or the trapeziums which 'explain' the overestimation of the horizontal with outward-pointing oblique lines in the Müller-Lyer figure, it is a question of three cases of a group of laws (the laws of these movements, of these angles, etc.) from which one then draws the law of over-estimation. It seems (but only at first) that for the experimentalist the idea of cause is confused with that of law, and it is just this confusion (often intentional under the influence of positivism) which one gets involved in when one confines oneself to defining the 'cause' as a 'regular succession'.

1 Analysis of an explanatory hypothesis

Let us look more closely at the eye movement hypothesis, which is seen to be false in the Müller-Lyer figure, by comparing it with an allied hypothesis shown as adequate in the case of another 'illusion': we shall try and discover, by comparing the two situations, what causal explanation adds to simply stating laws.

This second example of illusion (which demonstrates better than the first how the need to explain is essential in research) is that of the overestimation of the upper element A in the case of comparison between two equal vertical lines A and B, each in line with the other (Fig. 2). It is well known, in fact, that the two

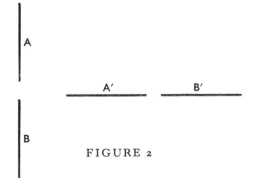

FIGURE 2

equal horizontal lines A' and B' do not produce systematic errors (except in individuals with problems of laterality), while the upper

Jean Piaget

vertical A is evaluated in relation to B. If the psychologist wishes to be more than a mere collector of facts, he must look for the reason. Thus, we have set up the hypothesis[4] that, the horizontal lines being perceptually symmetrical, the fixation points are distributed symmetrically over A′ and B′ (for example towards the middle of A′ and of B′) and that the comparison movements oscillating between these centerings over A′ and B′ would not then give place to distorting asymmetries; on the other hand the vertical lines A and B being perceptually asymmetrical (one directed towards the ground and the other towards the higher open space), the favoured fixation points would be situated at the summit of A and the summit of B: hence a sweeping movement between these two summits which would favour element A and largely ignore the lower part of element B. Cinematographic analysis of eye movements conducted by Vinh-Bang on these figures has effectively shown: 1) an accumulation of centering on the summit of the vertical lines A and B, but on the middle of the figure formed by the horizontal lines A′ and B′; 2) an equal distribution of comparison A′B′ and B′A′ in the case of the horizontal lines and unequal amount (BA > AB) in the case of the vertical lines.

Why, then, is the hypothesis of the part played by the eye movements explanatory in this situation and not in the form in which it was given for the Müller-Lyer figure? And what does this comparison teach us about the distinction between 'laws' and 'causes'?

The hypothesis might have succeeded for the Müller-Lyer figure (and it will certainly be tried again later on in a more appropriate form), but it failed for two distinct, but undoubtedly complementary reasons. The first is that the law of the distribution of eye movements in the exploration of this figure does not agree with the law of the overestimation of the segment of straight lines to be judged. Here are two laws, experimentally correct, but not mutually deducible; this simple fact is nevertheless fundamental and it shows immediately that the 'cause' is not to be sought at the level of the 'law' but rather at that of the deduction of one law from another, or from a number of others, i.e. at the deductive level (however simple and immediate these deductions might be). The second reason, parallel to the first, is that in the initial form of the hypothesis it is difficult to imagine the actual substrate (here physiological) which ensures the connection

[4] See Chap. 18, 6.

158

between an eyeball movement on the one hand and the organ specializing in recording the length of a straight line (retinal cells, etc.) on the other. In other words, so that there can be explanation, it is not sufficient to deduce the laws in a formal way. It is essential to rest this deduction on a substrate, either actual or 'model', concrete or abstract, which will allow one to re-construct the relations involved, and more generally, to co-ordinate the different levels of reality and introduce a hierarchical structure in the laws that have been established with regard to the areas to which they apply (conscious judgements, behavioural reactions, physiological laws, etc.).

If the eye movement hypothesis seems, on the contrary, to explain the case of the superimposed vertical lines, it is because these two conditions tend to be fulfilled. On the one hand, the laws of overestimation and those of the distribution of comparison movements as well as of the fixation points seem to agree, in such a way that one can deduce the first from the second, provided empirical laws describing the details of effects of overestimation by centering (Fauville, Hillebrand, Piaget and Morf, Fraisse, etc.) are introduced. On the other hand it is possible to construct designs or models which permit the co-ordination of diverse laws (general facts) observed by ordering their fields of application in a hierarchical structure. In this way one can make the over-estimations due to centering (inasmuch as perceptual reactions are conveyed by 'judgements' etc.) correspond to the probabilistic models of 'meets' (and of 'joins' or correspondence between 'meets'; see Chapter 18 under 3 and 4), which themselves would be made to correspond more or less to organic models (density of cells in the fovea, explanatory micromovements guided by rules of awareness or attention, etc.).

2   The three stages of research

So, from the discussion of these examples, we can conclude that it is essential to distinguish three stages in psychological research, the first of which is concerned with establishing general laws, while the other two relate to causal explanation:

1) There is first of all the establishment of general facts, or laws. In this connection, it must be realized that experimental findings always end in establishing laws. Even the third stage,

which consists of introducing a substrate or model and a sum of relationships between initial laws, comes back to establishing or assuming new laws, because these relationships continue to be altered by laws, though on a finer scale than that of explanatory laws.

However, the law in itself does not yet explain anything, since it is limited to verifying the generality of a factual relationship (succession, correlations, etc.). Explanation begins only with the co-ordination of laws, and that co-ordination may occur in two complementary ways (2 and 3).

2) Simple generalization is not enough. A new element, which cannot be contained within the idea of law must be introduced. That is deductive argument (however simple it may be in certain cases) by means of which one distinguishes the law requiring explanation from laws which are assumed to explain it (and which will explain it, in fact, if the argument is adequate from the deductive point of view, and if it is verified by the experiment). One law by itself does not comprise deductive measuring since it is derived solely from an inductive generalization even though this encompasses, it is true, a fairly large part of deductions which are probabilistic though drawn up specifically to establish the generality of the law in question. Explanation, on the contrary, presupposes a system of laws among which one can be constructed or reconstructed deductively from the others, and *there* is the first specific characteristic of explanation as opposed to simple generalization. But this is not its only characteristic, because the deduction of a law from a collection of other laws does not constitute a 'causal' explanation.[5]

3) We must now consider the third stage, which complements the previous ones, and which constitutes the second specific characteristic of causal explanation: the deduction of the law requiring explanation from the system of laws which account for it does not remain simply ideal or 'logical', but it can be applied to a 'real' or 'model' substrate which is assumed to support such a deduction and to 'represent' its various connections. For example,

[5] Such a deduction is sufficient in mathematics, where one does not usually speak of 'causes' but where nevertheless G. Bouligand uses the term 'causality' when this deduction provides the 'proof' of a theorem. This 'causality', compared with that of the experimental sciences, lacks only the second specific characteristic which we shall mention, and which relates to the type of reality invoked as substrate of the deduction.

in the case of the illusion quoted above, where the upper vertical line is overestimated in relation to the lower vertical line which it extends, there are three laws: a) that expressing this overestimation of the upper element; b) that describing the accumulation of centring points of regard at the top of the vertical lines (favouring the part between the two top ends as opposed to the middle or lower parts of the lower vertical and c) that expressing the fact that an element which is centred upon is automatically overestimated. Law a) can in fact be deduced from laws b) and c). That, however, is not enough to render the explanation 'causal' since it still remains to discover 'how', i.e. to furnish a 'real' model which must at the same time explain the apparent elongation resulting from the centring process and the manner in which this process is applied to the upper vertical line affecting the law (1). According to needs, this model will be either purely physiological or combined with a probabilistic schema, or simple a single schema etc. But, even in this last case, the model should not remain formal, otherwise it will be confused with deduction (2). It will consist in 'imagining' the 'how' part of the elongation by making an imaginative schema of the possible realities. Its meaing will always be 'real' even if it confines itself to schematizations which are ultimately regarded as extreme.

3   *The characteristics of causal explanation*

The ideal in causal deduction in psychology, as elsewhere, is a deductive argument applied to the production of phenomena. This argument is all the more satisfactory if deductive steps correspond to the links between the subject matter of the theory so that the order of the explanation reflects that of the antecedents and consequences involved in the actual and temporal unfolding of events. In other words, causal explanation will succeed insofar as each transformation involved in the relations between the objects corresponds to a transformation or operation in the deduction, this last being copied from reality. *Causa seu ratio*, said Descartes: the cause is a logical co-ordination (2) 'projected' on to a real co-ordination (3).

Seen like this, explanation presents the two characteristics classically attributed to causality, as opposed to simple generalization a) the *necessity* or relations between causes and effects, which arises from their *deducibility;* b) the *reality* of the causal tie underlying the measured phenomena (and thereby surpassing pure phenomenalism), which is assured by the *model acting as a substrate* of the deductive argument.

These two new characteristics of causal explanation which extend beyond the framework of simple generality, are distinguished from each other for the following reason. The interdependence of laws, which makes then deducible within the systems which they set up, rests solely on the rules of logico-mathatical deduction, which are formal. On the other hand, the models serving as substrates to the deductive process require co-ordination of the levels or areas of reality and, consequently, they are made up of a number of judgements about what exists. This second type of co-ordination, which is 'real' and not formal, gives rise especially to two important sub-varieties. The first proceeds by ranging the different levels of reality into a hierarchy: organic models would, for example be based on the representation of nervous connections which determine behavioural reactions and, in one limited sector, conscious epiphenomena; other models would be centred on the behaviour seen globally, etc. The second sub-variety proceeds by making mutually irreducible fields of reality isomorphic; it is here that the question arises of parallelism or isomorphism between the characteristic structures of states of consciousness and the concomitant organic structures.

3   The multiplicity of forms of psychological explanation

Unfortunately, there exists a great number of possible types of explanation in psychology, even more (and this is saying a lot) than in biology, and more than in the exact sciences such as physics or theoretical chemistry. This is not due to disagreements about the establishment of facts or laws; sooner or later agreement is reached on this level and, if there are still large areas where certain facts are recognized as such and considered to have general validity before being experimentally verified (in clinical psychology, for example), they always finish by becoming indispensable. The diversity of explanations stems mainly from the problem implicit in constructing a co-ordinated system of deductive principles, the deductive co-ordination of laws, not because the rules of deduction vary from one author to another, but because if some schools make a great effort at deductive coherence (for example, contemporary American learning theories), others are far less conscientious. But the main reason (by far) is the diversity of 'models', which at least shows that the difference between what we have called in Section 2 above logical co-ordination and real co-ordination in the stages of causal explanation exists. We must stress the fact that if the possible 'models' differ among themselves to the point where they are sometimes more of a hindrance than a help to the experimenter, this is essentially because of the difficulties arising from the need for a solution which is both theoretically acceptable and heuristically fertile (or at least suitable) for the problem of the relation between the structure of conscious reactions and organic structures. This question has been rejected as being outdated, badly presented, etc., and this is still the attitude taken by those who dictate the choice of explanatory models; hence their diversity, which arises more from the complexity of the proper area of psychology than from the incoherence of the theories or the method.

Having said this, let us try to classify, simply from the point of view of experimental psychology, the main types of explanation which the researcher can use. We shall not base this classification on the problem of psychophysiological parallelism, because the hypothesis which we have just developed on the part played by this question needs to be verified *a posteriori* and not to guide the analysis which follows *a priori*.

Nevertheless, the first point which arises in making such a classification is that there are two main types, or at least two extremes, in explanatory models, a) where they aim at a reduction from the most complex to the most simple, or again from the psychological to the extra-psychological or b) where they are directed towards a constructivism existing within the limits of 'conduct'. As the reductionist type of model may preserve a mainly psychological orientation or alternatively tend to reduce the mental to realities outside a certain framework, we finish up in fact with three main categories (A–C), the last two each comprising three varieties.

A) First there is what we call a psychological reductionism which consists of seeking to explain a certain number of varied reactions or conduct by reducing them to the same causal principle which remains unchanged throughout the transformation. An example of this sort of explanation by identification can be found in the recent experimental work of Freudian psychoanalysts on the development of 'object' relations.

B) We shall distinguish the diverse forms of reductionism which tend to explain reactions or conduct by referring to realities extending beyond the frontiers of psychology. Hence, three varieties:

B_1) Sociological explanations in psychology (psychosocial) which tend to interpret individual reactions as a function of the interaction between individuals or various levels of group structures.

B_2) Physicalist explanations which, starting from an isomorphism between mental and organic structures as in field models, rest briefly, on physical considerations (for example the Köhlerian Gestalt psychologists).

B_3) Organicist explanations in general, which insist on the reduction of the psychological to the physiological.

C) Finally, one could consider as 'constructivist' the types of explanation which, while giving a certain place to reduction (since it is one of the aspects of all explanation), mainly emphasize construction processes. This characteristic is quite distinct from type A and equally from type B, because insofar as one can give a constructive explanation of conduct or mental activity, a certain specifically psychological explanation is attained which is no longer reducible to social, physical or organic properties. We shall distinguish, in this connection three main types of models:

C_1) Models of the 'behaviour theory' type which, despite considerable differences existing between Hull and Tolman, for example, in fact have the common characteristic of co-ordinating diverse laws of learning in systems concerned principally with the acquisition of new conduct.

C_2) Models of essentially a developmental type which look for constructive processes in development which would account for innovatory behaviour without simply building on experience which has already been acquired.

C_3) Finally, 'abstract' models, whose name does not imply a rejection of any real substrate, in the sense of the presented causes we set out in Section 2 above as expressing the application of deduction such substrates, but rather because they refuse to choose between the diverse possible substrates, in order to define more clearly the way in which constructions themselves work in the most general form compatible with the demands of psychology.

Such a picture could not claim to be anything like complete without mentioning intermediate situations. If goes without saying that it is not a question of 'pre-explanatory' methods. For example, the so-called factor analysis method would be difficult to fit into any of the above categories, mainly because it does not in itself constitute an explanatory model. As a technique, it enables one to move from general to causal statements, but once the 'factors' are determined, the problem of assigning an explanatory meaning of them remains, and we know well enough how far a particular author can use them in one direction or another. Only one or two explanatory concepts are to be found to be in common between, for example, R. Meili, who combined factor analysis with Gestalt schemata, authors who sought to co-ordinate the same analysis with schemata of 'behaviour' (C_1) and (C). Spearman, the creator of the factorial method and originator of 'noögenesis'.

It is appropriate, then, to examine each of these seven categories of explanatory models, in such a way as to extract, by means of comparison, the aspects which they have in common or which are complementary.

1 Explanation by reduction to a psychogenetic principle

Let us briefly examine, as an example of this procedure, the method by which several present-day Freudian experimentalists (Hartmann, E. Kris, Spitz and K. Wolf, Glover, Th. Benedek, etc.) explain the formation of 'object relations' during the first few months of development. We shall choose as our main reference an excellent study made by Th. Gouin-Décarié on 90 subjects from 3 to 20 months, who were submitted simultaneously to a series of tests on the acquisition of the nature of a permanent object (through which the author arrived at the same succession of the stages of formation of the object as ours) and to parallel tests on the establishment of 'object' relations in the affective and Freudian sense of the word.

We have hitherto maintained that Freudian explanation in this connection follows the Meyersonian model of identification.

The same 'psychic' energy ('libido') at first centred on certain organic activities (oral and then anal stages), shifts to one's own total activity (narcissism) and finally to outside persons (choice of the 'object' and object relations), innovation thus resulting from a shift of affective charge or investment, and not from a change in its structure. It must be realized that the situation has become even more differentiated, since Hartmann took up his position on the independence of the 'ego' system and since the direct observation and experimental research which have characterized the re-examination of these first stages of affective development.

Broadly speaking, the present schema rests on the following three stages. In the first stage, the new-born child will be centred on himself, but as yet having no awareness of his own separateness. Physiological needs and the centres of interest which derive from them create 'isles of consistency' (Escalona) to which the psychic energy is directed, but which are not dissociated from the actual activity of the subject. In the course of the second stage, the reactions of anticipation and certain favoured perceptions (smiles) introduce the beginning of frontiers (albeit movable) between the actual activity and what one could call 'intermediary objects' such as 'the smiling human face' (Spitz). Lastly, the third stage will ensure a stable differentiation between subject and object with 'the flowering of all the elements whose seeds were planted in the previous stages' (Gouin): hence the consciousness of self and a 'cathexis which creates truly libidinous objects', and, similarly, the anguish allied to the loss of the loved object, etc.

It is evident from this that a structuring process takes place at the same time as the objects of affective energy are differentiated. Moreover, this structuring is necessarily accompanied by important cognitive modifications (anticipation, attention, understanding of the permanence of objects, etc.) which prudent authors may judge simply as parallel to the effective transformation, whilst others (Odier for example) would wish rather to treat as secondary. But the central question, from the point of view of this explanatory scheme, is to understand how such affective transformations occur. It appears that it is not yet possible to speak of a truly affective 'construct', for the same source of affective strength exists whatever the time but it simply changes its objectives; the qualitative change will be assumed to result from these simple shifts or redistributions, by means of 'flowering' and not by the inclusion of new elements.

Consequently, one has a choice: firstly to remain faithful to this scheme of identification, in which case the identity of the 'libido' will not explain development. An explanation will then be sought in the structural transformations of the whole (differentiation of self, etc.). The second possibility is to attempt to co-ordinate the process of cognitive construction with a truly affective construct at the time of each particular transformation and this would enable one to dispense with models of identification. In short explanation by identification completes and corrects itself by itself, under the influence of the internal modifications of Freudianism,[6] in the direction of a constructivist principle (cf. the models of type C and especially C_1 and C_2).

2 Explanation by reduction to psycho-sociological principles

If identification alone is insufficient, within the frontiers of psychology, it is because the logic of reductionism recognizes

[6] It is to show this internal evolution that we have quoted Freudians who have remained orthodox, rather than the English analysts (Bowlby, etc.) and Fromm, Alexander, Erikson, etc., and why we have not referred to the best explanatory theorist D. Rapaport. However, we must mention that psychoanalytical explanation is in Rapaport's view, oriented towards, if not abstract models, then at least a physicalism comprising theoretical extensions possible in all physicalism which has been elaborated on a little. Rapaport demonstrates, for example, that the constancy of cathexis (amount of psychic energy available) can indicate two distinct hypotheses: either this amount is theoretically constant with infinitesimal variations in the sense of D'Alembert's theorem or replacements of a physiological nature intervene to compensate the losses of the cathexis invested in the structures which is therefore 'tied'. In both cases a new series of distinctions must be introduced, and Rapaport reproached Freud for having distinguished only a mobile and a 'tied' cathexis: according to him one should differentiate between the structures which reduce the entropic discharge in order to neutralize the cathexis and the structural conditions which simply reduce the 'displaceability' of the cathexis and transform it into a 'tied' cathexis. Furthermore, if enough cathectic energy is invested in the formation of a structure, only one part of it becomes 'tied' while the rest is released: this liberation corresponds to the mobilization of energy. Rapaport (finally) states (all this appears in a study on Attention Cathexis, 1960 where he attempts to bridge the gap between the affective processes and the basic cognitive structures, such as attention) that structures activated by cathexis are modified and later stabilized, while the 'non-cathectised' structures (for a long time) lose their stability and cohesion: thus, according to this author, there is a parallel with Piaget's conceptions of the 'alimentation' of the sensori-motor schemata of assimilation, the 'alimented' schemes providing, through their results, an 'alimentation' for the others.

no limits to reduction. Thus, one could seek to reduce from the bottom: (organicism), or from the lateral point of view, regard the subject in relation to other subjects from his birth, hence explanatory models of a sociological type, which we will now examine.

Such an approach can be found today in the explanation of all areas of primary affective behaviour (so-called cultural psychoanalysis: Fromm, etc.), from conduct in general (R. Benedict, M. Mead, etc.) to cognitive reaction (from J. M. Baldwin and P. Janet to the works of Vigotsky and Luria on the role of language and, incidentally in our own early works) and primarily social conduct (sociometry etc.).

Its principle is as follows. When a new form of behaviour occurs to enrich the previous ones in the course of development, it is due less to an internal change than to the effects of social interaction. In this sense, the reduction of individual conduct of social structure does not exclude developmental schemata, but these are shifted to the area communal interaction from explanations in exclusively psycho-biological terms. When P. Janet, for example, explained the appearance of reflective thought (which was superimposed on direct or assertive thought) by reference to social conduct of deliberation and to its internalization in the form of a discussion with oneself, this was indeed a new behavioural development, but one on the inter-individual or collective plane, and the newness of such behaviour is reducible to an external mechanism, and need not be explained in terms of an earlier internal experience.

But two points must be made in connection with such a mode of explanation without, however, disputing its value. The first is that sooner or later it necessitates using a principle of internal development. For example, after believing that inter-individual co-operation was enough to explain the formation of logical structures occurring in the child's development (logic of the relations based on reciprocity, etc.), we have been obliged later: a) to admit that this formation also assumes, as an equally necessary condition, an internal constructive mechanism based on the co-ordination of the subjects' actions and their internalization in operations; b) to recognize that co-operation itself derives from co-ordinating actions and the same laws of operation as co-ordination between individuals, so that a circular relation and not a one-way association between co-operation between individuals and their co-ordination.

The second point is that, pushed to a certain degree of prediction sociological explanation (independently of reductions from the psychological to the social) falls back on abstract models, parallel with those used for psychological explanation (see C_3). All Claude Lévi-Strauss' work, particularly his excellent works on kinship, apply certain algebraic techniques (lattices, etc.) to social relations so that sociological explanation coincides with a qualitative enumeration analogous to that found in the construction of logical arguments. Obviously, when concrete microsociology takes its pattern from such models (and dispenses with Moreno's naive, and not at all sociological, conceptualization[7]), then psycho-sociological reductions will not only demand a certain principle of mental development (as in our first point) but will appear identical with modes of explanation using abstract models.

3 Explanation by reduction to physicalist principles

While it is natural that a reduction in a lateral direction, like that from the psychological to the social, will culminate in schemata of interaction and not of simple relationships (because this is naturally the point of the two remarks at the end of paragraph B_1), one might think that by contrast an explanation by reduction from higher to lower would mark a decisive victory for reductionism. A particularly daring and elegant model illustrating attempts of this kind is that of Gestalt theory, which tends not only to reduce mental phenomena (notably perception and intelligence) to physiological facts, but further to subordinate these to physical structures by using the concept of field. As a result, certain interpretations lead almost directly from the psychological to the physical, as in the case of 'good perceptual form', which is explained in terms of structures of 'physical Gestalts' and, like them, must submit to the principles of equilibrium and perfect immobility.

A celebrated example of this type of interpretation is that of after-effects, studied by Köhler and Wallach and consisting of modifications which take place in estimating the size or shape of a

[7] See Chap. XXXXIV of Maissonneuve, recording the progress made in this respect.

Jean Piaget

figure, when one's perception follows immediately after percepting another figure in the same region of the visual field. The explanatory hypothesis, once excitation is translated into potential differences and estimations of length into electrical resistance of the tissues, reverts to the observed effects to modifications in satiation. In permanent satiation (more frequent in the adult than in the child) the momentary and localized increase due to the inspection of figures, the restoration of equilibrium (more or less quickly according to the degree of satiation) by a homeostatic process and finally self-satiation depending on the point of fixation (less good in a child, and where there is a more extensive region capable of less satiation) should be differentiated. One arrives thus at an explanatory schema which takes account not only of the observed effects, but also of their evolution with age. It only remains to point out that owing to their orientation (Köhler was a physicist and Wallach a chemist before becoming psychologists), these authors tended to discount any effects arising from the functional behaviour of the subject and, in this respect, did not use the possibilities these would open up in connection with their homeostatic view of satiation or the relations between self-satiation and the fixation point.

It is not our place to judge the value of the theories we have mentioned, but simply to analyse the explanatory models they set forth. We shall confine ourselves to the following three points.

The first is that although physical models undoubtedly represent an essentially important ideal, they will be used with more conviction when biology itself makes them necessary, and when the possible reduction of certain psychological structures to physical structures is mediated by a preliminary distinct reduction of the former to biological structures. In this respect, it is possible that the use of specific forms of field equilibrium often conceals certain types of balance achieved by active compensation on the part of the subjects; it is still to be established, for example, with what frequency perceptual constancies end in 'over-constancy'.[8] One is often led to invoke over-compensation through precautions arising from the use of biological models rather than from any exact physical balance. But this does not necessarily lead us away from physicalism, as we shall see later.

[8] See Chap. 18, section 7.

170

In the second place, if the previous point seems to have a limited importance, one could set oneself to extend physicalism by quoting other models in addition to the Gestalt one. The physical characteristics which Gestalt psychology studies have been selected from among phenomena with non-additive components which are thus irreversible. Planck has demonstrated that the most important dichotomy which occurs in physics is that of irreversible (for example, thermodynamics) and reversible phenomena (cinematics, mechanics). To use physical analogies most efficiently one would have to find an analogous division in psychology, which would then oppose reversible structures composed of additive elements (operational structures of intelligence) and simple structures, such as that in Gestalt psychology. This no longer conforms to the Gestalt theory, but is undoubtedly inspired by an extended physicalism.

This gives rise to our third point. The most interesting thing as far as psychology is concerned in relation to physics is not perhaps reduction of a mental structure (perception, for example) to a physical structure (for example, electromagnetic field), but the analogy between the manner of composition of the first and that used by the physicist to attain knowledge of the second. In this connection, the rift between irreversible and reversible phenomena is also a rift between the domain of explanations, particularly probabilistic ones, and that of simple deduction. Physicalist analogies suggest, thus, not only actual reduction, but also the use of abstract models. We know, in particular what a close relationship exists between explanatory schemata of thermodynamics and those used in the theory of chance or the theory of decision and information theory.[9] So it is in precisely this direction that several authors are now seeking their explanatory models in the domain of perception[10]; moreover, our remarks above on perceptual over-constancies would easily lead to such models (as an example of 'decision' as a precaution against possible error or loss of information).

In brief, the two advantages of physicalist reduction are the precision which it can, in certain cases, add to organicist reduction

[9] The calculation of this information is, in fact, copied from calculations of entropy in thermodynamics.

[10] For example, W. P. Tanner and his team for the theory of thresholds (see above under C_3).

Jean Piaget

and the opportunities it affords to certain abstract models which
are among the most fruitful available to us today.

4   Explanation by organicist reduction

With the attempt to reduce mental phenomena to physiological
reactions we join one of the main streams of experimental psychology. For many authors, since the area covered by psychology is
that which divides biological from social methodology the best
form of psychological explanation (on points where he is not
subordinated to sociology) would be reduction from the higher to
the lower, i.e. assimilation of physiological models.

The examples of such reductionist approaches are numerous,
starting with the work of Helmholtz and Hering on perception.
We have selected one which is perhaps the most classical and also
the most instructive with regard to its central idea, which we
defend in this chapter, that of the complementarity of reductionist
and constructivist 'abstract' models. Associationist psychology
which, despite its 'simplistic' mechanism, has had considerable
influence on experimental psychology, sought to reduce mental
structures to the supposedly elementary mechanism of association.
But how does one account for this particularly in its most simple
form of association by contiguity? At first the answer was by
reduction to simple verbal physiological models, then Pavlov
put forward his theory of conditioned reflexes, which he considered
to be 'completely identical' with associations as defined by psychologists and even as covering 'what the genius Hemholtz described
(in the field of perception) by the celebrated phrase "unconscious
conclusion" '.

But the characteristic reduction is that it raises new problems
by its indefinite regression and, while psychologists discovered
the increasing complexity of association learning (the part played
by anticipation, reinforcement, motivation, problems of stability,
etc.), physiologists pursued their work by trying to answer the
many questions left unanswered by Pavlov's hypothetical interpretation (the theories of irradiation, induction, etc., were barely
within the framework of general laws.) Without listing all the new
techniques (notably electrophysiological) which made it possible to
progress, we should mention, following the excellent report by
A. Fessard and H. Gastaut, the two main themes which the

172

research touched on: the role of the main anatomo-functional structures (reticular formation, diencephalic integration and the cortical association system), and the scale interpretation of the neurone organization.

In connection with this last point, it is relevant to our present enquiry to examine how authors set about accounting for the fact that a signal *s*, usually associated with a response *r*, can be replaced by an unconditioned signal S to bring about a reaction R. On the one hand experimental evidence supplies a mass of important but limited information: for example that learning (at least in the adult) does not depend on the growth new nerve endings or on the formation of new synapses, but on a new function being established between already formed connections; that conditioning supposes a structure of the reticular type comprising numerous cells with star-like ramifications, etc. But, on the other hand, it is a question of making use of this information in an explanatory schema. Therefore, either the schema to be constructed must be devised in the form of an artificial model outlining (but with what ingenuity!) the conditions in which these results can be obtained: for example, Grey Walter's famous 'machines', or one can construct a theoretical model of the reticular field of neurons, like Fessard's idea of the lattice all of whose elements have identical properties, (where the choice of preferential routes in historically determined), but where the possibility of introducing a certain homeostatic stability can occur despite substitutions of routes. Obviously such models (the second, as much as the first) create a mass of logico-mathematical problems, some to do with structure and some with dynamics; their interdependence being stressed by Fessard.

From the dynamic point of view, first of all, it is a question of explaining the nature of the routes and one naturally resorts to a probabilistic schema. Fessard presented his lattice as a 'dependent stochastic lattice'; stochastic, because each neuron in the system had particular probability of discharge, which is a function of time, and dependent because it depends on the action of other similar neurons (A. Rapaport, Shimbel and others have tried to go even further in treating analagous problems mathematically).

Looking at the problem of structure (all structures being conceived from a genetic point of view as alternatively the cause or effect of dynamic function) it is obvious that the choice of a 'lattice' model leads to many fundamental implications, since it is one of the most representative structures of general (logical and mathematical) algebra and the basis of propositional logic. It is appropriate here to point out that W. McCulloch and Pitts have shown precisely where the diverse combinations of neural connections are isomorphic with relations in propositional logic[11] (and in a general way with those in Boolean algebra), which is enough to demonstrate how lattice models sooner or later may be considered among the most daring of 'abstract' models.

In brief, such an example indicates that organicist reduction does not conflict with the use of abstract models for the simple reason that, insofar as neurology tends to be precise (whether or not it duplicates mechano-physiological attempts) it overlaps with the treatment of probability and general algebra. This is why one of our colleagues, returning from a visit to McCulloch's term, described the workers as each sitting between two tables, on one of which he examines neurons through the microscope and on the other he carries out his logistic calculations.

5 Behavioural explanation

The three types of explanatory models remaining to be examined do not preclude any of the previous forms of reduction, but their specifically psychological form of construction, based on the laws of a single behavioural act (C_1), or of development which is both genetic and mental (C_2) or on abstract systems of mental activity (C_3) complement them.

At first one can only refer to the single behavioural act, which implies of course an underlying organicism, but also introduces the notion of new structures designed to operate at a higher level. For example, one of the central concepts of Hull's theory of learning is that of habit-family hierarchies. This is global a mechanism whose explanatory power is relatively independent of organicist reduction, which is not specifically demanded by this mode of explanation. In the same way Tolman's sign-gestalt-expectations consist, at an equally molar level of behaviour, of the organization of a number of relations between a sign, a signified object and the anticipation of the fact that a particular type of behaviour will lead from one particular aspect to another of the structured field.

[11] Conjunction, disjunction, incompatibility, exclusion, implication, etc.

What then does explanation consist of at this higher stage, in terms of neural connections? These, according to Hull, remain hypothetical and the subject of inference (at least those to which he himself referred); they are only intervening variables between the physical surroundings and observable reactions which make up behaviour: what must be explained, therefore, is the causal connection between the environmental conditions and these observable reactions. But what is the nature of this causal connection?

On reading Hull, whose interpretative system is by far the most developed, one at first has the impression that nothing else exists but laws, without any reference to causality: these are the laws of association, of drive reduction, the types of reinforcement (success, etc.) which consolidate association, of goal-gradients (acceleration of response near the goal), of the formation and structuring of habit-family hierarchies. But here, as everywhere, it is the deductive connection between these laws which supplies the causal explanation and which is applied to a real state of affairs. It is the sum of ideas describing responses on a scale of behaviour (what the behaviourists call 'conceptualization', as opposed to general descriptions). What does this deduction consist of, which in Hull's system is the operative part of a truly causal explanation?

Hull and his followers gave three successive answers to this question. The first simply consisted of co-ordinating the laws obtained using only ordinary language, i.e. by using the deductive mode which logicians (with some arrogance) call 'simple' deduction. This anticipated to some extent the second answer since Hull, in this first construction indicated the frequencies involved to an often disconcerting number of decimal places though without constructing probabilistic schemata.

The second solution was put forward by Bush and Mosteller in a fundamental study in which they outlined a probabilistic theory of learning. In this case the deduction of laws was presented *more mathematico:* given a particular situation characterized by particular parameters, it could be deduced, if certain laws applied, that the probability of learning would conform to a particular mode of calculation.

The third reply was made by Hull himself. Following discussions arising from his contribution to the International Congress of

Psychology in Paris in 1938, he visited England and met the logician, Woodger, a specialist in biological axiomatics. Under his influence Hull decided, with the help of Fitsch another logician, to construct a formalization of his explanatory system. The result was a deductive theory *more logico* which this time described all the processes involved in the system in an entirely explicit way. It has since been shown that it is easy to formalize Tolman's system in the same way, and our colleague L. Apostel has recently published in *Études d'épistemologie génétique* a comprehensive study supplying, among other things, the framework of a sort of algebra of learning and disentangling the formal laws used by those who are involved in interpretations of this kind.

Thus it is of interest to note that one of the most strictly experimental lines of thought in psychology came about through the use of abstract models, one of a probabilistic nature aimed at establishing statistical causality, the other logical revealing the deductive nature of the explanatory process. Moreover, this use of deductive schemata obviously does not in any way contradict the reductionist aspect of these systems since (as we saw under B_3) the eventual reduction to neural connections at this lower level raises questions of explanation for whose solution we must use analogous probabilistic or algebraic schemata.

6 Genetic explanation

This method is assumed, by learning theorists, to account for mental development in all its aspects, except for the effects of maturation which may be regarded as combining with the learning patterns in various ways. For certain developmental theorists, on the other hand, maturation and learning as a function of the environment consitute only two of the factors involved, and do not exhaust all the possibilities. Not being afraid of a certain 'mentalism' which the aforementioned theorists proscribe, they substitute for a single behavioural action the idea of 'conduct' which they define, in common with Janet and many others, as behaviour plus the internalized activity which accompanies various forms of 'being conscious'. Because of these nuances, one is confronted with modes of explanation distinct from the preceding one, (C_1) and equally distinct from the diverse varieties of reductionism (A to B_2).

176

We must first quote E. von Holst, K. Lorenz and N. Tinbergen, who represent a school of comparative psychology which is called 'ethology' or 'objectivism' and whose central idea is psychophysiological. It is the notion of 'spontaneous activity' of the organism, which is quite distinct from 'response' and which can be seen in the rhythmical movements of worms, (studied by von Holst) as well as in the movements of the new-born human child. But though these authors lay stress on the activities of the organism and the human subject, they do not, for all that, neglect the environmental situation, and their theory of 'innate releasers' and instincts (hereditary or specific perceptual signals which release for example the following of the mother in chicks, ducklings, etc.) introduces a close form of interaction between the subject and the object whose subtle causal nature deserves detailed analysis.

However, to draw out the parallel with the theorists of human learning, perhaps we might be allowed to quote from our own work as an example of the C_2 type of explanation, because if we too have emphasized the activity of the subject (and essentially in the development of cognitive processes) we have done so to extract an explanation of intellectual development. We would like to outline briefly the particular form of causal explanation which we have used.

Given that people's actions are structured from birth (initially not very well but hereditarily determined) their reactions to situations will be on the one hand assimilatory, in which they tend to incorporate objects into their structures, and on the other hand accommodatory, in which they tend to modify, i.e. to discriminate, these same structures in terms of the situation. It is therefore necessary to have at the outset a process of equilibration which will enable one to produce various combinations of assimilation and accommodation. The balancing mechanism thus consists of compensating for external disturbances till they are incorporated in the initial structures or into a transformation process the result being that the series of development arising from this interaction will rest on increasingly complex rules governing the co-ordination of actions. Since they are oriented towards an approximate reversibility, these rules are transformed finally by systems of operations, or internalized actions co-ordinated in a reversible way, and it will be because of this operational process diverse levels of intelligence occur successively.

Because it is concerned with establishing operational structures, this kind of interpretation arrives at logico-mathematical constructs. It must be noted however that it is not a question of an already existing logical system being used by the psychologist, as in the formalization of Hull's system: nor is it a question of the processes and the logic of the subject itself, since the central problem has all along been to know how that is constructed.[12] Before resorting to abstract models, an attempt was made to work out a developmental type of explanation and the model employed traced the effects of learning and social factors, as well as maturation, to account for a system of equilibrium, so that the whole process could be treated as a probabilistic sequence. Taking, for example, a problem of the conservation of matter where an object is simultaneously modified in the directions $+a$ and $-b$, one would want to know how the subject carries out the operation which describes the transformation of $+a$ and $-b$ in such a way that it will allow him to infer that the quantity remains the same despite the apparent modifications. The explanatory schema will consist firstly of determining why the initial reaction is not likely to be concerned with the transformation as such but only with one aspect of it (for example $+a$ but not $-b$); then it must determine why the most probable subsequent action (it is only the most probable after the first has been dealt with, not having been so all the time) will consist in noting the other aspect of the problem (previously neglected); then one must demonstrate how the oscillation between these two reactions renders it increasingly more likely that one will infer the relatedness of $+a$ and $-b$. This requires a shift from the initial emphasis placed on the single configuration to the whole transformation. Lastly one must determine why the reaction eventually becoming the most probable will consist of compensating one for the other, which means discovering the operation which mediates conservation.

It has been established, then, that this causal schema of equilibrium leads to an abstract probabilistic model and to models which are either algebraic or logical. But it remains for us to

[12] There have been attempts since to integrate these results into Hull's system of explanation: D. Berlyne endeavoured to do this (see 1960) by introducing 'response-transformations' to account for 'operations', and transforming one 'copy-reponse' into another.

establish by what inner necessity it is always so. This we shall attempt now on a more general plane.

7 Explanation based on abstract models

If causal explanation consists in deducing laws which link objects as functions of a certain substrate of reality, and if it supposes three conditions: 1) being in possession of laws; 2) choosing deductive schemata and 3) choosing a substrate to which the deduction applies (society, nervous system, behaviour, conduct, etc.), one can then define explanation based on abstract models in two distinct ways, one more general and the other particular:

a) In a general way one would say that abstract models are used when, instead of being satisfied with 'simple' deduction based on everyday language, one chooses a deductive scheme of a technical nature taken from probabilistic mathematics (the classical theory of probability, theory of chance, theory of decision, theory of information, etc.) or from general algebra comprising Boolean algebra and logic (theory of lattices, theory of groups, formalized propositional logic etc.). According to general acceptance the use of abstract models completes one or other of the explanations so far envisaged when a higher degree of precision than that currently being used is required. This means first of all that an exact language is substituted for the ordinary language, but it later leads to new developments in the explanation, insofar as the chosen deductive schema requires consideration of specific relationships which would be helpful: the introduction of a 'lattice' or 'group' structure for example enables one to perceive a richer mass of well-determined relations not noticed before. But, according to this definition a) the introduction of the abstract model changes nothing at the previously chosen substrate 3: it is still a question of the same neural systems, the same pattern of behaviour, etc., seen in detail.

b) More particularly one speaks of explanation by abstract model when a technical deductive schema 2 is employed for a collection of laws or general facts 1, without selecting an already defined substrate of reality 3 but trying instead to substitute what the possible different models may have in common for it. If this model is itself 'abstract', the term 'abstract' means simply 'common to the different conceivable real models'. Since the ideal in explanation consists of extracting the necessary and sufficient conditions for a collection of facts, the abstract model 3 aims at establishing these conditions and, even if it does not achieve this degree of generality, at least it succeeds in discovering a certain number of sufficient conditions. For example, to explain the perceptual effects of overestimation as a result of centring, we used a probability schema of 'meets' (between the elementary segments of the perceived line and the elements of the subject's receptor organs) and 'joins' (or correspondences between meets on different regions of the figure, these meets not having the same density in every region of the figure). Since we lacked certain data we refused to establish whether these meets were determined by the density of the retinal cells or the number of exploratory micromovements of the eyeball, etc. We even refused to establish whether the joins were due to neural links or whether they were to be found in abstractions which translate the connections which the subject makes consciously in perceiving. The model used suffices to account for the observed laws, not by choosing the real substrate 3, but by seeking what the various conceivable substrates have in common, and it is this which justifies its use, because, if it is correct it will sooner or later apply to one of the real substrates which are actually conceivable.

In these two forms a) and b) explanation by abstract models fulfils three uses. Firstly it makes precise otherwise imprecise deductions: it is this kind of service which Hull expected from the logical formalization of his theory, and he drew nothing else from it, but this in itself constituted an advance in explanation since it provides a deduction system of phenomena.

Secondly, the abstract schema enables us to discover new relations between general facts or laws which were not previously comparable. For example, in the development of a child's intellectual operations (see under C_2) a series of new thought processes is observed to occur between 11–12 years: the appearance of the idea of proportions, double reference systems comprehension of physical relations between actions and reactions, etc. It seems that nothing can explain the simultaneous occurrence of these developments, whose relation to each other is imperceptible. But to account for the operational nature of propositional logic, we formed a 'group' of four transformations (isomorphic with the Klein group) whose existence had eluded logicians: given relation such as implication (p implies q) one can: (1) invert by negation, N (p and non-q); (2) transform it into its reciprocal R (q implies p); (3) transform it into its dual and correlative C (non-p and q); and (4) leave it unaltered, I. One then has $NR = C$, $CR = N$, $CN = R$ and $NRC = I$. This group is interesting from the psychological point of view in that it fuses in a single system the two previously separated forms of reversibility (between 7 and 11–12 years): the inversion N and reciprocity R. It can be said, then, that it simultaneously expresses the natural outcome of operations which develop earlier and the moment when propositional operations begin to occur between 11–12 and 14–15 years. So, it transpires that the new operational schemata which we have just discussed (proportions, etc.) is exactly reducible to such a group! The abstract schema enabled us therefore to discover a close relationship which was missed by the 'simple' and non-algebraic type of investigation.[13]

Thirdly, the abstract schema can supply causal links which were previously overlooked. For example, von Neumann and Morgenstern constructed, for the use of economists, a probabilistic model called the theory of chance or decision, permitting one to calculate the 'strategy' a gambler should adopt in various situations to obtain the *maximum* gain with the *minimum* loss (Bay's criterion) or to minimize to the *maximum* the losses due to the astuteness of his opponent (*minimax* criterion). This can also be applied to losses and gains of information. So, taking up the theory of thresholds of perception (which has not so far managed to be sufficiently precise in its mathematical calculations) W. P. Tanner (of Michigan) succeeded in applying the theory of chance to the discrimination of objective indices and of 'noise' by adapting the computation tables. This success was enough to modify the causal interpretation: instead of explaining it in terms of very fine adjustments of perception one can use the concept of 'decision' to suggest the mediation of unconscious inductive inference, which to a certain extent goes back to Helmholtz . . .

Generally speaking, we maintain that the use of abstract schemata tends to set a certain standard of legitimacy and precision to constructive explanations by stressing the activity of the subject. Whereas reductionist hypotheses subordinate the higher to the lower, the abstract schema, and while not denying that links with

[13] See Chap. 24, Intellectual operations and their development.

the organism are important, reveals the uniqueness and the novelty of developments occurring at the level of behaviour and conduct. Moreover, as neurology (a factual science) cannot explain why $2 + 2 = 4$ or why $A = A$ (equivalences whose necessity rests not on facts but on deductive principles) the fact remains that the implications of consciousness, while reflecting organic connections, could not be understood in developmental terms without resorting to abstract models whose very force depends on their deductive necessity. But isn't this a series of vicious circles, since these models are the products of certain deliberate actions and since they are used in neurology, which is expected to explain psychological facts? These circles would, in fact, be vicious if the discussion of the problem of psychophysiological parallelism did not enable us to define their nature precisely.

4 Psychological explanations and the problem of psychophysiological parallelism

From what has gone before at least two conclusions can be drawn. It is essential that a) psychological explanation allows a certain reduction to take place from the higher to the lower, since its organicism provides an irreplaceable model (capable of leading to physicalism); b) in order to interpret the higher forms of conduct (including their characteristic of 'self awareness') one resorts to a certain form of construction, with all its technical demands (abstract models). There cannot be any contradiction between these conclusions a) and b) and the best proof of this is that when the neurologist studies the nervous system he uses, as an active and intelligent subject, the higher forms of conduct and deductive schemata whose logical necessity is not reducible to material facts.

1 The problem of parallelism

To overcome these difficulties it is necessary to foresee, in aiming at a system of reduction, a method permitting one to respect the uniqueness of conscious necessity, while ensuring that it will continue to reflect its factual origins to which it will be eventually reduced. For example, if the truth of $2 + 2 = 4$ is inconceivable except in the consciousness of a mathematician (be he aged 7 years), a system of neural connections must exist to enable him to recognize this. What, then, is the nature of the link between the conscious judgement and the physiological connections which underlie them? Is it a causal relationship or should we use other categories such as correspondence, parallelism, or isomorphism? This is the eternal problem which forms of psychological explanation have come up against and which we find again simply in comparing these various forms.

First of all, let us note that this problem is not, as is sometimes claimed, one of mind and body, but exclusively that of consciousness and the underlying physiological structures. To speak of the mind is either to reify consciousness, which amounts to prejudging the solution, or to the assign to the whole concept the global designation of 'higher nervous activity plus consciousness' and the problem then reappears in the contents of that 'mind'. This is why to dispute the nomenclature of a certain form of medicine which some call 'psychosomatic' and others 'corticovisceral' amounts to no more than a verbal argument: it is generally agreed that psychological treatment can in certain cases act on a somatic affective state, but this by no means settles the question of knowing whether consciousness has acted causally or the subject has 'taken note' of the nervous activity.

Consequently, the various solutions which have been put forward to account for the relations between the consciousness and its accompanying nervous mechanisms can be reduced to two (excluding idealism, which is not concerned with psychological theories, since the same problem occurs in its own field): either there is interaction between the consciousness and corresponding nervous processes, or it is a question of two parallel series of phenomena whose basic differences prevent their acting causally upon one another.

2 The interactionist solution

The interactionist solution seems confirmed by current observation: when a glass of wine makes us euphoric, we are tempted to see this as a direct action of the organism on the consciousness, and when one moves one's arms to the side after having consciously decided to do so there seems to be direct control of the organism by the consciousness. But as soon as we seek to analyse these causal relations they become utterly incomprehensible, in both directions.

In the first place, to say that the consciousness can direct a physiological process is either to endow it with force, in whatever form (strength, work, power, etc.) or to presuppose a sort of 'psychic energy', which then poses the question of the relation existing between them. A force is a measurable quantity originating in the physical world, and to talk of energy in order to gloss over the difficulties merely increases them tenfold since it implies two consequences of the mutual transformation of the forces and the conservation of energy, neither of which are relevant to the eventual control of consciousness over the body. Actually, when one tries to envisage such an action, one imagines a sort of ethereal or material lining underlying the consciousness which acts in its name when it releases an organic action. So it is obvious that it is not consciousness which 'acts' in this instance, but rather the concomitant nervous activity, it being understood that a nervous actions accompanied by consciousness are not identical with those unaccompanied by consciousness (cf. electrophysiological studies of awareness, etc.). But if these two functions are different does it not assume that interactionism depends on consciousness modifying the function? The problem of 'how' reappears: either the nature of consciousness is simply to 'be conscious' of reasons or causes (or a part of them) or it is a cause which must be given power energy, etc., with all the difficulties mentioned above.

Secondly, the direct causal action of an organic process on consciousness is no easier to understand. Such a process consists of material sequences involving mass, force, resistance, energy, etc. For these material sequences to modify consciousness they would have to find a point where contact could be made with consciousness whose nature was homogeneous with theirs, in the form of displacement of mass, speed of a moving body, diminution of resistance, etc., otherwise the modification would remain unintelligible. Therefore, if a glass of wine makes us gay, this is translated into an increase in the speed of association, by a lowering of inhibition etc. But is this an action '*on* the consciousness' or on a collection of neural connections, with consciousness confined to 'being conscious' of them according to the role which even its name specifically evokes?

3 The parallelist solution

These insurmountable difficulties drive most authors to admit two distinct kinds of phenomena, one consisting of states of conscious-ness and the other of concomitant nervous processes (each state of consciousness corresponding to such a process, but without the reverse being true), and to consider that the relations between elements in one series and the other are never causally connected, but simply correspond or, as it is generally called exist 'parallel' to each other.

In this second solution several sub-varieties can be distinguished. For example,the classic parallelism was atomistic and sought a correspondence between each element (in other words a physiolo-gical concomitant for each sensation, each 'association', etc.). *Gestalt* theory (see 3, under B_2) on the other hand invokes an 'isomorphic' principle by admitting a correspondence between structures. Another subdivision, independent of the former, divided authors with dualist tendencies (the body and 'mind') from those favouring monism who saw the two as two sides of the same coin, which could be known internally (consciously) or externally (physiologically). Moreover, organicist monism put the accent on physiology and regarded consciousness merely as an 'epiphenomenon', etc.

This second group of solutions effectively disposes of the diffi-culties involved in interactionism. But, in the form in which it is usually presented, other equally serious problems arise. In fact, if consciousness is nothing but the subjective aspect of certain nervous activities, it has no distinct function, since these activities can cope with everything. The fact that an external stimulus releases an adaptive reaction and that a problem of higher mathe-matics can be solved by the real brain in the same way as by an 'electronic brain' suggest that these questions can all be explained without recourse to consciousness. One could, of course, maintain that the problem is badly formulated and that consciousness has no more functional significance than a neutral (or *a fortiori* lethal) mutation in the field of biogenetics. But it could be objected that consciousness obeys many laws and that, in psychogenesis as in sociogenesis, the construction of increasingly complex conduct is accompanied not only by an extension of the conscious area, but also by an ever more refined structuring of it. The history of science, to take but one example, is a history of the progress of conscious knowledge. This is true even of the history of behaviourist psychology (cf. C_1), which disregards consciousness by a curious usage of its own conscious thought.

All this then presents a problem and, so that the parallelist solution provides an adequate explanation of admitting two 'parallel' or isomorphic series, it would be desirable for neither of the two types of phenomenon to cease to be functionally significant. It should be understood, at least how these heterogeneous phenomena can be complementary, without being causally interconnected.

5 Isomorphism between causality and 'implication'—conclusions

Sciences more advanced than ours have realized long ago that progress, in moments of crisis, is generally associated with retroactive criticism of the ideas that have been used and so to epistemological criticism which is internal but independent of philosophy. This is appropriate when one is confronted by the problem of consciousness, and it makes it possible to do justice to the ideas of parallelism and isomorphism and, perhaps, to overcome the difficulties which they usually raise.

1 States of consciousness and causality

Thus we are immediately led to suppose that the principal difficulties arise from poor definition of specific ideas which apply to the unique consciousness and for which one has substituted current ideas which are more or less adapted to material causality (physical or physiological), but which are perhaps meaningless in the case of 'states' of mind and even more so in that of the products of the mind (concepts, values, etc.).

In fact it is remarkable how carelessly so many great psychologists have used physical concepts to talk of consciousness. Janet used the terms 'force of synthesis' and 'psychological force'. The expression 'psychic energy' is frequently employed and 'work' is commonplace. Therefore, either one refers implicitly to physiology and must therefore define and measure, or one talks of the consciousness and immediately resorts to metaphors for lack of any clearly defined concepts comparable to those about physical laws and causality. These concepts all presuppose, directly or indirectly, the notion of mass or substance, which has no meaning as far as consciousness is concerned.

We can now define our previous points more accurately by saying that the idea of causality does not apply to consciousness. It does, however, apply to behaviour, and even to conduct, giving rise to different types of causal explanation which we have already differentiated. But it is not 'relevant' in the sphere of consciousness as such, because one state of consciousness does not 'cause' another, but implies it according to other categories. Among the seven forms of explanation which we have recognized only abstract models (under C_3) apply to conscious processes precisely because they can disregard what we have called the real 'substrate'; but, for causality to exist, deduction must apply to such a substrate, which is distinguished from the deductive process in that it is represented in material terms (even when it is a question of behaviour or conduct). Furthermore (and this verifies our argument), the difficulties of interactionism arise from the fact that one is seeking to extend the sphere of causality to the consciousness itself.

2   States of consciousness and implication

Consequently, if none of the constituent ideas of physical causality, except time, applies to facts of consciousness and particularly that of substance (the only one which experimental psychology refused to inherit when philosophical psychology bequeathed its burden), the only choice left is between the following alternatives: either consciousness is nothing, or it arises from original and specific categories which by their very nature ignore material facts. These categories do exist. Let us start with the facts of consciousness occurring in the higher forms of conduct (because here they are in their most characteristic form), the truth of $2 + 2 = 4$ is not the 'cause' of the truth of $4 - 2 = 2$ in the same way that a cannon causes the movement of two billiard balls, or a stimulus is one of the causes of a reaction: the truth (we use the word 'truth' since it refers explicitly to the consciousness of the author of the judgement) of $2 + 2 = 4$ 'implies' that of $4 - 2 = 2$, which is quite a different matter. In the same way the value

187

Jean Piaget

attributed to an aim or moral obligation is not the 'cause' of the value of the means or of an action connected with the obligation: one of the values implies the other in a way similar to logical implication, and one can call this implication between values.

We claim then that however high one climbs towards simple states of consciousness one finds relations of this type. In fact, the most general characteristic of states of consciousness is undoubtedly that they consist of 'meanings' of a cognitive nature (translated in terms of truth or falsehood) or an affective nature (values) or more probably, both at the same time. So, neither the connection between meanings nor the relation of the significant to the signified object arises from causality.

We will use 'implication in the wide sense' therefore to characterize these two sorts of connections including the second (which can be distinguished by the term 'designation') and we hypothesize that the mode of connection proper to phenomena of consciousness is implication in the wide sense, of which implication in the strict sense is a particular case.

Thus presented, the activity of the consciousness is no longer negligible and unimportant. For example, all the deductive sciences, (logic and mathematics), the fine arts, ethics and law arise from diverse forms of conscious implication, and if the nervous system is perfectly capable of rendering them possible, since it is responsible for the effective production of their material substrates, the fact remains that consciousness is essential in order to judge truth and value, i.e. to reach the implications which specifically characterize them.

3 Isomorphism between causality and implication

This leads us to the problem of parallelism, the hypothesis being that the parallelism between states of consciousness and their concomitant physiological processes are in effect isomorphism between systems of implication in the wide sense and causal system. To justify this, recourse to mechanistic physiology supplies the clearest examples. An 'artificial brain' is in effect capable, not only of conducting amazingly complex calculations, but even of working out new demonstrations.[14] Each operation which it

[14] A machine has recently demonstrated a theory of Euclid in a way that one is ashamed to say is new. Given an isosceles triangle ABC whose apex is B and

uses is isomorphic with a logical or mathematical operation and there is a complete isomorphism between the conscious system of operations and the mechanical system. But there remains this difference: the mathematician judges the truth and falsehood of propositions and then evaluates their validity and that of their implications; the machine, on the other hand, is confined to producing results, which have an exact significance from the point of view of its constructor, but to which the machine itself remains indifferent because it is strictly determined and proceeds only by simple causality. True, it is capable of correction and regulation (feedback), but again without evaluation and as a function of single results determined causally by its programming. There is therefore only an objectively negligible difference: mathematics is a science because of the validity of its implications, while the machine acts causally with the same detachment as a pebble takes on the form of a beautiful crystal if the conditions are right.

It can now be seen why neural connections, whose isomorphism with the propositional operations was demonstrated by McCulloch, can well culminate in causally producing a combination of the same kind as $2 + 2 = 4$, but without producing a necessary truth, because logical necessity does not arise from a question of fact but from conscious necessity inherent in implication. One could thus conceive of a completely isomorphic relationship between the causal system of neural connections or behaviour, culminating by successive adjustments in the construction of 'groups' of 'lattices', etc., and the conscious system of implication and judgement using the same structures to validate and make deductions without losing the originality and functional specificity of the system.

4 Conclusion

What is equally evident, and this will be our conclusion, is the complex nature of explanation and of causality in general. We have seen that causality presupposes, 1) laws; 2) a deduction from these laws but 3) applied to a real substrate. Elements 1 and 3 of

whose sides AB = BC. To be demonstrated that the angle BAC equals the angle ACB. Euclid drew a bisector, etc. The machine, when questioned, simply replied: the side AB equals the side CB beginning from the same point B; the side AC is common to the two angles, therefore BAC = ACB because they can be placed symmetrically one upon the other.

189

causality belong to the actual event to be explained (some of the conceptualization coming from the theoretician) while element 2 is introduced by the theoretician (as subject-author of the explanation). Briefly, causality is an assimilation of material actions between objects to the operations of the subject-theoretician. So, of the seven types of explanation which we have distinguished, the first six (A to C_2) are based on causality and are distinguished from each other essentially by the real substrate 3, which is invoked, whilst abstract models (C_3) are distinguished by the type of deduction (2) which is used and are based on deductive implication. Hence their possible application to the conscious structures (an application, moreover, which is not exclusive since this abstract deduction can also be applied to the real substrates (3) by virtue of the principle of isomorphism).

The essential results of our analysis are then: a) that the favoured and dominant directions of explanation in psychology are organicist reduction and interpretation by abstract models; and b) that these two orientations, organicist and deductive, are in no way contradictory, but rather complementary. Until now we have justified this complementarity by stating how much each type of explanation refers, on the one hand to an explicit or implicit organicism while at the same time referring to abstract models; and added to this that the more exact neurology becomes the more it will need deductive models. We can now interpret this complementarity by basing it on deeper reasons: if parallelism between facts of consciousness and physiological processes is isomorphism between the implicative systems of meanings and the causal systems of the material world, it is then evident that this parallelism involves equally, not only a complementarity, but in the final analysis the hope of isomorphism between the organicist schemata and the logico-mathematical schemata used in abstract models.

Bibliography

APOSTEL, L., 'Logique et apprentissage', *Études d'Épistém. génét.*, vol. III, (*Logique, apprentissage et probabilité*) 1959, pp. 1–38

BERLYNE, D. E., 'Les équivalences psychologiques et les notions quantitatives', *Études d'Épist. génét.*, vol. XII (*Théorie du comportement et opérations*), 1960, pp. 1–103

BUSH, R. R. and MOSTELLER, F., *Stochastic models for learning*, Wiley and Sons, 1955

FESSARD, M.-A. and GASTAUT, H., 'Corrélations neuro-physioloques de la formation des réflexes conditionnels', in *Le conditionnement et l'apprentissage*, Paris, Presses Universitaires de France, 1958

GOUIN-DECARIÉ, TH., *Intelligence et affectivité chez le jeune enfant*, Neuchâtel and Paris, Delachaux and Niestlé, 1962

HULL, C. L., *Principles of Behavior*, New York, Appleton Century Crofts, 1943

JANET, P., *De l'angoisse à l'extase*, vol. II, Paris, Alcan, 1926

KÖHLER, W. and WALLACH, H., 'Figural after-effects', *Proc. Amer. Philos. Soc.*, vol. 88, 1944, pp. 269–357

LÉVI-STRAUSS, C., *Les structures élémentaires de la parenté*, Paris, Presses Universitaires de France, 1949

LORENZ, K., *Vergleichende Verhaltenslehre*, Vienna

MCCULLOCH, W. S. and PITTS, W., 'A logical calculus of the ideas immanent in nervous activity', *Bull. math. Biophys.*, vol. V, 1943, pp. 45–133

PIAGET, J., *Introduction à l'épistémologie génétique*, Bk. III (*La pensée biologique, la pensée psychologique et la pensée sociologique*) Paris, Presses Universitaires de France, 1951

—'Logique et équilibre dans les comportements du sujet', *Études d'épistém. génét.*, vol. II (*Logique et équilibre*), 1957, pp. 27–118

—'The problem of consciousness in child psychology' in *Problems of consciousness*, Macy Foundation Conference, New York, Bk. IV, 1953, pp. 136–77

RAPAPORT, D., 'The theory of attention cathexis', forming part of various writings distributed in duplicated form (1960) and which are to be published posthumously

SPEARMAN, C., *The nature of intelligence*, London, 1923

TANNER, W. P., JR. and SWETS, J. A., 'A decision-making theory of human detection', *Psychol. Rev.*, vol. 61, 1954, pp. 401–9

Chapter 4

Measurement in psychology

Maurice Reuchlin

In its most general sense the word 'measurement' designates the operation by which numbers (or at least numerals) are assigned to things. Obviously this can be valuable only if it is carried out according to certain rules.

These rules always consist of establishing a correspondence between properties of numbers and properties of things. They form the basis of the value of measurement in the sense that it is often much easier to verify or to use the properties of numbers than to verify or use directly the corresponding properties of things.

Certain of these rules are relatively easy to respect, others more difficult.

It would be relatively easy for example to find an experimental criterion enabling different observers to agree in general on the meaning of an expression such as the following: 'These two actions (or two symptoms, or skills) belong to the same class of actions (or symptoms or skills)'. This done, it would be easy for them to decide upon a symbol, for example, a number, to designate all the things placed in the same class, using different numbers for different classes. Thus the property of things to be different or not would have been made to correspond to the same property in numbers. Such a method of 'measurement' can be applied to many circumstances. It is very general, because the rules on which it is based are easy to respect. But the arithmetical treatment of the numbers which designate the classes would, of course, be completely absurd, and would teach us nothing about the things which corresponded to them: this method of measurement is as *weak* as it is *general*.

It would be more difficult for observers to find an experimental means of general agreement on the meaning of expressions such as 'of these two different responses, the latter is the better one; of these two different skills, the second is better'. If they succeeded they could designate the responses or the skills by numbers, using two of their properties instead of one: not only would they decide that the different responses and the different skills would be designated by different numbers, but moreover, that the better response or the skill would be allocated higher numbers than those where the response was not so good or the skill less. Numbers thus assigned would obviously present wider possibilities of application, since they possess more properties. The use of such a method of measurement demands a more precise specification of the experimental operations involved. It will be more *specific*, but also stronger, more *powerful*.

It is often experimentally possible, in physical measurement, to use fairly strict rules so that the numbers assigned to things express all their properties arithmetically. On the other hand, in the present state of psychological knowledge it is generally impossible to discover, for all arithmetical operations, experimental operations which when carried out on two things produce an empirical result which one would have been able to foresee from the corresponding arithmetical operation on numbers assigned to those things. The psychologist, more often than the physicist, runs the risk of carrying out an arithmetical treatment of his measurements which is entirely meaningless. It is therefore very important to grasp thoroughly the connection which is established between the properties of things (which are experimentally determined) and the properties of the numbers which can be assigned to them; between the experimental conditions of measurement and the properties of the numbers which it supplies.

The only reply one can give to the question of whether or not measurement is possible in psychology is to show the experimental and mathematical techniques which up till now have allowed a correspondence to exist between the properties of things and those of number, thus giving a double reading, psychological and numerical, in one formal system of relations. This correspondence, this double reading, can be carried out at different levels, from the weaker and general to the more powerful and specific. It is convenient to distinguish four levels which we call, so as to conform with terms already used, by S. S. Stevens (1951) in particular, *nominal scales, ordinal scales, interval scales* and *ratio scales*.

1   Nominal scales

They are obtained by using the most general and weakest of the methods which assign numbers to things, and the use of the word 'measurement' at this level can be justified only by giving the word the extremely general definition which we have chosen. However, nominal scales permit the numerical treatment of psychological observations in quite a number of cases, and it makes for coherence to present them with other methods permitting the same treatment, though starting from more rigorous rules.

1   Experimental conditions

To construct and use a nominal scale, the experimenter must be able to *classify* his facts, that is to define experimentally a *relation of equivalence* enabling him to divide his facts into a certain number of 'independent' classes: each fact must find a place in one class and one only. This supposes first of all that these data be dissociated from each other, as elements of a whole; and subsequently that an experimental criterion be found which makes it possible to assign each fact to one class. Here are several examples:

During the determination of the threshold of tactile discrimination using Manouvriez' aesthesiometer (Fraisse, 1956, p. 96) the subject's responses constituted the elements to be classified. Two classes were used : 'Perception of two points' and 'Non-perception of two points'. A response such as 'doubtful' was a drawback to the criterion of classification and demanded a modification of the experimental technique. instructions to the subject to use only one or the other of the two original responses; or, preferably, the adoption of three classes. Evidently, in this example, the 'non-perception of two points' class does not, by definition, include all the responses other than 'I feel two points'. Hence, the necessity of limiting, by an experimental technique (here, instructions to the subject) the number of possible responses.

A finer distinction could be made by sub-dividing one of these classes. Thus, a subject who had been asked to compare a variable stimulus with a fixed stimulus could be told to use only one of three categories of response: 'smaller' 'equal' or 'greater'. But one can make the classification still finer by subdividing the first class into 'smaller', and 'perhaps smaller' and proceeding in the same way for the third class.

It can be made less refined by the opposite method or by a particular convention designed especially with the nature of observation in mind. For example, 'perhaps smaller' can be suppressed by attributing half to the 'smaller' class and half to the 'equal' class.

The above examples demonstrate that the refinement of a classification can only be made by a modification of experimental conditions, while the regrouping of several classes can be made either at the experimental stage or in the numerical treatment. It appears from this that it is always possible to use as fine an experimental division as possible. In fact, if this method were to be generally followed, account should be taken of other factors in the assessment. The setting up of experimental conditions which permit a very fine classification is costly, in the general sense of the word, and the experimenter must always draw dividing lines with the strategy of his whole plan of work in mind, and not simply as a function of a particular measurement taken out of its context. It might happen, for example, that a larger number of relatively rough divisions might be more useful than a small number of finer ones. Moreover, in many cases where the experimental operation, which provides the basis for measurement, consists of the classification of stimuli by a human observer, increasing the number of classes does not mean an indefinite increase in the information which the observer can transmit: many faults cancel out the benefit which can be expected from this refinement. To determine the optimum number of classes the idea of 'equivalent number' borrowed from information theory is useful (Faverge, 1953, p. 468–9). We shall return to the problem of the necessary fineness of divisions at the experimental stage after quoting some examples which will illustrate better the difficulties which can arise from the distinction of elements to be classified and the definition of criteria of classification.

Quantitative analysis of clinical interviews between the psychologist and a subject has often made use of nominal scales, and numerous examples can be found in a critical review by J. Cambon (1955). The element to be classified can be the portion of one individual's conversation contained between two interruptions by the other; or the 'exchange', i.e. the interruption of the psychologist following a reply from the subject. The subject's remarks can be classified in categories such as 'abandonment or pursuit of self-exploration', 'being aware of the situation', etc.; those of the psychologist as 'interpretations', clarification', 'reformulation', etc. The recording and typing of each interview facilitates this classification.

Dissociating the elements to be classified can be more difficult in experiments which involve observation of behaviour, for example in administering individual tests (Reuchlin, 1950). One decides to isolate a certain number of 'characteristics' in the subject's behaviour, that is elements of behaviour whose unitary character is established by the fact that two independent observers agree in noting their appearance: 'asks a question', 'drops something', 'replaces the material', etc. Each of these characteristics fall into position on a nominal scale of two classes: present or absent.

Similarly one can differentiate and classify practical observations of patients. But when this analysis is done from the files on these patients (Bacher, Reuchlin, 1956) one must be able to take for granted the fact that when a trait is not actually noted it was in fact absent in the patient, and cannot always be sure that this is so.

Frequently, in certain spheres of psychology, one has to take account of the subjects' professions or, if they are children, of their fathers' professions. This information can be used only through the intermediary of nominal scales, which is difficult. In fact, current terminology is very imprecise in this sphere, and a term such as 'mechanic' can cover extremely diverse occupations. This first difficulty can only be smoothed out if one obtains a sufficiently detailed description of the subject's actual activity from him. Moreover, this activity always presents multiple aspects which can be classified in many ways, of each category being fairly finely distinguished from others.[1] Obviously one must choose the system which one feels will be of most use to the

[1] By socio-professional categories: farmers, farm workers, employers, the professional classes and higher ranks, middle ranks, employees, etc.; by categories of collective activity, agriculture and forestry, the mining industries, building and public works, transport, commerce, etc; or by status: self-employed, employers, domestic workers, apprentices, those employed at home, etc. (from the Institut National de la Statistique et des Études Économiques).

psychological problem being studied, and from this point of view the level of qualification and area of activity, for example, cannot be used without due consideration. Moreover, it is desirable to use a classification which has already been used during other investigations or for which one can use statistical information obtained in the general population census, such as the classifications of the Institut National de la Statistique et des Études Économiques.

The problem of the degree of fineness of a nominal scale must be reconsidered now in greater detail. During the setting up of such a scale one is often led to subdivide certain of the originally planned classes and to regroup certain other classes.[2]

These subdivisions and regroupings will be dictated by two types of considerations.

Some concern the power of the observational method which has been used and the cost of setting it up: for instance, if two observers could not agree on a particular subdivision of behaviour traits, that subdivision will be abandoned; e.g. a subdivision of the scale of professions which required each subject's employer to be interviewed.

Others, perhaps more important, concern the content of the information which one seeks to collect. They are of two kinds.

On the one hand it must be realized that in many cases the degree of fineness the distinction cannot be modified without involving a change in the content of the information which not only becomes more or less precise, but actually different. To subdivide the action 'asking a question' into 'questions relating to the understanding of instructions' and 'questions relating to the value of the result obtained' does not introduce a more precise fashion of counting the questions, but rather introduces a new dimension into the analysis.

Moreover, it is often difficult to use a classification which is not similar to others. To classify subjects according to their profession is also to distinguish them according to their average cultural level, living standards, amount and kind of leisure time,

---

[2] All the subdivisions thus constitute, from the point of view of fineness, a partially ordered whole, a *lattice* (Faverge, 1959): in considering two of them one can set up either a subdivision more or less as fine as the finest (taking the classes after subdivision, and before regrouping) or a subdivision more or less as broad as the broadest.

etc. The words used to designate the classes must not be misleading: the names of professional activities, for example, must be taken as symbols, whose significance is not perhaps limited to their meaning in everyday language. This difficulty can be lessened or avoided in certain spheres by a more rigorous determination of the conditions of observation and 'measurement'. In other cases, experimental analysis can be clarified by later treatment of the numbers which it has produced, as long as this has been previously planned so that it will be possible. This point, which does not apply to simple nominal scales, leads us in particular to examine the numerical properties which these scales enable us to assign to things.

2   Numerical properties

The numbers finally used to designate the classes have no property other than being different from each other, and it is obviously not these which are used. All numerical treatment based on nominal scales has a bearing on the number of observations arranged or effective in each class. The methods applicable to this treatment are sometimes called 'statistics of attributes' (Yule and Kendall, 1949, Chapters I to V).

Since no experimental technique has laid down an order between these classes, there is no sense in considering the complements in any particular order. There is every reason to limit the form of the histogram of the distribution to the characteristics which remain true for any permutation of classes. Similarly, statistics ranged around a measure such as the median have no meaning here. This is especially true of statistics based on the distance between two measurements such as the standard deviation.

By contrast, one can determine which class contains the most frequent instances and call it the *mode* of the distribution. The mode would be a statistic of 'central tendency', taking this expression in its wide and somewhat incorrect sense, since a distribution of this type does not, in fact, have a 'centre', as its classes are not in order. Supposing that one continues to make observations without changing the conditions which make up the distribution, then the mode represents the most probable observation.

According to this hypothesis, the uncertainty as to the class which the next observation will belong to will depend simply on the number of classes and their complements and this can be determined. It is a question of the *entropy* of the distribution, in the sense of information theory as expounded by Shannon and Weaver (1949), which the psychologist can study in Faverge's publications (particularly in 1953 and 1954*b*). Entropy defines dispersion in the widest sense. It increases with the number of classes and, for a given number of classes, is at its maximum when all the complements are equal. Thus it may be seen that it varies as also does the observer's uncertainty as to the next stimulus he is going to perceive. But one could say that the more uncertain the observer is, the greater is the value of the information provided by observation. Hence this seemingly paradoxical assimilation between uncertainty and information: the entropy of a distribution of observations measures the average value of the information contributed by one of them. Experiments on language, in particular, make great use of the idea of entropy, and several examples can be found in the article by Bresson (1954). The absolute threshold might equally be defined as the value of the stimulus for which the entropy of the distribution of the responses (shared between the two classes 'stimulus perceived' and 'stimulus not perceived') is greatest.

If two different experimental criteria were used to classify the same collection of experimental data according to two different nominal scales, an appropriate numerical treatment of the results of these 'measurements' would enable one to know whether the two experimental criteria were independent.

For example, the choice of occupation by children and the occupation which their fathers follow are independent of each other if the children's choice is distributed among the different classes according to the same proportions as the fathers' occupations. A statistic such as χ^2 makes it possible to know whether the actual distribution of observations deviates from that theoretical distribution, from that model, sufficiently for one to reject, without too great a risk of error, the hypothesis of independence thus formulated. Thus, in the examples quoted above, the behaviour traits and symptoms were associated with each other.

Here is an example in which χ^2 has been used to this end (Reuchlin 1950). For each subject of a group of 97, an observer noted the number of times during the application of a test that actions such as 'asking a question', 'acting straight away' etc.

Measurement in psychology

appeared, each one of these actions having already been explicitly defined. The frequencies with which each action appeared were grouped in two classes, chosen so as to contain as near as possible the same number of subjects. For example, for the action 'asking a question' one class was made up of the 47 subjects who did not ask questions, another of the 50 subjects who asked one, two, three or seven questions. For each pair of actions one could then draw up a 2×2 contingency table and the independence of these two actions, *thus divided in 2*, can be tested by use of χ^2.

Obviously the use of dichotomy was not essential in this example. It is explained by the desire to speak unambiguously of the *sense* of the connection between the two traits, an idea which can lose its meaning if the contingency table is larger than 2×2. Moreover, if dichotomization of the scale is accepted, it could be done in many other ways, each of which would correspond to a different value of the contingency.

In certain other cases, the dichotomy becomes essential in a less arbitrary way. Such is the case where a symptom has been noted *present* or *absent* by the doctor who examined a patient (Bacher and Reuchlin, 1956).

It might be said also that children's choice of occupation is independent of that of their parents if the psychologist's uncertainty as to the occupation which the child will choose remains the same, on average, whether or not he knows the father's occupation. The comparison of measurements of entropy present in the two hypotheses will enable one to know whether the two scales are independent in this sense. If they are not, a certain quantity of information is transmitted from one scale to another, i.e. from system of observation to another. The quantity of information transmitted (R) constitutes a measure of the degrees of association between the two distributions, a 'contingency co-efficient' (Faverge 1959), among possible others.[3] The quantity of information transmitted has been used in experiments on language, learning and, in a completely different psychological area, in the analysis of information collected through an examination of the professional orientation of the subjects and comprising very different types of observations (Bacher, 1957), etc.

[3] The expression 'contingency coefficient', used without any other definition, is usually applied to the C coefficient of K. Pearson or the coefficient of the average square of the contingency (Yule and Kendall, 1949, p. 68).

In this last work, contingency tables were drawn up between a great number of raised items in notation scales. Here are two examples:

Past scholastic record (from the point of view of irregularity)

a) No changes of primary school, no prolonged or frequent absence

b) Several changes (in all three establishments); a certain irregularity in attendance

c) Numerous changes, changes of country, prolonged absence (several months), great irregularity of attendance (absence every month).

Youth groups

a) Belongs to a group (scouts, club, church club)

b) Did belong to a group, but does so no longer

c) Has never belonged to a group.

It can be seen that the scales used here are in fact ordinal scales. They are treated as nominal scales because, for certain observations, an ordinal relation could not be established. Moreover, it will be seen that the contingency tables go beyond the dimension 2×2, which involves the necessity of describing for each division the deviations between the observed complements and the theoretical complements and interpreting the associations noted.

The great advantage of using the quantity of information transmitted R on the χ^2 test depends on the brevity of the calculations. If N is the total number of observations, the calculation of NR simply requires the summing of the numbers read in the table of $n \log_2 n$, a sum comprising as many terms as there are complements in the contingency tables (including the marginal complement and the total complement): say 16 terms for the two variables given in the example.

However, we must never lose sight of the close connection which is necessarily established between, on the one hand, the experimental operation which produces the distribution and on the other the significance of the results obtained at the end of the numerical treatment.

It could help for example, in understanding the variation of a measure of contingency between two partitions when its fineness varies—a property stressed by Faverge (1959). One could attempt to reconcile these variations by the fact that, in the majority of cases, a partition can only be made finer by introducing experimental criteria of a different nature from those previously used. In the same way one understands the recommendation of Yule and Kendall (1949 pp. 74–5) not to speak of association or contingency except in connection with *homogeneous* classifications, i.e. those in which the refining of the partition is carried out by applying the same principle of subdivisions to all classes at a certain level.

Generally speaking, it is always through this inevitable connection that one is able to understand that numbers assigned to things by rules as general as those used at this level can supply only very general answers to the questions one attempts to solve by such 'measurement' processes. Thus, the quantity of information transmitted, R, permits one to know whether the psychologist's uncertainty about the occupation chosen by the child diminishes *on average* when the father's occupation is known. But the psychologist who knows only this quantity R is not able to say whether the range of choice of the children whose father is in a certain occupation is less than the general range he is incapable of saying which occupation is most often chosen by that particular class of children. The answer to these questions demands careful analysis of the frequency table. However we realize that it is sufficient, to know the normal correlation coefficient, r, calculated between two interval scales under the required conditions to find out the mean and the standard deviation of the measurements affected on one of the scales for all the elements with a given value on the other.

This comparison illustrates the limitations of 'weak', general models, and justifies the psychologist's desire to use, in certain cases, scales of measurement which are more powerful than nominal scales.

2 Ordinal scales

Measurements derived from ordinal scales have all the properties of the above scales in addition to new ones. This is due to the fact that the experimenter who uses them is first capable of establishing a relation of equivalence and, further, an ordered relation between the things. For this he would need to have discovered an experimental method (an apparatus which permits the comparison of two

Maurice Reuchlin

sensations; a test allowing one to compare two subjects) allowing him to say that A is superior to B in that it has certain properties. This operation should exclude the possibility of one being able to assert simultaneously that A is superior to B and B superior to A; the operation enabling one to say that A is superior to B and B superior to C must also enable one to say that A is superior to C. The search for means of constructing an ordinal scale with these properties involves experiment. If this search succeeds, one can then assign to each thing a symbol taken from a collection which express ordinal relations so that two symbols always relate to each other in the same way as the two things which they symbolize. Certain operations carried out with the help of symbols will permit one to foresee the results of others carried out on things, and it is only these properties of symbols which are of interest to the experimentalist.

1 Experimental conditions

In different spheres of psychology operations have been found which allow one to establish ordinal relations experimentally with an acceptable degree of accuracy. Here are several examples.

A) ORDERING OF SENSATIONS

A subject is asked to place in order the sensations which he feels when submitted to a stimulus of varying physical degree. It is noticed that the subject generally has no difficulty in understanding the nature of the task and that, if it is decided to mark each sensation by a physical measure of the stimulus, he arranges the sensations according to the measure, establishing an ordinal relationship between the sensations which verifies the two general properties remarked on above. At least, this is what happens as long as the difference in the physical stimuli remains above a certain value, the differential threshold. This fact can be illustrated by the table of results obtained during a measurement of the kinesthetic differential threshold with the gravimeter of Piéron, a table reproduced by Fraisse (1956, p. 299). It involved comparing the weight of a variable stimulus to a fixed weight of 15 g. For each of the values between 146 g. and 158 g. the weight of the variable was sometimes stated as lower than the fixed

204

stimulus and sometimes higher, which contradicts the first property of the ordinal relation. Outside this margin, however, this did not happen. Such an experiment was aimed at determining the limits between which it is possible to establish experimentally an ordinal relation between sensations with the help of apparatus which includes the subject himself.

B) ORDERING OF MENTAL ABILITIES

A subject doing a test which sets out to define a mental ability operationally must accomplish a series of tasks ('items' or, more commonly 'questions') in well defined conditions. These conditions are selected, in such a way as to permit unambiguous classification of the subjects results into one or other of the classes: 'positive response' or 'negative response' (for example, the right answer and the wrong answer). The result of the test is made up of all the responses to the questions. Different subjects should, as often as possible, obtain different results in the test. The different possible results in the test must be arranged so that the subjects who have obtained these results can be ranged in the same way; this can be done by two methods, according to whether or not one wishes to take the speed of execution into account.

If it is a 'speed' test a series of identical tasks can be used, for example a series of screws to be turned, a series of arithmetical operations of the same nature and difficulty, etc. In this case the different results of the test (and the subjects who have obtained them) could be ordered according to the number of positive responses obtained in a given time.

The time of execution need not necessarily be considered (test of 'level'), the subjects being left to work as long as they wish, or at least long enough for it to be improbable that the results can be modified later. Scales of mental level like Binet's, and numerous collective tests aimed at more specific abilities are of this type. The questions are presented to the subject in increasing order of difficulty. This ordinal relationship between the questions is established by defining the difficulty according to proportion of subjects in the population who do not manage to supply a positive response. Theoretically, if the test is homogeneous, it is to be expected that all subjects solving a question of difficulty p should also solve all the questions of a difficulty below p (Loevinger 1948;

Maurice Reuchlin

Faverge 1958). The ability of a subject will be greater according to the degree of difficulty of the last question he has answered. The level of difficulty will be estimated by the position which the question holds in the test, i.e. by the number of questions solved. It will then be possible to order the subjects according to their ability as defined by the test, in the same way as the number of positive responses which they have supplied.

c) THE ORDERING OF ATTITUDES

The ordering of subjects according to their attitudes involves also ordering the questions which are put to them, by a technique such as the Guttman scale (Stouffer, 1950). In this technique a provisional hypothesis is adopted that the following three questions, for example, have been taken from the same 'universe of content', the universe of questions whose reply (yes or no) depends on the attitude of the subject to Negroes (Stouffer, 1950, p. 13):

a) Would you want one of your relations to marry a Negro?
b) Would you invite a Negro home to dinner?
c) Would you give Negroes the vote?

If these three questions can be ordered as to the attitude implied by a positive response, it can be expected that all the subjects who reply positively to the question implying the most favourable attitude will reply positively to the two others; that all the subjects who reply negatively to this first question, but positively to the question on the next line will reply positively to that on the third line; that all the subjects who reply negatively to this last question will reply negatively to all the others. The construction of the scale will then consist of determining whether there exists a classification of both subjects and questions which satisfies these conditions. If this were possible for the three questions in the example, a rank would be assigned to them (Q_1, Q_2, Q_3) so that the replies given by four groups of subjects (designated by G_0, G_1, G_2, G_3) could be represented by the following table:

The groups will then be ordered as a function of their attitude, from the least favourable (G_0) to the most favourable (G_3). A more detailed guide to the techniques used to effect the double simultaneous classification of subjects and questions will be found

206

in Guttman (1947), Suchman (1950), Kahn and Bodine (1951) and Moscovici (1954).

But the examples we have just given raise at least two more general points.

Firstly, it must be understood that the properties by which the ordinal relation is formally defined will hardly ever be strictly verified by experimental data. This can be seen, for example, in the construction of a Guttman scale by the appearance of certain responses which do not fit the parallelogram in the theoretical

	Yes to Q_1	Yes to Q_2	Yes to Q_3	Yes to Q_1	No to Q_2	No to Q_3
G_3...	×	×	×			
G_2...		×	×	×		
G_1...			×	×	×	
G_0...				×	×	×

arrangement of the preceding table. It would be convenient to study, in each particular case, *in what measure* the ordinal relation is verified experimentally. Methods applicable to this study as far as the Guttman scales are concerned have been put forward by Durain and Moscovici (1956), Moscovici and Durain (1956) and Moscovici and Vibert-Durain (1958).

Secondly it must be noted that the experimental conditions which we describe above only have meaning for certain subjects in certain situations, subjects and situations necessarily playing complementary and reciprocal roles: in the test, it is the responses of the subjects which define the order of difficulty of the questions as a function of which the subjects are finally classified; in the Guttman scale, the order of the questions is only significant if it leads to the classification of the subjects, and vice versa. This reciprocal and simultaneous determination of the means of measurement and of the object to which it applies is a step of which the psychologist must be aware, even though it is not proper to psychology.

2 Numerical properties

The properties of numbers assigned according to an ordinal scale are those which remain unchanged when these numbers are replaced by others ordered in the same way (monotonic transformation).

It will be noticed that two objects which were expressed by different numbers before the transformation will automatically be given different numbers after. So numbers ranged according to an ordinal scale also have the properties of those ranged according to a nominal scale. They have others in addition.

We can consider here the order in which the complements of the different classes fall, since the order of these classes is defined by the experimental operation. However, on the histogram which represents the distribution graphically, the interval chosen on the *x*-axis to represent each class remains arbitrary. The shape of the histogram should not then give rise to interpretation other than that which would be equally true if the *x*-axis were expanded or contracted to varying degrees.

These transformations will not affect the point at which 50 per cent of the distribution (the median) falls. It would be useful to know the value assigned to it, the number which one calls the *median* and which can be regarded as a statistic of central tendency.

The distribution of measurements can be described, fairly finely, by tables of numbers called *centilage, decilage* or *quartilage*. The centilage is made up of the series of 99 numbers assigned to the 99 elements which have been exceeded by 1 per cent, by 2 per cent . . ., by 99 per cent of the elements. From this one can easily deduce the definition of decilage (9 numbers) (Faverge, 1954a, p. 51) and quartilage (3 numbers). The numbers in these tables are called centiles, deciles, quartiles. It can be seen that the median, the 50th centile, the 5th decile, the 2nd quartile, is the same number.

The median is often used in the determination of thresholds. The value of an absolute threshold is that of the stimulus which has been perceived in 50 per cent of the cases, that is the median of the distribution of the 'stimulus perceived' responses in classes ranged in order of the degree of the strength of the physical stimulus (Fraisse, 1956, p. 293). Similarly, during the measurement of a differential threshold, a 'higher or lower liminal value' is determined which represents the value of the stimulus perceived as greater or smaller in 50 per cent of the cases (Fraisse, 1956, p. 300). The decilage is used in the psychology of individual

208

differences to place a subject according to the mark he has obtained in a test out of a population of similar subjects who have done the same test. If the subject has done many tests, for example, his degree of superiority in test A would be considered greater than that in test B if he had only been surpassed by 20 per cent of the population in A but 40 per cent in B. The direct comparison of marks in the two tests would be meaningless, since a numerical transformation compatible with the experimental properties of an ordinal scale could arbitrarily change the result.

If each element of a certain group has been measured on two distinct ordinal scales, it must be determined whether or not these two scales are independent. In this case the Kendall's correlation coefficient by ranking (1955) could be used. Having noted, for example that two elements, A and B measured on the scale x can be written A > B, one determines what relation is established between these elements on the scale y. If the two scales are independent, there is an equal chance of either A > B or A < B occurring only. The pairs of elements are successively considered and the coefficient τ sums up the collection of statements (Festinger and Katz, 1959, p. 650–4).

In the above treatment no arithmetical operation like addition has been used on the measurements: all these methods would still be possible if the numbers assigned to the object or classes were replaced by another system conventionally arranged symbols, for example, letters which, like numbers, would allow one to make comparisons. Possible arithmetical operations, as at the level of nominal scales, would only concern the complements of the classes. When arithmetical operations are carried out on the measurements themselves one is going beyond the experimental properties of ordinal scales, and since this upsets the fundamental balance of the experimental and numerical relationship it always requires theoretical consideration.

This occurs when one attempts to determine the value of a median, or of centiles, deciles and quartiles, by interpolation. For example, given that in a test (Faverge, 1954a, p. 53) 8 subjects out of 126 have marks above 44·5, 16 subjects out of 26 have marks above 43·5, and that one wishes to calculate the first decile, i.e. the mark which would be exceeded by 12·6 subjects out of 126. Linear interpolation comes down to allocating the *distance* between 43·5 and 44·5 proportionally to the numbers (12·6——9) and (16————12·6). But if we consider the marks 43·5 and 44·5 simply as ordered symbols, this idea of distance has no meaning. We can certainly interpolate as many ordered symbols as we wish between 43·5 and 44·5. But the problem of knowing which of these symbols occupies a particular 'position' in the 'interval' between 43·5 and 44·5 has absolutely no meaning since we can always consider a moving of these symbols as long as their order is preserved. Graphic interpolation does not solve this problem either, since it uses a representative curve whose shape is undetermined because of the 'elastic' and 'compressible' character of its co-ordinate axes, which represents the ordinal scale. In practice, it is often enough to know that the decile one is looking for falls between 43·5 and 44·5. It can be useful in certain cases to introduce the complementary hypothesis of an arbitrary metric between these two values, for example, supposing them to be separated by nine equidistant degrees, 43·6, 43·7 . . . 44·4, thus permitting interpolation.

Another discussion of the same kind should, for the same reasons, be associated with the use of quartile or semi-interquartile distances, the latter being derived by halving the difference between the first and the third quartile. Here again, an arithmetical operation is concerned with the ordered symbols between which one has no experimentally defined distance. It might be thought that such a statistic supplies some information on the extent covered by the numbers used as ordered symbols. But obviously two equal semi-interquartile distances can comprise quite different numbers of classes: moreover, this statistic teaches us nothing about the distribution of the complements among these classes. It is independent of the entropy of the distribution, and it is not of much use in the case of strictly ordinal scales, where it seems to be impossible to define what is meant by the 'distance' between measurements.

Finally, Spearman's correlation coefficient by ranking (Faverge, 1956, p. 175) is in fact simply a Bravais–Pearson coefficient calculated on ranks. In using it, it is assumed that the ranks have the properties required to make the calculation of the Bravais–Pearson coefficient meaningful, i.e. that one can assign certain properties to the distances between the measurements. When one wishes to avoid assumptions of this kind, it is convenient simply to use the Kendall τ.

Measurement in psychology

These discussions show how the absence of an experimental definition of distance, of intervals between measurements, limits the properties of numbers assigned to things. It is natural, then, that attempts should have been made to establish such a definition, attempts which we shall now consider.

3 Interval scales

In constructing interval scales an experimental operation must be found which permits a definition of what is meant when one says that the distance (or the difference) between two things is equal to the distance (or difference) between two others. If such an operation can be found, numbers can be assigned to things in such a way that two numerical differences would correspond to two experimentally equal distances (or differences).

The empirical definition of the equality of two distances or differences is difficult, and psychologists have often had to use not only experimental results, but also certain postulates. We will distinguish the experimental, or mainly experimental, definitions from those which make wider use of the language and method of statistics, particularly in the formulation of postulates.

1 Experimental definition of the equality of two intervals

A) OPERATIONS OF EQUAL DIVISION

a) *Equalization of distances between sensations.* The principle of these experiments, first carried out by Delbœuf at the suggestion of Plateau, is well known. They consisted first of supplying a painter with a white sample and a black sample and asking him to make up a grey which seemed to him to be equally distant from them both. The progress of experimental techniques later permitted numerous experiments concerning diverse sensory modalities to be carried out on the same principle. The method they employ is the method of 'equal sensory distances' or 'average gradations'.

If such an experimental operation is to permit us to define the equality of two or more intervals satisfactorily, the responses must satisfy the following experimental control. A sensory interval AE

Maurice Reuchlin

is first subdivided into two equal intervals by a stimulus C, chosen by the subject. The subject then defines in the same way a stimulus B dividing AC equally and a stimulus D dividing CE equally. Then comes the crucial test: the mean of BD must be C. Gage (1934) carried out these verifications in the auditory and visual senses. The expected coincidence did not in fact occur. Piéron explained this failure by the ambiguity of the task presented to the subject. He was asked to judge the intensity of his sensations, though usually he would judge the intensity of the physical stimulus which aroused them.

b) *Attitude scales of apparently equal intervals.* The method of equal sensory distance was adapted by Thurstone to the measurement of appreciation or attitudes. This method could, for example, be applied to the determination of intervals judged equal on a scale of scholastic behaviour (S. Larcebeau, 1955). Phrases describing the behaviour of primary school children from a particular point of view were written on cards. A large number of 'judges' (schoolteachers) were asked to arrange these phrases into five categories which seemed to them to correspond to five equidistant points on the scale. For this to be done unambiguously, all the judges would have to put a given phrase in the same place. In fact, certain phrases did command substantial agreement, but for others the judgements were widely disparate and they had to be discarded.

In this work, 218 phrases were used, drawn from 'cutting up' 162 'portraits' of good, middling and bad pupils obtained from 54 teachers after elimination of duplications and manifestly ambiguous formulations, etc. The phrases were first placed in 15 categories. One of them concerned, for example, 'attention'. The phrases relating to this were reproduced on cards and given to the judges (44 schoolteachers) with the following instructions: 'You are asked to classify these phrases in five equidistant columns. In the first column you will place the phrases which express the highest levels of attention. In the second column you will place the phrases which, in your opinion, express a lesser degree of attention. And so on, until the fifth column in which you will place the phrases expressing the minimum or absence of attention'. A phrase could have been added inviting the judges to verify their classification afterwards by immediately re-examining all the cards thus classified. For each phrase the semi-interquartile

212

distance and the mean was calculated. The mean determined the classification of each of the phrases on the scale.

B) FECHNER'S LAW

By taking a certain stimulus as standard, one can determine the stimulus which is perceived as greater (or smaller) in 50 per cent of cases. This new stimulus can be taken as the standard and a series of stimuli can thus be more and more closely determined. The methods employed to draw up this scale are described in the determination of differential thresholds. Fechner considered as equal all the intervals separating sensations aroused by stimuli thus determined (differential increments).

As for the preceding methods, the first question is how far the obtained results vary when the same subject repeats the experiment or when the experiment is repeated with different subjects. Piéron (*Actes du XVe Congrès international de psychologie*, 1959, *p*. 101) held that this variability was about 10 per cent, that is to say fairly weak in relation to that observed in other methods. If, then, Fechner's affirmation is simply an assumption, a convention of language, this assumption at least seems clearly defined.

But, equally, its degree of generality can be questioned. It is seen that it only needs a variation of the receptor involved for the assumption to cease to apply (Piéron, 1951, p. 19 and 1951, p. 448). This is particularly apparent in experiments of comparison of sounds of different frequencies, like those carried out by Fletcher and Munson in 1933. Two sounds, A and B, of different frequencies are equalized at a certain level of intensity. Two others, A' and B' whose frequencies are equal respectively to those of A and B are equalized at another level of intensity. It is seen that the number of differential increments which can be distinguished on AA' is in general different from the number on BB'.

Despite these limitations, Fechner's postulate has a 'certain practical value' (Piéron, 1951, p. 63). The results obtained by the equal distribution method are frequently in agreement with this postulate. Similarly, scales of the degree of perception of sensory data constructed without using the method of determination of differential thresholds, are in agreement with Fechner's definition. This also applies to scales of grey used in engraving, the scale of the thickness of wool, or the scale used to judge the apparent brilliance of the stars (Piéron, 1955, p. 475).

The convergence of these different results or observations is demonstrated by the fact that the physical intensities of the stimuli chosen to indicate equal sense intervals are, in all these cases, in geometric progression.[4]

The postulates introduced in defining the equality of intervals takes a statistical form in other cases.

2 *Statistical definition of the equality of two intervals*

A) THE FORM OF THE DISTRIBUTION

a) A postulate on the form of the distribution of a series of measurements carried out on an ordinal scale suffices to define the equality of the intervals on that scale, then to transform it into an interval scale.

Let us suppose that an ordinal distribution is drawn on an elastic surface, using class intervals of an arbitrary width, the area of each class being proportional to its complement, imagining that the distortions necessary to give the distribution its chosen form are imprinted on this surface. Once this result is obtained, the class intervals take the values determined by the form of distribution which has been selected and in this sense one can speak of equal or unequal intervals.

It will be seen that any form of distribution supplies a definition of the equality of intervals. Naturally, these definitions are different and it is desirable to choose a postulate which appears to fit in with one's knowledge of the field studied and which offers, if possible, certain methodological advantages. Psychologists usually choose the 'normal' distribution of Laplace and Gauss.

b) It has often seemed likely that the distances from the central value may be as rare as they are important. A given stimulus, perceived several times under the same conditions, tends to arouse a sensation of the same intensity. Equally, different members of an homogeneous group, in comparable living conditions,

---

[4] The numbers attributed to sensations on a scale composed of equal intervals are necessarily in arithmetical progression. The result is a logarithmic form for the law which relates the intensity of the stimulus to the intensity of the sensation.

tend to exhibit each of their characteristics to the same degree. The measurements carried out in non-psychological spheres (measurement of height, for example) confirm this hypothesis and have often led, empirically in several cases, to distributions very near to that of Laplace and Gauss.

Moreover, normal distribution possesses a formal property which also favours its adoption. As Faverge (1954b, p. 423) recalls, Shannon has shown that, if several distributions have the same variance, those possessing the greatest entropy are those with normal distributions. Obviously, it is always desirable to choose the scale of measurement which best differentiates the things measured.

Finally, normal distribution has often been studied, and a great number of statistical techniques are available which apply to this distribution.

c) To transform a distribution of any kind into a normal distribution, one can first of all use methods which modify the experimental conditions of measurement.

A case in which this method is often used in psychology is the construction of mental tests. In effect, the nature of the questions asked, the time allotted for their solution, the criteria defining a positive response can all be modified. The form of the distribution of scores in the test depends on the difficulty of the questions and the links which exist between them. In practice, one notes by observing the distribution that the test is 'too easy' or 'too difficult' and then proceeds empirically to alter the questions as necessary. These modifications supply a test better adapted to the population being examined, i.e. they avoid the use of a test in which most of the answers would be wrong (or right). Such tests would provide less information than those whose difficulty is well adapted. The methods of transformation in the following paragraph are easy to use, but they do not have this advantage.

d) A distribution can simply be 'normalized' by a transformation of the original scale of measurement using a statistical or mathematical treatment taken from the results already obtained, without modification of the experimental conditions.

α) *Normalization on the complements* (Faverge, 1954a, p. 55). The distribution of results is divided into a certain number of classes (5, for example). The proportion of elements in each class is chosen in such a way that the boundaries of these classes would be equidistant from each other in a normal distribution. Starting from an ordinal distribution, the required complement is assigned to each class. Each boundary between two classes can be defined by an intermediary number assigned to the lower element of the upper class. These numbers are considered as equidistant on the scale of intervals, and thus a *normalized scale* has been constructed.

β) *Normalization on the variable* (Faverge, 1954a, p. 49; Fautrel, 1952). By applying a non-linear mathematical transformation to the numbers assigned on an ordinal scale, it is possible to modify the relative importance of the differences calculated between these numbers. If the transformation is suitably chosen, these modifications can balance or normalize an asymmetrical distribution. The experiment shows in particular that the transformation:

$$x' = \log (x + c)$$

can in certain cases perform this function, for a value matched to c (x denotes the original variable and x' the transformed variable). Normalization on the variable is advantageous in a case where automatic methods of calculation are used.

e) The choice of the normal curve to determine intervals between measurements is by far the most frequent, for the reasons which we have given, but any curve can, formally, perform the same function.

Thus, if one calculates the differences between quartiles, deciles or centiles, one accepts the definition of intervals by assigning a rectangular form to the distribution. By definition, all the classes have the same complement in this type of scale. G. A. Ferguson (1949) has put forward theoretical arguments putting himself on the level of the ordinal relationship favouring the adoption of a rectangular distribution for test scores: this distribution minimizes the number of pairs of individuals where it would be impossible to know which individual was the best.

In examinations, a cut can be made dividing those to be admitted and those to be refused. The errors of classification would be more numerous when the complements were greater in the region of the cut-off front. One would thus be led to seek a bimodal curve, with a minimum at the point where it reaches its lowest level. One would see that a normal distribution with a cut at the level of the average constitutes exactly the opposite of a desirable condition.

Measurement in psychology

B) OTHER STATISTICAL DEFINITIONS

We shall arrange under this heading statistical methods of defining intervals which do not make use (or, at least, not only) of the form of the distribution.

a) *Intelligence quotient.* This is only of interest insofar as each value defined by the I.Q. is reached, at all ages, by the same proportion of the population. One can attempt, as did Terman (1919) and Terman and Merrill (1937) to modify the experimental conditions by successive approximation in order to obtain this, but it is an extremely costly and inadequate process. It is much simpler to transform distributions of the scores obtained for the representative groups, in increasing age, chosen in such a way that the transformed score is, in all the age groups, normally distributed with the same average (100) and the same standard deviation (15) (Wechsler, 1944). The intervals are then defined on each distribution by the general properties limiting the variable I.Q. (Reuchlin, 1959).

b) *Intra-individual heterogeneity.* The problem here is to define intervals between several measurements carried out on the same individual, but in different experimental conditions. For example, to define the distances between the scores an individual obtained in different tests (Piéron, 1945). A population of individuals who have done all the tests serves as a standard. If all the inter-individual distributions are of the same type (normal), one can transform an individual's raw score by expressing it in the form of a reduced measure; the distance between that score and the average score, which is measured in units of the standard deviation of the interindividual distribution. The distances are comparable if it is assumed that the different tests have the same inter-individual dispersion in the population. It is evident here that the intra-individual distances are defined as a function of inter-individual dispersion. This thus transforms each subject into a variable and one can then calculate correlations and 'inter-personal' factor analysis, an idea which occured almost at the same time to Thomson (1935) and Stephenson (1935).

c) *The method of paired comparisons.* If it is possible to range a number of things in order, one can say, for each pair of elements selected, which is better than the other. These judgements must be consistent so that the whole series can be arranged in order of

217

elements thus compared. Thurstone (1927) proposed the adoption of several supplementary postulates which would allow one to define the distances in similar experimental conditions, between what was being compared. The postulate was based on the assumption that the distribution of perceptions aroused by repeated presentation of the same stimulus to different individuals was normal. Other postulates concerned the correlation between the observed distances, for the compared stimuli during successive presentation and on the dispersion of distributions. These postulates give direction to the definition of intervals between two stimuli, starting from the proportion of cases in which one is considered superior to the other. As in simple ordering, the intervals thus determined between the pairs of elements must constitute a coherent whole. If the scale is to be linear, it is especially important to be able to prove the equality AB + BC = AC, between three points A, B and C.

These possibilities of proof are indicated in a method which is explained in more technical detail by Thurstone (1952, p. 167) and Faverge (1954a, p. 62). The method of paired comparisons has been used in psychophysics (scale of weights), in experimental aesthetics, in social psychology (scale of seriousness for different offences), etc.

The subject is presented with all the possible pairs of stimuli in the series of stimuli which are to be placed on the scale. The task demanded of the subject can be fairly long if these stimuli are numerous, and this a practical disadvantage of this method (there are $n(n-1)/2$ pairs for n stimuli). For each pair one marks which of the stimuli is declared superior to the other (heavier, more pleasant, more serious etc.). By repeating the experiment on several subjects it can be ascertained, for each pair (A, B) what proportion of the subjects prefer A to B. The calculations start with a table of the proportions established for all the pairs (each stimulus appearing at the same time in one row and one column).

d) *Multidimensional scales.* It can happen that the distances obtained by the preceding method are not consistent with the assumption of a linear scale. But if the distances between the different points are such that all the points do not fall in a straight line, perhaps they can be represented in 2, 3 . . . n dimensions. Techniques have been developed called multidimensional scales, which define distances in such cases, first by Young and

Householder (1938) at the suggestion of M. W. Richardson (1938) and more recently by others such as Messick (1956). For example, the objects to be measured can be presented to the judges in threes, and questioning can be confined to asking which of objects B and C most 'resembles' object A. It is not necessary to specify from which viewpoint the 'resemblance' should be considered, since the possible existence of several standards of comparison will be evident from the necessity to resort to distances measured in several dimensions. We cannot describe here the complex method of analysis. Like the method of paired comparisons, it has been used in psychophysics (where it has been used to find 'reflectance' and 'purity' dimensions in Munsell's Atlas cards), and in social psychology (dimensions used in common language to describe other people in everyday life, etc.).

3 Numerical properties

The properties of the numbers on an interval scale are those which remain after linear transformation: $y = ax + b$. Similarly it can be said that on such a scale the point of origin (parameter b) and the unity (parameter a) are also arbitrary. The order of elements ranged according to the x variable will remain unchanged if ranged according to y, and these numbers have at least linear properties of an ordinal scale. But besides this, it is clear that if two intervals are equal on the variable x, they remain equal on y, which shows that linear transformation preserves the numerical property corresponding to the experimental property on which the scale rests.

The fact that one can define the distance between two things justifies numerical treatment using the difference between their measurements, the numbers being such that equal distances correspond to equal differences.

It is useful to calculate the arithmetic mean of such measurements, since it is defined by the fact that the sum of the distances between the different elements and the mean is zero. If the variable undergoes a linear transformation, the numerical value of the mean itself will be transformed, but the new numerical value will preserve its property in the new distribution.

Equally, there is some sense in calculating a statistic of dispersion derived from enumerating the distances, for example, the standard deviation. In a linear transformation $y + ax = b$, the standard deviation will be multiplied by a, but will preserve its property. Moreover, if the interval scale in question fits into normal distribution (which is necessarily the case if the intervals have been defined with reference to such a distribution) the mean and standard deviation will enable one to use a table of the reduced law of normality. In this case especially it may be useful to express the measurement of each element in the form of a reduced distance (distance from the mean measured in units of the standard deviation): a simple reading of the table will give the proportion of elements exceeding a particular reduced distance. A table can be constructed for a particular distribution giving, for each value of the variable, the corresponding reduced distance, or multiple of it. We sometimes speak of a 'reduced scale', of '*tétronage*' (Weinberg 1937). Obviously the use of these tables does not modify the nature of the distribution, but on the other hand linear transformation of the variable has no effect on the reduced distance of an element.

In fact these tables supply only an approximation to the reduced distance or one of its multiples. For example, *tétronage* uses classes whose interval is equal to a quarter of the standard deviation. The limits of class 0 are selected to include all the elements whose distance from the mean is not more than an eighth of the standard deviation. The limits of the classes -1, -2 etc. are obtained by cutting away a quarter of the standard deviation from the lower limit immediately above. *Tétronage*, then, supplies the quadruple of the reduced distance with an approximation of about an eighth of the standard deviation.

For the same reason it is useful to calculate a correlation coefficient between two quantities starting from distances from the mean measured on each internal scale. This coefficient is obtained by calculating the mean product of the reduced distances, each elementary product being derived from two noted differences for the same element of the whole. Linear transformation of the two variables will leave their coefficient unchanged, since it has no effect on the reduced distances. Generally, this calculation is only made in cases where it has been possible to introduce supplementary conditions, some of which concern only one variable (that it should be normally distributed) and others which concern the variables as a whole (partial means must fall on a 'regression line'; partial distributions should all be normal and have the same variance). If the empirical data satisfies these new conditions experimentally ('normal, bivariate distribution') their numerical treatment will enable one to obtain a Bravais–Pearson correlation coefficient having new properties, if one compares it to previously discussed coefficients. It is enough to know the value of the coefficient to deduce the most probable value of the reduced distance, in one of the variables, and of an element of known reduced distance in the other variable; and the degree of error involved in this prediction; the proportion of elements exceeding at any particular time a particular reduced distance in one or other of the variables.

These new properties of the correlation coefficient, which are jointly responsible for new specifications of the conditions which must be empirically verified by measurement, are yet another illustration of the main theme of this explanation. This is to enable us to understand the role of postulates which are introduced in the definition of interval scales. If they constitute a way of defining the meaning of the terms we use to describe experimental operations, the meaning of these terms describing our numerical procedures is limited by these definitions. Thus we can say, with Fechner, that the experimenter who has discovered two different scales has defined two 'equal' intervals of sensation. But our later confirmation depends on certain numerical treatment, according to which sensation evolves according to the logarithm of the intensity of the stimulus, and this depends entirely on our original definition of 'equality' of sense intervals. The same point would be valid for the assumption of normality which is often involved in the definition of interval scales.

Consideration of such kinds of argument can be found at two levels. Firstly, one can consider the weakness of the connection between each preliminary empirical condition and the conclusion. This is more tenuous in some cases than in others. For example, we have listed above the conditions of a normal distribution with two variables to which the Bravais–Pearson correlation coefficient applies. A statistician like Hotelling (1955, p. 123) admits, however, that in many cases the separate construction of a normal distribution of each of the two variables is sufficient for it to be treated as a normal bivariate distribution.

At another level one could see that the system made up of certain postulates and their conclusions does not constitute an isolated system, but necessarily fits into the larger whole of observations, theories and applications of the rest of psychology. That whole is not structured in a sufficiently precise way for us to know clearly if a particular partial construction is consistent with the rest. However, it can offer the opportunity to introduce—more or less decisively according to each individual case—the notion of 'success' of such a system; it may or may not happen that results or theories, which have till then been isolated, are fitted into it; it may or may not lead to effective applications. Stevens (1951, p. 28) considers that the postulate of a normal distribution of psychological measurements has a certain usefulness (and this testimony is all the more worth quoting since Stevens himself hardly ever made use of this postulate).

In concluding this explanation of the properties of numbers in an interval scale, it will be seen that the majority of methods which psychologists use are legitimate at this level. It seems that research must concern itself more with the methods by which one can define what constitutes equality in intervals than with the means of working out, by more specific operations, better methods of measurement. However, we should mention that Stevens suggested experimental techniques whereby one could assign numbers whose origin was no longer arbitrary, as it was in the case of all the methods of measurement we have examined so far.

4   Ratio scales

The method put forward by Stevens consists of defining experimentally what one means by saying that the ratio between two things is equal to the ratio between two others. Once this is achieved, one can assign to those things which have this property numbers whose ratios are equal.

1   Experimental definition of the equality of two ratios

Although Stevens emphasized the possibility of constructing a ratio scale starting from judgements of equality, first on intervals and then on any ratios (1951, p. 29 and 41), the methods which he used do not in general consist of making directly equal two ratios.

Thus, in 1957, he made the following classification of the experimental procedures he advocated: methods of *estimation of ratios*, in which two stimuli are presented to the subject who states directly the numerical value of the ratio of the corresponding sensations; methods of *production of ratios* in which the subject himself adjusts the stimulus in such a way that the ratio of the sensation aroused is of a predetermined value in relation to another, constant, sensation; methods of *estimation of loudness*, which require the subject to make a direct numerical estimate of each of the sensations produced by a series of stimuli; methods of *production of loudness* in which the subject is asked to regulate a variable stimulus in such a way that the sensation represents a value which seems to him to correspond to a given number.

The use made of numbers in the experimental stage of measurement is of obvious importance. We repeat, that it seems that Stevens only made use of them, at this stage, because of their convenience as a language, and the principle on which he learned could be set in motion by the simple equalization of intervals and ratios of any size. Undoubtedly certain criticisms made of his method on logical grounds (British Assn. for the Adv. of Science, 1939–40, p. 337, 345, etc.) would have been less justified if the experimental operations had only used such equalizations.

On the strictly experimental level, another criticism has been made of Stevens' methods: the considerable variability of the results of this type of experiment, as much for the repetitions in estimation by the same individual as for repetitions made by different individuals. Piéron has noted that the use of logarithmic units could mask the extent of this variability. For instance it must be remembered that an error of 2 bels or 20 decibels consists of confusing two stimuli, one of which is physically 100 times greater than the other. Thus, margins of variability of this order, that is about 10,000 per cent are met in the assessment relating to this type of scale (Piéron, 1954, p. 101).

These experiments have hardly been carried out until recently, except in psychophysics. However, we can mention an isolated attempt by Reese (1943) to transpose them into the area of tests. For example, he asked subjects who had learned two series of figures if the difficulty they had found in memorizing the second had seemed to them to be half that of the first, or higher or lower than half.

223

2 Numerical properties

Let us suppose, for example, that in a certain sense modality the method of production of ratios had been used. The experiment could then supply, for each stimulus x, the value of the stimulus y for which the sensation had been considered, let us say, double that aroused by x.

By arbitrarily assigning a number to the sensation aroused by one or other of the stimuli, the experimental results will make it possible to determine which stimulus must be regarded as double the number of the first, and then which stimulus should be regarded as double the number of the preceding one, and so on.

Obviously, it is sufficient for a number to be arbitrarily assigned to a thing (which comes back to choosing the order of the size of the units), so that all the numbers can be determined before being assigned to the other things. This was not true for the previous scales.

The properties of the numbers here, then, are those which are preserved by the transformation $y = ax$. The disappearance of the parameter b, present in the transformation which applies to interval scales, emphasizes the fact that in this case the origin is fixed. Such psychological measurements, if they were carried out decisively on the experimental plane, would have all the properties of the 'strongest' physical measurements, such as length, or mass. All arithmetical operations on such numbers are valid. In practice, the methods of the psychologist will scarcely be enriched if he changes from interval scales to ratio scales. Let us point out that a coefficient of variance (ratio of the standard deviation to the mean) is only valid for measurements based on a fixed point of origin (a displacement of the origin would affect the mean but not the standard deviation).

5 Derived scales

In the different scales which we have just described, there is no intermediary between the experimental operation and the allocation of numbers. But in certain cases such scales constitute only a first step in the measurement procedure. This can be designed to translate numerically certain aspects of experimental data, which have been brought to light by preliminary calculations. This

Measurement in psychology

technique depends directly on which aspect of the facts one seeks to describe. As we have already seen, numbers must only be utilized within the limits of their actual properties. To designate things, this technique supplies a new series of numbers, which one could say constitute a derived scale, which varies in the same way as the original scales.

1 Prognosis

Some of these derived scales can effect only a very elementary improvement on the original scales. If, for example, for each subject in a group we use one test score and one score according to a criterion of professional or scholastic success, we can construct a derived scale, the prognosis of which will enable us to assign to each subject of the population from which the group is taken, a number varying with the test score, which will be the most probable score of professional or scholastic ability of this subject. We know that one need only multiply the reduced distance in the test by the Bravais–Pearson correlation coefficient between the two variables, to obtain the reduced distances in the prognosis. This prognosis can be more precisely calculated with several tests. The derived scale would in this case be a well-balanced sum of the original scales (equations of multiple regression) (Faverge, 1954a, Chapter 10).

2 Factorial scoring

Through factor analysis a derived scale can be obtained, factorial scoring, starting from several original scales which are most often the test scores. Several factor scores can be obtained for the same subject, from the same series of scores in the tests. The choice between these scores (that is between different mathematical functions) depends on the nature of the fact one wishes to isolate, and the functions (in the general sense) that one assigns to the factorial scores. It might merely be a means of reducing the volume of data available.

Supposing that 15 test scores are required to identify an individual in a population as unambiguously as possible (very few individuals having obtained the same series of 15 marks), one may wish to identify the individuals from a number of more

225

restricted factorial scores, knowing that such a restriction entails a loss of precision in identification. However, it is desirable that this loss be as small as possible. If only a single variable is used it should be the best, and similarly if there are two, three variables, etc. The sequence of derived scales to be used in this case is determined by the 'principal components' of Hotelling, each of which is a function of the 15 original scales (Faverge, 1954a, p. 218).

But factorial scoring can perform quite another function. It may be, that the organization of correlations observed between the tests fits a particular hypothesis explaining the existing causes of the variations, each common to several tests. It would seem as if each individual possessed to a fairly developed degree factors responsible for his success, each of which would determine his replies in several tests. Factorial scores thus have to be derived from the test scores in such a way that each is an estimate of the strength of these factors. These factorial scores could then be used in the same way as the test scores: in studying the distribution in the population; to compare sub-groups of individuals from the point of view of each factor; to describe an individual in terms of the factors, etc. (Bernyer, 1947, 1948).

Technically the problem of estimating factors from test scores is confused with that of prognosis based on several tests; in both cases correlations between the tests are used: the 'saturations' of the factorial tests here replace the 'validities' of tests in terms of the criterion.

3 Discriminating functions

It may be that two groups of subjects, for example, a group of mental patients and a group of normal people, can hardly be differentiated by considering variables in isolation, such as the results of a psychological examination. But, in certain cases, it is easier to differentiate between the two groups if one considers all the results obtained for each subject: although in each of the two groups some individuals can be found who have the maximum possible marks in each test, certain combinations of these marks characterize one group while certain other combinations are found mainly in the other group. The problem here is to find a function of the original scores which maximizes one's powers to discriminate between the two groups.

This 'discriminating function' can be considered as a derived scale whose role is to reveal the distinctive characteristics of the two groups from the sum of scores when looked at altogether. Knowing the marks an individual obtains on the original scale, the psychologist could, by placing this individual on such a derived scale, state that he is more likely to belong to one or other of these groups and he would then be able to use this in order to make a diagnosis or prognosis.

Discriminating functions were first studied by Fisher, and their use in psychology has been demonstrated by Garrett (1943) and by Pichot and Perse (1952).

The problem of which of the derived scales which have discussed should be used presents the psychologist with a similar situation to where he has to choose an experimental operation suitable for the establishment of a particular relationship definitive postulate the freedom of his choice, i.e. his apparent indetermination, is in fact limited by the role he intends to assign to the measurements he makes.

6 The problem of precision in measurement

1 The meaning of the problem

Generally speaking, the problem of the precision of a measurement can be considered in two ways.

A) Firstly one can consider that the process of measurement applies to an object whose existence and invariance is postulated, an object which possesses certain characteristics which could be discovered by other means than measurement and which, in this sense, are independent of it. In this case, it would be possible to measure the same object several times. If the numbers thus successively assigned to it were not equal, one would conclude that each was composed of two numbers, one of which represented the true measurement and the other the error. Since the true measurement is, in such a situation, by definition identical for all effective measurement, the range of errors supplies a measure of the extent of the variation of error. The existence of a 'systematic error' which does not vary during repeated measurement is not excluded. It will be seen that it corresponds to a displacement of the origin of the scale of measurements used and that it will not, consequently, affect the properties of scales with arbitrary origins (interval scales and scales of lower order), where, of course, these properties are used for a number of objects measured with the same systematic error.

In such a case, one can compare an estimate of the dispersion of true measurements with an estimate of the variations of the error. If the measurements have been approached with a view to differentiating the objects, measurement could fulfil this function more precisely if the ratio between the dispersion of the measurements and that of the errors (or the estimate of this ratio) were greater.

The problem has been presented in these terms, in particular, by certain methods of estimating the precision of tests, using analysis of variance.

In this conception of the problem of precision, stable characteristics are attributed independently to the measured object and to the instrument of measurement: a subject has a certain degree of ability whether or not he is doing a test; the test possesses a certain degree of accuracy, independent of the individuals to whom it is applied (in populations where the true dispersion remains the same).

B) Another conception of the problem, which has been maintained in the sphere of the epistemology of the physical sciences by certain philosophers, can also be used in psychology.

If it is considered that ideas such as sensory threshold or degree of aptitude can be defined in a precise way only by describing a particular experimental operation (the apparatus used for the measurement of the threshold, the test) one can no longer assign to the threshold or to the aptitude an absolute measure independent of the operation, nor can one assign to the process of measurement an absolute characteristic independent of the object to which it is applied. In fact, measurement and its object are one, and it can be said that an object exists only if a relation is established between several repeatable measurements: for example, one would speak of sensory threshold only if it were possible to find the same relations several times between the variations of the physical measurement of the stimulus and the variations of the subjects' responses. Experimental relations properly observed are, in fact, repeatable to a greater or lesser degree. For example the first perception of the two points of the aesthesiometer will not always occur at exactly the same distance apart, in a particular subject or in subjects in general. Also, one could say that an object appears to a greater or lesser degree at a definite threshold which has been determined by an experimental procedure which was more or less easy to establish with a particular subject.

When one or other of these two approaches is adopted, it is seen that to obtain precision a measurement must first of all be experimentally repeated and an appropriate numerical treatment should then be carried out on these repeated measurements.

1 Experimental repetition of measurement

A) In the determination of sensory thresholds, it is usual to repeat several series of presentations of the stimuli on the same subject, each series defining an 'instantaneous threshold' (Fraisse, 1956, p. 284). This expression must not be taken literally, and can only determine the result obtained after a series of presentations with different thresholds over a period of time. During this there will have been, variations in the excitability of the peripheral receptors, changes in the attitude of the subject, differing degrees of influence of the series of measurements.

To this intra-subject variability is added an inter-subject variability, which is considerable.

Finally, research, such as that of Fechner or Stevens, which is concerned with the general form of the law relating physical intensity of the stimulus to intensity of the sensation, assumes that this law is more or less valid on repeated occasions, not only when the presentations and the subjects vary, but also when the physical nature of the stimulus varies.

B) As far as tests are concerned, three methods are usually employed in the repetition of measurements aimed at establishing their accuracy.

One is to apply the same test to the same subjects two or more times in succession, after a certain time lag. This can produce learning whose effect one can control when one treats the results or whose width or generality one can confine experimentally by lengthening the interval between presentations or by using 'parallel' tests.

The parallel test method involves using at least two different tests which are regarded as interchangeable. Though the theoretical

definition of such tests is easy, their construction is difficult
(Gulliksen, 1950, Chapter 14). The two parallel tests are successively applied to the same subjects, and this is regarded as a
repetition of the measurement.

These two methods involve a certain time lag between repetitions. During this period, according to the first of the two views
of accuracy we have distinguished, variations of the true measure
may arise which will then be treated as variations of the error.
Then one might consider a test consisting of a series of questions
as two parallel tests overlapping in time: the questions of even
numbers supplying one measurement, and the questions of odd
numbers supplying another. This is the 'odd-even' method or,
more usually, the 'split-half' method.

3 Treatment of results

The dispersion of the 'instantaneous thresholds' supplies a simple
means of determining the accuracy of the measurement of an
individual's threshold. Just as the threshold is the median of
the instantaneous thresholds, so its variability is often expressed
by the corresponding quartile distance. If several subjects are used,
one would give the dispersion of the distribution of thresholds.
When a single law is proposed to account, in a general way, for
the relation between the physical measurement of the stimulus
and the measurement of the sensation, special experiments must
be carried out aimed at establishing the law for each sensory
modality, the intra- and inter-individual variation of which we
have just mentioned. In a case where the proposed law contains a
parameter which varies from one sensory modality to another,
the dispersion of the value of this parameter calls for further
comment.

In the sphere of tests, one has long been limited to calculating a
correlation between the two series of measurements obtained, by
one of the three experimental methods of repetition, this correlation
coefficient being called the 'coefficient of reliability' and being
considered as a characteristic of the test. The introduction of the
statistical method of analysis of variance into psychology by
Fisher has helped to solve this problem. It has made it possible to
estimate the relative importance of the fraction of variance
explained by 'true' differences between the subjects and that

simply due to temporary fluctuations. But it is immediately obvious that one cannot talk of 'true' variance and 'error variance' in an absolute sense, and that these two expressions are simply names by which each of the experimental repetitive procedures classify the different variation factors (Cronbach, 1947). This technical development may lead to the adoption of the second view of accuracy rather than the first.

The interpretation and use of estimates of accuracy depend, implicitly or explicitly, first of all on which of these two views is adopted. They depend, moreover, on which method of experimental repetition is chosen.

7 Conclusion

In conclusion, we shall examine the general significance of measurement in psychology, i.e. its general role in the process by which the psychologist extends his knowledge. It is by consulting the whole of this *Treatise* that the reader will find a detailed reply to this question. But several more general points would be in order here:

A) Starting from the level of each particular use made of measurement procedures, we maintain that these procedures can never be considered as standardized operations, inserted like prefabricated wheels into the machinery of an experiment. In each case the selection of a measurement procedure must be made with two considerations in mind: firstly, the conditions existing before a measurement is made are defined by the provisional limits of experimental knowledge which may or may not make it possible to define a relation of equivalence, a relation of order, the equality of two intervals or two ratios; and secondly, conditions applying after the measurement have been made which concern the use one plans to make of them within the framework of the experiment.

The examples given above show how these two considerations combine. If the experiment is aimed at determining the most likely of a number of possible outcomes, or their entropy, it would be necessary—and sufficient—to define experimentally a relation of equivalence. But if the experimenter makes his measurements with a view to seeing whether or not certain underlying factors

231

contradict observed correlations, he will have to use interval scales of normal distribution. Other relationships can be established between the various considerations which affect measurement operations. For example, if the same treatment must be applied to different variables, it will sometimes be necessary to adopt the weakest since it alone, applies to one of the variables. In this way one can be led to use nominal scales in spheres where the means of defining an ordinal relation experimentally is known (see for example, Bacher 1957).

B) But this complication of considerations preceding and following measurement procedures takes up only a moment of the psychologist's progress. It determines the character of a particular experiment, which is merely a step in this progress. From one experiment to another, and even from one phase of the same experiment to another, the knowledge and aims of the experimenter develop and constraints arise from them in such a way that the use of a particular method of measurement contributes to creating the conditions favourable to its development. Examples of these successive approximations can be cited from different fields.

Stevens (1955) asked his subjects to adjust three sounds of variable physical intensity in such a way as to establish four apparently equal intervals on a scale of sensation within the range of two sounds of fixed intensity. Each adjustment being repeated several times he had, at the end of the experiment, to calculate for each of them the physical measurement of the stimulus corresponding to the mean of the sensation aroused by the different trials. Therefore, he knew only the different physical measurements chosen by the subjects during the trial and could only postulate with certainty that the sound of average physical intensity will arouse a sensation of average intensity. To solve the problem he would have to know the relation between the physical intensity and the intensity of the sensation, the discovery of which is precisely the object of the experiment. He therefore proceeds by successive approximation: the average of the physical intensities supplies him with an approximate form of the relationship, from which he can obtain a better estimate of the value of the stimulus corresponding to each average sensation, and so on. The gradations of the sensory scale are thus obtained by provisional forms of this scale.

In the construction of Guttman scales, the provisional use of a series of questions to a provisional sample of subjects enables one to try to classify these questions and subjects according to the model of a parallelogram. The necessity of eliminating any response which does not fit into the parallelogram leads to the elimination, by successive approximations, of particular subjects and questions, and to the construction of the improved or definitive version of a scale which can be used on a well defined population.

A provisional system of grading enabled Terman to arrange the scores in an attainment test according to age. The means and standard deviations observed supplied him with the elements necessary for the selection of modifications to be applied to the questions, so that all the I.Q.s had the same mean and same standard deviation.

C) The progress made by the application of measurement in each particular experimental field thus developes the content of measurement operations by a series of approximations unfolding within its limits. But the field itself is not isolated, it constitutes only a fragment of the general sphere of psychological knowledge. Scales which are progressively defined within this field are related to other scales. These relationships, established explicitly by new experiments, or considered likely in cases where explicit experiment has been impossible, contribute to the clearer definition of the scales and permit the 'interpretation' of the measurement and of its results.

In this way one can seek to connect the results of psychophysical measurement and the knowledge which other types of research have enabled to be established in nerve physiology. H. Piéron (1955, Part 4, Chapter 6) worked out a general schema of the physiological mechanisms involved in intensive appreciation, he introduced between the two variables by the psychophysical experiment (the acoustic pressure of the sound and the response of the subject, for example) a chain of other variables: frequency of potentials in the afferent fibres, linked to the recruitment of aesthesions, with a normal distribution of excitability to explain the sigmoid relation between the size of the stimulus and that of the sensation.

Measurements made with the help of tests or attitude scales are similarly related to other, more or less precisely defined observations, sometimes expressed in the form of measurement scales, sometimes not. Numerous works in applied psychology therefore consist of calculations of correlations between test scores and the criteria of academic or professional success. When explicitly defined variables are revealed as being associated with each other and relatively distinct from other variables, one attempts to discover whether this 'factor' can explain the common characteristics, which are often difficult to define clearly.

In all these cases where one seeks to 'interpret' the result of a measurement, variables are introduced which cannot always be defined as explicitly as those dealt with by the processes we have considered. These intermediary or peripheral variables are, or appear to be, associated with the variables measured by associations which cannot always be expressed numerically. Uncertainties are inevitable: on the one hand the different ideas of the psychologist are not made properly explicit, or different methods of explanation are used; on the other hand psychological ideas are inserted among others—physiological, economic, social—and cannot always be translated into the same language. But it would not be right to consider that the least explicit variables are more 'real' than those which are better explained, or to say that one must necessarily, for example, 'interpret' the test score as a function of a semi-intuitive criterion of 'success', a term resonant with all the complexities and ambiguities of everyday language. The syncretism of ordinary language is not to its advantage and the answer to the question 'What are you measuring'? cannot be rendered in it.

This question is, in fact, meaningless if it implies the existence of essential realities existing before measurement and independent of it, which could be entirely known without being measured. It makes the same mistake as that of demanding that the experimenter define once and for all the object of his experiment, or of the psychologist that he give an exhaustive *a priori* definition of psychology. Measurement constitutes only one phase in the process of successive approximations by which knowledge is enriched and ordered. This phase is interdependent with those which precede it and those which follow it and cannot be defined outside them. It is, like them, part of a continuous movement of reorganization in which each stage is at the same time the means and the end.

Bibliography

Actes du XV² Congrès international de Psychologie, 658 pp. Amsterdam, North Holland Publishing Co. 1959

BACHER, E. and REUCHLIN, M., 'Analyse statistique de "tableaux cliniques" ', *Biotypol.*, 1956, 17, 205–15

BACHER, F., *Étude sur la structure de l'information apportée par l'examen d'orientation professionnelle*, B.I.N.O.P., 1957, 13, special number

BAMBON, J., 'L'entretien: quelques applications des techniques récentes d'analyse quantitative', *Année psychol.*, 1955, 55, 103–8

BERNYER, G., 'L'estimation des facteurs psychologique par la régression', *Année psychol.*, 1947, 43–4, 299–322

—'Distribution des facteurs psychologiques dans une population', *Année psychol.*, 1948, 45–6, 16–28

BODINE, A. J., Cf. KAHN, L. A.

BRESSON, F., 'Langage et communications', *Année psychol.*, 1953, 53, 477–502

BRITISH ASSOCIATION FOR THE ADVANCEMENT OF SCIENCE, "Quantitative estimates of sensory events', *The Advancement of Science*, 1939–40, 1, 311–49

CRONBACH, L. J., 'Test reliability: its meaning and determination', *Psychometrika*, 1947, 12, 1–16

DURAIN, G. and MOSCOVICI, S., 'Quelques applications de la théorie de l'informations à l'étude des quasi-échelles', *Bull. Centre. Et. Rech. psychotechn.*, 1956, 5, 33–40

—Cf. MOSCOVICI, S.

FAUTREL, M., 'La validation de l'examen psychotechnique préalable à la formation professionnelle accélérée', *Bull. Centre Et. Rech. psychotechn.*, 1, no. 2, 1–13

FAVERGE, J.-M., 'La théorie de l'information en psychologie expérimentale', *Année psychol.*, 1953, 53, 463–76

—*Méthodes statistiques en psychologie appliquée*, 2 vols. Paris, Presses Universitaires de France, 1954a

—'Sur la mesure en psychologie', *J. Psychol.*, 1954b, 47–51, 417–30

—'La définition des variables en psychologie', *Bull. Psychol.*, 1958, 11, 181–5

—*Sur la notion de contingence*, B.I.N.O.P., 1959, 15, 75–84

FERGUSON, G. A., 'On the theory of test discrimination', *Psychometrika*, 1949, 14, 61–8

FESTINGER, L. and KATZ, D., *Research Methods in the Social Sciences*, New York, Holt, 1959

FLETCHER, H. and MUSON, W. A., 'Loudness, its definition, measurement and calculation', *J. acous. Soc. Amer.*, 1933, 5, 82–106

FRAISSE, P., *Manuel pratique de psychologie expérimentale*, 312 pp., Paris, Presses Universitaires de France, 1956

235

Maurice Reuchlin

GAGE, F. H., 'An experimental investigation of the measurability of auditory sensations', *Proceedings of the Royal Society of London*, B, 1934–35, 116, 103–122; 'An experimental investigation of the measurability of visual sensations', ibid., 123–37

GARRETT, H. E., 'The discriminant function and its use in psychology', *Psychometrika*, 1943, 65–79

GULLIKSEN, H., *Theory of mental tests*, 486 pp., New York, Wiley, 1950

GUTTMAN, L., 'The Cornell technique for scale and intensity analysis', *Educ. psychol. Measurem.*, 1947, 7, 247–79

HOTELLING, H., 'Les rapports entre les méthodes statistiques récentes portant sur des variables multiples et l'analyse factorielle' in *L'analyse factorielle et ses applications*, 431 pp., Paris, Centre Nationale de la recherche scientifique, 1955

HOUSEHOLDER, A. A., Cf. YOUNG, G.

KAHN, L. A. and BODINE, A. J., 'Guttman scale analysis by means of I.B.M. equipment', *Educ. psychol. measurem.*, 1951, 11, 298–314

KATZ, D., Cf. FESTINGER, L.

KENDALL, M. G., Cf. YULE, G. U.

—*Rank correlation methods*, 196 pp. London, Griffin, 1955 (2nd edn.)

LARCEBEAU, S. *Éléments de construction d'une fiche scolaire*, B.I.N.O.P., 1955, 11, 133–43

LOEVINGER, J., 'The technique of homogeneous tests compared with some aspects of "scale analysis" and factor analysis', *Psychol. Bull.*, 1948, 45, 507–29

MERRILL, M. A., Cf. TERMAN, L. M.

MESSICK, S. J., 'Some recent theoretical developments in multidimensional scaling', *Educ. psychol. Measurem.*, 1956, 16, 82–100

MOSCOVICI, S., 'L'analyse hiérarchique', *Année psychol.*, 1954, 54, 83–110

—DURAIN, G., 'Quelques applications de la théorie de l'information à la construction des échelles d'attitude', *Année psychol.*, 1956, 56, 47–57

—VIBERT-DURAIN, G., 'Analyse non paramétrique des échelles', *Psychol. française*, 1958, 3, 27–34

—Cf. DURAIN, G.

MUNSON, W. A., Cf. FLETCHER, H.

PERSE, J., Cf. PICHOT, P.

PICHOT, P. and PERSE, J., 'L'applications des fonctions discriminantes au diagnostic individuel en psychologie', *Rev. Psychol. appl.*, 1952, 2, 19–34

PIÉRON, H., 'L'hétérogenéité normale des aptitudes', *Année psychol.*, 1945, 41–42, 1–13

—*Les problèmes fondamentaux de la psychophysique dans la science actuelle*, 63 pp., Paris, Herman, 1951

Measurement in psychology

—*La sensation, guide de vie*, 626 pp., Paris, Gallimard 1955 (2nd edn.)

REESE, T. W., 'The application of the theory of physical measurement to the measurement of psychological magnitudes, with three experimental examples', *Psychol. Monogr.*, 1943, 55, No. 3, 89 pp.

REUCHLIN, M., 'Contribution aux méthodes d'observation du comportement', *Année psychol.*, 1950, 49, 119–57

—'La définition du quotient d'intelligence', *Biotypol.*, 1959, 20, 13–24

—*Les méthodes quantitatives on psychologie*, 454 pp., Paris, Presses Universitaires de France, 1962

—Cf. BACHER, F.

SHANNON, C. E. and WEAVER, W., *The mathematical theory of communications*, 117 pp., Urbana, the Univ. of Illinois press, 1949

STEPHENSON, W., 'The invected factor technique', *Brit. J. Psychol.*, 1935–1936, 26, 344–61

STEVENS, S. S., *Handbook of Experimental psychology*, 1436 pp., New York, John Wiley, 1951

—'On the averaging of data', *Science*, 1955, 121, 113–16

—'On the psychophysical law', *Psychol. Rev.*, 1957, 64, 153–81

STOUFFER, (Ed.) *Studies in social psychology in World War II, Measurement and Prediction*, 756 pp., Princeton, Princeton Univ. Press, 1950.

SUCHMAN, E. A., 'The scalogram board technique for scale analysis', in STOUFFER (Ed.) *Measurement and prediction*, 756 pp., Princeton 1950 (pp. 91–121)

TERMAN, L. M., *The measurement of intelligence*, 362 pp., London, Harrap, 1919

—MERRILL, M. A., *Measuring intelligence*, 461 pp., London, Harrap, 1937

THOMSON, G. H., 'On complete families of correlation coefficients', *Brit. J. Psychol.*, 1935–1936, 26, 63–92

THURSTONE, L. L., 'A law of comparative judgment', *Psychol. Rev.*, 1927, 34, 273–286

—'Les méthodes psychophysiques', in ANDREWS, T. G., *Les méthodes de la psychologie*, Fr. translation, 2 vols. 882 pp., Paris, Presses Universitaires de France, 1952

VIBERT-DURAIN, G., Cf. MOSCOVICI, S.

WEAVER, W., Cf. SHANNON, C. E.

WECHSLER, D., *The measurement of adult intelligence*, 258 pp. Baltimore, Williams and Wilkins, 1944

WEINBERG, D., *Méthodes d'unifications des mesures en biométrie et biotypologie. Le tétronage*, 64 pp., Paris, Herman, 1937

YOUNG, G. and HOUSEHOLDER, A. S., 'Discussion of a set of points in terms of their mutual distances', *Psychometrika*, 1938, 3, 19–22

YULE, G. U. and KENDALL, M. G., *An introduction to the theory of statistics*, 570 pp. London, Griffin, 1949

237

Index

Index

Index